Patagonia

Ben Box

Credits

Footprint credits

Editorial: Felicity Laughton
Maps: Kevin Feeney

Managing Director: Andy Riddle
Commercial Director: Patrick Dawson
Publisher: Alan Murphy
Publishing Managers: Felicity Laughton,
Nicola Gibbs, Jo Williams
Marketing and Partnerships Director:
Liz Harper
Trade Product Manager: Diane McEntee
Advertising: Renu Sibal, Elizabeth Taylor
Trade Product Co-ordinator: Kirsty Holmes

Photography credits

Front cover: Dreamstime
Back cover: Shutterstock

Printed in the United States of America.

Publishing information

Footprint *Focus Patagonia*
1st edition
© Footprint Handbooks Ltd
September 2012

ISBN: 978 1 908206 81 7
CIP DATA: A catalogue record for this book
is available from the British Library

® Footprint Handbooks and the Footprint
mark are a registered trademark of Footprint
Handbooks Ltd

Published by Footprint
6 Riverside Court
Lower Bristol Road
Bath BA2 3DZ, UK
T +44 (0)1225 469141
F +44 (0)1225 469461
footprinttravelguides.com

Distributed in the USA by Globe Pequot Press,
Guilford, Connecticut

The content of Footprint *Focus Patagonia*
has been taken directly from Footprint's
South American Handbook which was
researched and written by Ben Box.

Every effort has been made to ensure that
the facts in this guidebook are accurate.
However, travellers should still obtain
advice from consulates, airlines, etc about
travel and visa requirements before travelling.
The authors and publishers cannot accept
responsibility for any loss, injury or
inconvenience however caused.

Contents

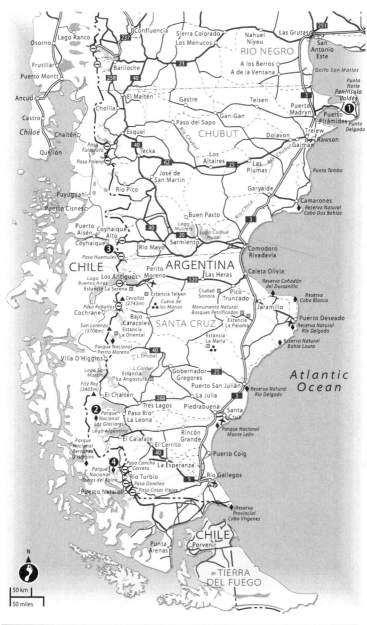

Squeezed between two oceans and split by the tail of the Andes, Patagonia is a land of vast horizons and limitless possibilities. Unvanquished by the conquistadors, it has developed in isolation, attracting brave pioneers, hardy Welsh settlers, Wild West outlaws on the run and Ernesto 'Che' Guevara on a pre-revolutionary jaunt. Head south on the ultimate road trip until, rising up from the flat lands, you see Fitz Roy's spires, or the granite turrets of Torres del Paine. Sculpted glaciers cleave with a roar and the raw power of nature is palpable. Seals and migrating whales animate the deserted beaches of the Atlantic, while on the Pacific coast, the land splinters into a labyrinth of islets, fjords and looming icebergs. The oceans meet at the tip of Patagonia – the Land of Fire is a final frontier at the end of the world.

Planning your trip

Getting to Patagonia

Air
Unless you are arriving from the Falkland Islands, it is not possible to fly directly to Patagonia from outside Argentina or Chile. Instead you must choose to fly into either Buenos Aires' **Ezeiza International Airport** (EZE) or Santiago's **Aeropuerto Arturo Merino Benítez** (SCL) and pick up onward transport there. There are several flights a day between Santiago and Buenos Aires, operated by **LAN, Aerolíneas Argentinas, Air Canada** or the Brazilian airline, **Gol**.

Fares vary from airline to airline and according to the time of year. Discounted fares are offered through specialist agencies but always check the reservation with the airline concerned to make sure the flight still exists. Note that citizens of Albania (US$30), Australia (US$95), Canada (US$132), Mexico (US$23) and the USA (US$140) are charged a one-off reciprocal entry tax on arrival by air in Chile, valid for the lifetime of the passport.

Transport in Patagonia

Air: onward flights to Patagonia
From Buenos Aires All domestic flights from Buenos Aires (as well as some flights to/from neighbouring countries) are handled from **Aeroparque**, situated 4 km north of the centre of Buenos Aires. **Manuel Tienda León** ① *T0800-888 5366, www.tiendaleon.com*, runs efficient buses between the two airports (US$16) and from Aeroparque to the city centre (US$5.75). They have a desk inside the arrivals hall, where you can also book a *remise* taxi. From Aeroparque, the main air routes to Patagonia are to **Bariloche** (2½ hours), **San Martín de los Andes** (two hours), **Trelew** (two hours), **El Calafate** (3¼ hours) and **Ushuaia** (three hours 20 minutes).

From Santiago You will go through customs and immigration in international arrivals before transferring to the domestic section of the same terminal. LAN (www.lan.com) flies between Santiago and major cities under the banner **Lan Express**. **Sky Airline** (www.skyairline.cl) also serves the main destinations but less frequently. Return flights are often cheaper than one-way tickets. The most important routes from Santiago are to **Temuco** (1½ hours), **Valdivia** (summer only, 1½ hours), **Osorno** (2½ hours), **Puerto Montt** (1¾ hours), **Balmaceda** (for Coyhaique, 2½ hours, can be cheaper with stopover in Puerto Montt) and **Punta Arenas** (4½ hours).

Rail
The touristy *Tren del Fin del Mundo*, www.trendelfindelmundo.com.ar, travels from Ushuaia to the Parque Naccional Tierra del Fuego (see page 60).

Road
Internal flights are fast, but not green, so consider long-distance buses for some of your journey. Argentina and Chile have very comfortable buses that travel overnight, enabling

Don't miss ...

you to sleep. However, the 24-hour bus ride along the Ruta 40 from Los Antiguos to El Chaltén has fantastic views that you'll want to stay awake for. On long bus journeys, carry small packs of tissues and bottled water; toilets on buses can be unpleasant. Also take a jumper to combat the fierce air conditioning.

Buses in Argentina The country is connected by a network of efficient long-distance buses, which is usually the cheapest way of getting around. They run all year, are safe and comfortable, and travel overnight, which saves time on long journeys. The main operators are **Andesmar**, www.andesmar.com, **TAC**, T011-4312-7012 and **Via Bariloche**, www.viabariloche.com.ar. Book seats a day in advance in January. Regional services to tourist destinations within Patagonia tend to be limited after mid-March.

When choosing a bus, bear in mind that *común* buses have lots of stops, are uncomfortable and not recommended for long journeys. *Semi-cama* have slightly reclining seats, meals and a toilet onboard. *Coche-cama* have fully reclining seats, meals, a toilet, only a few stops and are worth the small extra expense for a good night's sleep.

Bus companies may give discounts to students with ID, and to teachers with proof of employment. Discounts aren't usually available December to March. Make sure your seat number is on your ticket. Luggage is safely stored in a large hold at the back of the bus, and you'll be given a numbered ticket to reclaim it on arrival. *Maleteros* take the bags off the bus, and may expect a small tip – 50 centavos or a peso is fine.

Buses in Chile Bus services in Chile are frequent and comfortable. Buses tend to be punctual, arriving and leaving on time. Along the Carretera Austral, however, services are far less reliable, less frequent and usually in minibuses. Services improve again between Punta Arenas and Puerto Natales in the far south. In addition, there are long-distance international services from Santiago to Buenos Aires, from Osorno to Bariloche, from Coyhaique to Comodoro Rivadavia and from Punta Arenas to Río Gallegos and Ushuaia.

When choosing a bus in Chile, remember *clásico/salón-ejecutivo* are comfortable enough for daytime travel but are not ideal for long distances. *Semi-cama* have more leg room and fewer stops but are 50% more expensive. *Salón-cama* are similar to a *coche-cama* in Argentina (see above), and *cama premium* have flat beds. *Salón-cama* are the most spacious, with dinner available on overnight services. They are 50% more expensive than *semi-cama*. The premium service with fully reclining seats runs between Santiago and the lakes (30% more expensive than *salón-cama*).

Apart from at holiday times, there is little problem getting a seat on a long-distance bus and you only need to reserve ahead in high season. Prices are highest from December to March but competition between bus companies means you may be able to bargain for a lower fare, particularly just before departure; discounts are also often available for return journeys. Students may also get discounts out of season. Most bus companies will carry bicycles, but may ask for payment.

Car Hiring a car is an excellent idea if you want to travel independently and explore the more remote areas of Patagonia, although it can be complicated to take a hire car across the border between Argentina and Chile (see below). The most important routes in Argentine Patagonia are Ruta 40, which runs along the west side of the Andes and faster Ruta 3, which runs down the Atlantic coast. Santiago is linked to the Chilean Lake district by the paved toll road, the **Pan-American Highway** (or Panamericana), marked on maps as Ruta 5, which runs all the way from the Peruvian frontier south to Puerto Montt. The **Carretera Austral**, a mostly *ripio* (gravel) road marked on maps as Ruta 7, runs south of Puerto Montt, punctuated by three ferry crossings as far as Villa O'Higgins, from where the southbound boat does not carry cars. There is an excellent paved road between Punta Arenas and Puerto Natales from where there are two *ripio* roads to Torres del Paine.

Generally, main roads are in good condition but on some *ripio* roads, particularly south of Puerto Montt, a high-clearance, 4WD vehicle is required, as road surfaces can degenerate to earth (*tierra*). Most roads in Patagonia are single lane in each direction. There's little traffic and service stations for fuel, toilets, water and food are much further apart than in Europe and the US, so always carry water and spare fuel and keep the tank full. Safety belts are supposed to be worn, if fitted.

Car hire Car hire is slightly more expensive in Chile than in Argentina. There are few hire cars available outside the main tourist centres in either country, although small towns will have cheaper deals. Hiring a car from one place and dropping it off in another is rarely practical since very high penalties are charged. The multinational companies (**Hertz**, **Avis**) are represented all over Patagonia but local companies may be cheaper and usually just as reliable. You must be 25 or over in Argentina and 22 or over in Chile to hire a car; a national driver's licence should be sufficient. Vehicles may be rented by the day, the week or the month, with or without unlimited mileage. Rates quoted should include insurance and VAT but always check first. Note that the insurance excess, which you'll have to pay if there's an accident, can be extremely expensive. Check the vehicle carefully with the hire company for scratches and cracks in the windscreen before you set off, so that you won't be blamed for them on your return. Hire companies will take a print of your credit card as their guarantee instead of a deposit but are honourable about not using it for extra charges. Ensure that the hire company gives you the vehicle's ownership papers, which have to be shown at police and military checks.

Fuel Petrol (known as *nafta* in Argentina, *petróleo* in Chile) becomes more expensive in Chile the further south you go, but in Argentine Patagonia, fuel prices are a third lower than in the rest of the country. Diesel (*gasoil* in Argentina, *bencina* in Chile) is available in both countries and is much cheaper than petrol. Cars in Argentina are increasingly converting to gas GNC (*gas natural comprimido*), which is about 25% the cost of petrol. However, you will not be able to hire a GNC car outside Buenos Aires and fuel stations offering GNC are very limited in Patagonia. What's more, if you're taking a gas-run vehicle from Argentina into Chile, check that it will run on Chilean gas; there is a difference.

Crossing between Argentine and Chilean Patagonia

The main routes between Argentine and Chilean Patagonia are by boat and bus between Bariloche and Puerto Montt in the Lake District; by road from El Calafate to Puerto Natales and Torres del Paine or by road and ferry from El Calafate via Río Gallegos to Tierra del Fuego. There are many other crossings (some little more than a police post), which are detailed throughout the guide. For some crossings, prior permission must be obtained from the authorities. Note that passes across the Andes may be blocked by snow from April onwards. See also Visas and immigration, page 16.

→ Crossing the border is not a lengthy procedure unless you're on a bus, when each individual is checked. It is your responsibility to ensure that your passport is stamped in and out when you cross borders. Do not lose your tourist card; replacing one can be inconvenient and costly. Immigration and customs officials are generally friendly, helpful and efficient, however, the police at Chilean control points a little further into the country can be extremely bureaucratic.

→ Tourist card holders returning across a land border to Argentina will be given a further 90 days in the country. Visa holders should check regulations with the Chilean/Argentine embassies.

→ Fruit, vegetables, meat, flowers and milk products may not be imported into Chile; these will be confiscated at all borders. Searches are thorough.

→ There are often no exchange facilities at the border so make sure you carry small amounts of both currencies. Remember to change your watch if crossing the border between ear y March and September/October.

Crossing the border Obtain an authorization form from the hire company. This is exchanged at the outgoing border control for another form, one part of which is surrendered on each side of the border. If you plan to leave more than once you will need to photocopy the authorization. Make sure the number plate is etched on the car windows and ensure that the hire company gives you the vehicle's ownership papers, which have to be shown at police and military checks. At some crossings, you must pay for the car's tyres to be sprayed with pesticides.

Useful contacts

Automóvil Club Argentino (ACA), Av Libertador Gen San Martín 1850, Buenos Aires, T011-4808 4000, www.aca.org.ar. This motoring association has hotels, *hosterías* and campsites as well as a useful route service.

Automóvil Club de Chile, Av Andrés Bello 1863, Santiago, T02-431-1117 (calling from Chile) www.automovilclub.cl. Car-hire agency with discounts for members or affiliates. Also provides road maps.

Hitchhiking This is relatively easy and safe (although you should always exercise caution) and often involves an exhilarating ride in the back of a pickup truck. However, traffic is sparse in the south, and roads in places like Tierra del Fuego rarely see more than a few vehicles per day.

Taxis, colectivos and remises Taxis usually have meters and can either be hailed in the street or booked in advance, although they tend to be more expensive when booked from a hotel. Surcharges are applied late at night and at weekends. Agree fares beforehand for long journeys out of city centre or for special excursions; also compare prices among several drivers.

Collective taxis (*colectivos* in Chile, *remise* in Argentina) operate on fixed routes (identified by numbers and destinations) and are a good way of getting around cities. They are usually flagged down on the street corner, but make sure you have small notes and coins to pay the driver. In Chile, *colectivos* also operate on some inter-urban routes, leaving from a set point when full; they compete favourably with buses for speed but not for comfort.

Sea
Ferries In the south of Chile, maritime transport is very important. The main transporter/car-ferry operators are Naviera Austral, Transmarchilay and Navimag. **Puerto Montt** is the hub for boat services south, with regular sailings to Chiloé, Chaitén, Puerto Chacabuco, Puerto Natales (one a week, year round) and the San Rafael glacier. **Punta Arenas** is the departure point for ferry services to Porvenir and Puerto Williams on Tierra del Fuego as well as the Crucero Australis service to Ushuaia. Reservations are essential for the ferries in high summer. Details of all routes are given under the relevant chapters.

Where to stay in Patagonia

Tourist destinations in Patagonia have a good range of hotels and *hosterías*, although on the Chilean side, there is good-value budget accommodation and some relatively high-end hotels, but not much choice in between. **Hosterías** have fewer than 20 rooms; rather than being lower quality, they are often family-run and can be very good value in more remote areas. **Residenciales** and **hospedajes** tend to provide simpler accommodation, often with full board offered. **Hostales** traditionally offer dorm beds but most also have double rooms for couples and may also offer services geared specifically towards foreign backpackers, such as internet access, tours, bicycle hire, etc. **Cabañas** are more or less well-equipped self-catering cottages, cabins or apartments, often in superb locations. They're very popular among Chilean and Argentine holidaymakers and are a great option if you have your own transport and are travelling in a small group. Camping is popular and there are many superbly situated sites with good facilities, although official Chilean campsites can be surprisingly expensive, with no reductions for single travellers or couples. There are also **refugios** (refuges) for walkers in national parks and reserves; standards of comfort and facilities vary hugely. Camping wild is generally safe, even in remote areas, but always consult *guardaparques* (park rangers) before pitching your tent in a national park.

Accommodation in Argentina is excellent value for visitors from Western countries, while accommodation in Chile is just a little more expensive. Prices also tend to be higher in Santiago and the further south you go from Puerto Montt. However, single travellers do not come off too badly in southern Chile, as many *hospedajes* charge per person (although you may have to share your room). The Chilean government waives the VAT charge (IVA 19%) for bills paid in dollars (cash or traveller's cheques) at designated high-end hotels, but some establishments may get round this apparent discount by offering you a low dollar exchange rate. Prices often rise in high season (*temporada alta*), especially during January and February, but off-season you can often bargain for a discount (*descuento*) if you are staying

Price codes

Where to stay

$$$$	over US$150	**$$$**	US$66-151
$$	US$30-65	**$**	under US$30

Prices are for a double room in high season, including taxes.

Restaurants

$$$	over US$12	**$$**	US$7-12	**$**	US$6 and under

Prices are for a two-course meal for one person, excluding drinks or service charge.

for two or more days. The ski resorts are more expensive during the winter school holidays. During public holidays or high season you should always book ahead. Few places accept credit cards. In both countries you should establish clearly in advance what is included in the price before booking. For further information on accommodation, see: www.interpatagonia.com, www.backpackerschile.com and www.i-escape.com.

Estancias

Estancias are the huge sheep and cattle ranches found all over Patagonia, and many of them now welcome paying guests. They offer a marvellous way to see remote landscapes and enjoy horse riding and other activities, as well as providing an authentic experience of rural Argentine life.

You'll need to stay at least two or three nights to make the most of an estancia, as they are often off the beaten track. Hire a car, or arrange with your hosts to be picked up in the nearest town. Estancias can be more expensive than hotels, but they offer a unique experience and, once you add the activities, meals and wine, are often good value.

Estancias vary enormously in style and activities: **Helsingfors** is a giant sheep farm close to glaciers; **Viamonte** and **Harberton** on Tierra del Fuego are infused with history; while on the mainland, **Monte Dinero** has a colony of Magellanic penguins on its doorstep.

Food and drink in Patagonia

Buffet-style 'American breakfasts' are served in international hotels but elsewhere, breakfast (*desayuno*) is a very simple affair. Lunch (*almuerzo*) is eaten any time from 1300 to 1530 and is followed, in Argentina (but not Buenos Aires), by a siesta. At around 1700, many Argentines go to a *confitería* for *merienda* (tea, sandwiches and cakes), while Chileans have a snack meal known as *onces* (literally elevenses). Restaurants open for *cena* (dinner) at about 2000 in Chile but rarely before 2100 in Argentina, where most people don't eat until 2230 or later. Many restaurants in Chile serve a cheaper fixed-price meal at lunch time (US$3.50-5), called *la colación* or *el menú*. In Argentina this is known as *el menú fijo*. Those on a tight budget should also try *tenedor libre* (free fork) restaurants, where you can eat all you want for a fixed price. Some hotels will offer a packed lunch to take on hikes; ask the night before.

Food and drink

In the last few years Argentina has become known for its fresh and sophisticated cuisine; especially salmon and wild game from Patagonia. In general, the meat is legendary. The classic meal is the *asado* – beef or lamb (in Patagonia) cooked over an open fire. In rural areas, a whole lamb is splayed out on a cross-shaped stick at an angle over the fire. *Parrilla* restaurants, found all over Argentina, grill cuts of meat in much the same way; they can be ordered as individual dishes or as *parrillada* (basically a mixed grill). Other food to try includes salmon in Patagonia, wild boar in Bariloche and even guanaco. Italian immigration has left a legacy of pizza, *pasta casera* (home-made pasta) and *ñoquis* (gnocchi). Perhaps the most outstanding ingredient in Chilean cuisine is the seafood. Some of the best is to be had at Angelmo (Puerto Montt). The most popular fish are *merluza* (a species of hake, better the further south it is fished), *congrio* (ling), *corvina* (bass – often served marinated in lemon juice as *ceviche*), *reineta* (a type of bream), *lenguado* (sole), *salmon* and *albacora* (sword fish). There is an almost bewildering array of unusual shellfish, particularly *erizos, machas, picorocos* and *locos*. The local *centolla* (king crab) is also exquisite.

Both Argentine and Chilean wines are excellent, and even the cheapest varieties are very drinkable. Also try the home-brewed beer around El Bolsón in Argentina. Cider (*chicha de manzana*) is popular in southern Chile. The most famous spirit in Chile is *pisco*, made with grapes and usually drunk with lemon or lime juice as *pisco sour*, or mixed with Coca Cola or Sprite. The great Argentine drink (also widely drunk in Chilean Patagonia) is *mate* (pronounced mattay), an important social convention. Dried yerba leaves, similar to tea, are placed in a hollowed-out gourd into which hot water (not boiling) is poured, and the resulting infusion is drunk through a metal straw with a filter at the bottom. The cup is filled with water for each person in the group, who then drinks in turn. If offered, give it a go, but be prepared for the bitter taste; you can add a little sugar to make it more palatable. The experience of sharing a *mate* is a great way to make friends and transcends social boundaries.

National parks and natural phenomena

The snow-capped mountains, sheer cliffs and deep valleys of Patagonia are home to stunning national parks and incredible natural wonders. There is an extensive network of reserves and protected areas, the most important of which are designated national parks (additional areas are designated as natural monuments and natural reserves). From glaciers and waterfalls to fjords and ancient land marks, Patagonia is a great place to enjoy nature in all its fabulous forms.

Petrified forests

Some 130 million years ago during the Jurassic period, parts of southern Patagonia were covered in forests of giant *araucarias* (a version of today's monkey puzzle trees), and the climate was moist and stable. Then, at the beginning of the Cretaceous period, intense volcanic activity resulted in these forests being buried in ash – a natural preservative. The remains of these petrified forests can be seen today in two areas of Argentine Patagonia: Monumento Nacional Bosques Petrificados (halfway between Caleta Olivia in the north and San Julián in the south, see page 32) and Bosque Petrificado José Ormachea (Saramiento, see also page 32). Lying, strewn along the ground are large tree trunks which look like wood, but are actually stone.

Patagonian national parks

Patagonia has an extensive network of reserves and protected areas, the most important of which are designated national parks (PN). Additional areas have been designated as natural monuments (MN) and natural reserves (RN).

Argentina The main office of the Administración de Parques Nacionales is at Santa Fe 680, near the Plaza San Martín in central Buenos Aires T011-4311 0303, www.parquesnacionales.gov.ar. Most parks have *guardaparque* (ranger) offices at the main entrance, where you can get advice and basic maps. They are usually knowledgeable about wildlife and walks. Parks in the Lake District are particularly well set up for trekking, with signed trails, *refugios* and campsites.

Chile All reserves and national parks in Chile are managed by CONAF (Corporación Nacional Forestal), Avenida Bulnes 285, 1st floor, Santiago, T/F02-697-2273, www.conaf.cl. It maintains an office in each region of the country and kiosks in some natural areas. Most of the parks have public access; details are given in the text. Camping areas are usually clearly designated, wild camping is discouraged and frequently banned.

Southern Patagonian Ice Field

With an area of over 16,800 km (of which 14,200 km belongs to Chile and 2600 km to Argentina) and extending 350 km, the Southern Patagonian Ice Field is the third biggest extension of continental ice after Antarctica and Greenland. The ice field feeds many of Patagonia's glaciers such as Upsala, Viedma, Bruggen, Grey and the famous Perito Moreno (the world's only advancing and receding glacier), and is home to several volcanoes that lie undisturbed under the ice. Spread over three national parks, this enormous ice field is one of two remnants of the Patagonian Ice Sheet, which was a narrow sheet of ice that covered southern Chile during the last ice age. The other remnant is the much smaller Northern Patagonian Ice Field found within the borders of Laguna San Rafael National Park.

Volcanoes

Patagonia marks the end of the so-called Pacific ring of fire and is home to over two dozen active volcanoes running in a chain along the west of the Andes. Volcán Chaitén, little known and generally thought to be extinct, roared into life in 2008 and again in 2009, drowning the nearby village of Chaitén under a muddy mix of ash and water. In 2011 government plans were afoot to rebuild Chaitén the northern part of the old town. Make enquiries before going to this area.

Hot springs

The western edge of South America is geologically very active. The same tectonic forces that created the Andes and gave Chile so many volcanoes and the occasional destructive earthquake, is also responsible for the abundance of natural hot springs.

Many people swear by the medicinal properties of the springs due to their temperature and high mineral content, and every year Chileans flock from the capital to 'take the waters'. They may or may not be a cure for rheumatism, but what is certain is that there is nothing better after an arduous day's Patagon an trekking than a long soak in a thermal bath.

Essentials A-Z

Accident and emergency

Argentina: Ambulance T107, Coastguard T101, Fire service T100, Police T101, Air Rescue Service T101.

Chile: Ambulance T131, Coastguard T138, Fire service T132, Police T133, Air Rescue Service T138.

Contact the relevant emergency service and your embassy. Make sure you obtain police/medical reports required for insurance claims.

Electricity

220 volts AC. **Chile** has 2- or 3-round-pin European-style plugs. **Argentina** has European-style plugs in old buildings, Australian 3-pin flat-type in the new. Bring a universal adaptor, as these are not readily available.

Embassies and consulates

For all Argentine and Chilean embassies abroad and for all foreign embassies in Argentina and Chile, see http://embassy.goabroad.com.

Health

No vaccinations are demanded by immigration officials in Chile or Argentina, but you would do well to be vaccinated against typhoid, polio, hepatitis A and tetanus. Children should, of course, also be up-to-date with any immunization programmes in their country of origin. See your GP or travel clinic at least 6 weeks before departure for general advice on travel risks and vaccinations. Try contacting a specialist travel clinic if your own doctor is unfamiliar with health in the region. Make sure you have sufficient medical travel insurance, get a dental check, know your blood group and, if you suffer a long-term condition such as diabetes or epilepsy, obtain a Medic Alert bracelet/necklace (www.mediband.com.au).

Health risks

Temperate regions of South America, such as Patagonia, present far fewer health risks than tropical areas to the north. However, travellers should take precautions against: **diarrhoea/intestinal upset**; **hanta virus** (carried by rodents and causing a flu-like illness); **hepatitis A**; **hypothermia**; **marea roja** (red tide); **rabies**; **sexually transmitted diseases**; **sun burn** (a real risk in the far south due to depleted ozone); and **ticks.**

Further information

www.cdc.gov US government site that gives excellent advice on travel health and details of disease outbreaks.

www.fco.gov.uk British Foreign and Commonwealth Office travel site has useful information on the country, people, climate and a list of UK embassies/consulates.

www.fitfortravel.scot.nhs.uk A-Z of vaccine/health advice for each country.

Language

Although English is understood in many major hotels, tour agencies and airline offices (especially in Buenos Aires and Santiago), travellers are advised to learn some Spanish before setting out. Argentines and Chileans are welcoming, and are very likely to strike up conversation on a bus, in a shop or a queue for the cinema. They're also incredibly hospitable (even more so away from the capital cities), and may invite you for dinner, to stay or to travel with them, and your attempts to speak Spanish will be enormously appreciated. Spanish classes are available at low cost in a number of centres in Chile and Argentina.

Large cities all offer Spanish classes, see individual chapters for recommendations.

Money

Argentina → £1 = Arg $7.15; €1 = Arg $5.63;
US$1 = Arg $4.57; Ch $1000 = Arg $9.48 (Aug 2012).
The unit of currency is the peso ($) = 100
centavos. Peso notes in circulation are 2, 5,
10, 20, 50 and 100. Coins in circulation are
1, 5, 10, 25 and 50 centavos and 1 peso.

Chile → £1 = Ch $754; €1 = Ch $594;
US$1 = Ch $482; Arg $1 = Ch $105 (Aug 2012).
US dollar bills are also widely accepted.
The unit is also the peso ($). Peso notes in
circulation are 1000, 2000, 5000, 10,000
and 20,000; coins come in denominations
of 1, 5, 10, 50, 100 and 500.

ATMs and credit cards

In general, the easiest way to get cash while in
Patagonia is to use an international credit or
debit card at an ATM (cajero automático). These
can be found in every town or city.

Argentina Visa, MasterCard, American
Express and Diners Club cards are all widely
accepted in the major cities and provincial
capitals, though less so outside these. There
is a high surcharge on credit card transactions
in many establishments; many hotels offer
reductions for cash.

Chile The easiest way to obtain cash is by
using ATMs which operate under the sign
Redbanc (www.redbanc.cl, for a full list); they
take **Cirrus** (MasterCard), **Maestro** and **Plus**
(**Visa**) and permit transactions up to 200,000
pesos chilenos per day. Instructions are
available in English. Note, though, that ATMs
in Chile charge 4000 pesos commission and
1800 pesos fees (US$12 in total) for each
transaction. This charge is not made in ATMs
of **BancoEstado** (Banco del Estado) or
Servi-Estado in **Líder** supermarkets. Note also
that **Banco del Estado Redbanc** ATMs take
only MasterCard. Visa and MasterCard are
common in Chile. American Express and
Diners Club are less useful.

Changing money

Most major towns in both countries have
bureaux de change (casas de cambio). They
are often quicker to use than banks but may not
have the best rates, so shop around. US dollars
(US$) and euro (€) are easier to change than
other currencies but will only be accepted if in
good condition. Travellers to rural areas of Chile
should carry supplies of small denomination
notes, as larger notes are difficult to change.
Traveller's cheques (TCs) are not very
convenient for travel in Patagonia. The
exchange rate is often lower than for cash
and the commission can be very high.

Cost of travelling

Argentina You can find comfortable
accommodation with a private bathroom
and breakfast for around US$50 for 2 people,
while a good dinner in the average restaurant
will be around US$10-15 pp. Prices are
cheaper away from the main touristy areas:
El Calafate and Ushuaia can be particularly
pricey. For travellers on a budget, hostels
usually cost between US$10-20 pp in a
shared dorm. A cheap breakfast costs US$4
and set meals at lunchtime about US$7. Fares
on long-distance buses increase annually and
very long journeys are quite expensive. Even
so it's worth splashing out an extra 20% for
coche cama service on overnight journeys.
Domestic flight prices were raised by 20% in
February 2012. The average cost of internet
use is US$0.50-2 per hr.

Chile The average cost for a traveller on an
economical budget is about US$40-45 per day
for food, accommodation and land trans-
portation (more for flights, tours, car hire, etc).
Breakfast in hotels, if not included in the price,
is US$2.50-4 (instant coffee, roll with ham or
cheese, and jam). Alojamiento in private houses
and hostels (bed, breakfast and often use of
kitchen) starts at about US$12. Internet costs
US$0.60-1 per hr. Southern Chile is much more
expensive between 15 Dec and 15 Mar.

Safety

Buenos Aires is much safer than most Latin American cities, but petty crime can be a problem in busy tourist areas in Buenos Aires, especially La Boca and Retiro. Travelling in Patagonia itself is very safe indeed. Chile is generally a safe country to visit but, like all major cities, Santiago does have crime problems. Elsewhere, the main threats to your safety are most likely to come from natural hazards and adventure activities than from crime. Don't hike alone in remote areas and always register with *guardaparques* (rangers) before you set off.

Time

Argentina is 3 hrs behind GMT. Chile is 4 hrs behind early Mar to Sep/Oct and 3 hrs behind mid-Sep/Oct to early Mar.

Tourist information
Argentina

Tourism authorities in Argentina are generally better equipped than their Chilean counterparts. The major centres of Puerto Madryn, El Calafate and Ushuaia all offer good tourist resources. Staff in these popular tourist areas usually speak some English and opening hours are typically 0800-2000 in summer although they may close at weekends or during low season. Provincial websites, with information on sights and accommodation, can be accessed via www.turismo.gov.ar.

Chile

The national secretariat of tourism, **Sernatur** (www.sernatur.cl) has offices in Puerto Montt, Ancud, Coyhaique, Punta Arenas and Puerto Natales. These can provide town maps, leaflets and other useful information, otherwise contact head office in Santiago. Other towns have municipal tourist offices.

Visas and immigration

Visa and immigration regulations change frequently so always check with the Argentine and Chilean embassies before you travel. Keep photocopies of essential documents and some additional passport-sized photographs, and always have a photocopy of your passport with you.

Argentina

Visitors from neighbouring countries only need to provide their ID card to enter Argentina. Citizens of the UK, Western Europe, USA, Australia, New Zealand and South Africa (among other countries) require a **passport**, valid for at least 6 months, and a **tourist card**, which is given to you on the plane before you land. This allows you to stay for a period of 90 days, and can be renewed for another 90 days (US$70)at the **Dirección Nacional de Migraciones** at Av Antártida Argentina 1355, Buenos Aires, T011-4317 0234 (Mon-Fri 0800-1400) or any other office (www.migraciones.gov.ar). No renewals are given after the expiry date. Other foreign nationals should consult with the Argentine embassy in their home country about visa requirements.

Chile

Carry your passport (or at least a photocopy) at all times; it is illegal not to have ID handy and thorough searches are not unknown. Citizens of the UK, Western Europe, USA, Canada, Australia, New Zealand and South Africa require only a **passport**, valid for at least 6 months, and a **tourist card**, which is handed out at major border crossings and at Chilean airports. This allows visitors to stay for 90 days and must be surrendered on departure from Chile. Other foreign nationals should consult with the Chilean embassy in their home country about visa requirements. After 90 days the tourist card must either be renewed by leaving and re-entering the country or extended (US$100) at the **Departamento del Extranjería** in Santiago or (preferably) from any local government office (*Gobernación*), where the procedure is slightly less time-consuming.

For the latest information, see www.minrel.cl.

Contents

Footprint features

Argentine Patagonia

Patagonia is the vast, windy, mostly treeless plateau covering all of southern Argentina south of the Río Colorado. The Atlantic coast is rich in marine life; penguins, whales and seals can all be seen around Puerto Madryn. The far south offers spectacular scenery in the Parque Nacional Los Glaciares, with the mighty Moreno and Upsala glaciers, as well as challenging trekking around Mount Fitz Roy. The contrasts are extreme: thousands of prehistoric handprints can be found in the Cueva de las Manos, but in most of Patagonia there's less than one person to each square kilometre; far from the densely wooded Andes, there are petrified forests in the deserts; and the legacy of brave early pioneers is the over-abundance of tea and cakes served up by Argentina's Welsh community in the Chubut valley.

Patagonia's appeal lies in its emptiness. Vegetation is sparse, since a relentless dry wind blows continually from the west, raising a haze of dust in summer, which can turn to mud in winter. Rainfall is high only in the foothills of the Andes, where dense virgin beech forests run from Neuquén to Tierra del Fuego. During a brief period in spring, after the snow melt, there is grass on the plateau, but in the desert-like expanses of eastern Patagonia, water can be pumped only in the deep crevices which intersect the land from west to east. This is where the great sheep estancias lie, sheltered from the wind. There is little agriculture except in the north, in the valleys of the Colorado and Negro rivers, where alfalfa is grown and cattle are raised. Centres of population are tiny and most of the towns are small ports on the Atlantic coast. Only Comodoro Rivadavia has a population over 100,000, thanks to its oil industry. Patagonia has attracted many generations of people getting away from it all, from Welsh religious pioneers to Butch Cassidy and the Sundance Kid, and tourism is an increasingly important source of income.

Arriving in Patagonia

Getting there

Air There are daily flights from Buenos Aires to Viedma, Trelew, Comodoro Rivadavia, Río Gallegos, El Calafate's airport, Lago Argentino, and Ushuaia. It is vital that you book these flights well ahead in the summer (December to February) and the winter ski season for Ushuaia (July and August). **Aerolíneas Argentinas** (AR) and **LADE** (contact details on page 21) fly these routes and flights get booked up very quickly. At other times of the year, flights can be booked with just a few days' warning. The Chilean airline, **LAN**, flies to Ushuaia from Argentine destinations as well as Punta Arenas (for connections to Puerto Montt and Santiago) in summer.

Flying between Patagonian towns is complicated without flying all the way back to Buenos Aires, since there are only weekly flights with **LADE**, whose tickets must be booked in advance from the flight's departure point. The baggage allowance is 15 kg. Flights are often heavily booked, but check again on the day of the flight even if it is sold out. Overnight buses may be more convenient.

Road The principal roads in Patagonia are the Ruta 3, which runs down the Atlantic coast, and the Ruta 40 on the west. One of Argentina's main arteries, Ruta 3 runs from Buenos Aires to Ushuaia, interrupted by the car ferry crossing through Chilean territory across the Magellan Strait to Tierra del Fuego. It is paved in Argentine territory, but sections on Chilean Tierra del Fuego (Cerro Sombrero to San Sebastián) are *ripio*. Regular buses run along the whole stretch, more frequently between October and April, and there are towns with services and accommodation every few hundred kilometres. Ruta 40, however, is a wide unpaved *ripio* track which zigzags across the moors from Zapala to Lago Argentino, near El Calafate, ending at Cabo Vírgenes. It's by far the more interesting road, lonely and bleak, offering fine views of the Andes and plenty of wildlife as well as giving access to many National Parks. A number of companies run daily tourist bus services in summer between Los Antiguos and El Chaltén. The east–west road across Patagonia, from south of Esquel in the Lake District to Comodoro Rivadavia, is paved, and there's a good paved highway running from Bariloche through Neuquén to San Antonio Oeste.

Many of the roads in southern Argentina are *ripio* – gravelled – limiting maximum speeds to 60 km per hour, or less where surfaces are poor, very hard on low-clearance vehicles. Strong winds can also be a hazard. Windscreen and headlight protection is a good idea (expensive to buy, but can be improvised with wire mesh for windscreen, strips cut from plastic bottles for lights). There are cattle grids (*guardaganados*), even on main highways, usually signposted; cross them very slowly. Always carry plenty of fuel, as service stations may be as much as 300 km apart and as a precaution in case of a breakdown, carry warm clothing and make sure your car has anti-freeze. Petrol prices in Chubut, Santa Cruz and Tierra del Fuego provinces are 40% cheaper than in the rest of the country (10-15% for diesel).

In summer hotel prices are very high, especially in El Calafate and El Chaltén. From November onwards you must reserve hotels a week or more in advance. Camping is increasingly popular and estancias may be hospitable to travellers who are stuck for a bed. Many estancias, especially in Santa Cruz province, offer transport, excursions and food as well as accommodation: see www.estanciasdesantacruz.com and www.interpatagonia.com/estancias. ACA establishments, which charge roughly the same prices all over Argentina, are good value in Patagonia. As very few hotels and restaurants have air conditioning or even fans, it can get uncomfortably hot in January.

Viedma, Carmen de Patagones and around

These two pleasant towns (*Phone code: 02920*) lie on opposite banks of the Río Negro, about 27 km from its mouth and 270 km south of Bahía Blanca. Patagones is older and charming, but most services are in Viedma (*Population: 80,000*), capital of Río Negro Province. A quiet place, its main attraction is the perfect bathing area along the shaded south bank of the river. **El Cóndor** is a beautiful beach 30 km south of Viedma, three buses a day from Viedma in summer, with hotels open January-February, restaurants and shops, free camping on beach 2 km south. And 30 km further southwest is the sealion colony, **Lobería Punta Bermeja**, daily bus in summer from Viedma; hitching easy in summer. **Provincial tourist office** ① *Av Caseros 1425, T422150, www.rionegrotur.gob.ar, Mon-Fri 0700-1400, 1800-2000*. **Municipal tourist office** ① *Av Francisco de Viedma 51, T427171, www.viedma.gov.ar, Mon-Fri 0800-2000, Sat-Sun 1200-1900*. Another office is open at weekends at El Cóndor.

Carmen de Patagones (*Population: 18,190*) was founded in 1779 and many early pioneer buildings remain in the pretty streets winding down to the river. There's a fascinating museum, **Museo Histórico Regional 'Emma Nozzi'** ① *JJ Biedma 64, T462729, daily 0930-1230, 1900-2100, Sun afternoon only*, with artifacts of the indigenous inhabitants, missionaries and gauchos; good guided tours. Helpful **tourist office** ① *Bynon 186, T462054*, is more dynamic than Viedma's. On 7 March the Battle of Patagones (1827) is celebrated in a week-long colourful fiesta of horse displays and fine food. The two towns are linked by two bridges and a four-minute frequent ferry crossing (US$1).

Bahía San Blas is an attractive small resort and renowned shark fishing area, 100 km from Patagones (tourist information at www.bahiasanblas.com); plentiful accommodation. Almost due west and 180 km along the coast, on the Gulf of San Matías, is **San Antonio Oeste** (*Phone code: 02934*), and 17 km south, the popular beach resort, **Las Grutas**. The caves themselves are not really worth visiting; but the water is famously warm. Las Grutas is closed in the winter, but very crowded in the summer; accessible by bus from San Antonio hourly US$2. San Antonio is on the bus routes north to Bahía Blanca and south as far as Río Gallegos and Punta Arenas.

Viedma, Carmen de Patagones and around listings

For hotel and restaurant price codes and other relevant information, see pages 10-12.

🛏 Where to stay

Viedma *p20*
$$$ Nijar, Mitre 490, T422833, www.hotelnijar.com. Most comfortable, smart, modern, good service.

$$$-$$ Austral, 25 de Mayo y Villarino, T422615, viedma@hotelesaustral.com. Modern, with well-equipped if rather old-fashioned rooms, Wi-Fi.

$$ Peumayen, Buenos Aires 334, T425222, www.hotelpeumayen.com.ar. Old-fashioned friendly place on the plaza.

Camping Good municipal site near the river, US$2 pp.

Restaurants

Viedma *p20*

$$ Parrilla Libre, Buenos Aires y Colón. Well-priced *tenedor libre* steaks in a cheerful atmosphere.

Transport

Viedma *p20*

Air Airport 5 km south. LADE (Saavedra 576, T424420, www.lade.com.ar) fly to **Buenos** Aires, **Mar del Plata**, Bahía Blanca, **Comodoro Rivadavia** and other Patagonian destinations.

Bus Terminal in Viedma at Av Pte Ferón y Guido, 15 blocks from plaza: taxi US$2. To **Buenos Aires** 13 hrs, daily, US$89-122, Don Otto and others. To **San Antonio Oeste**, 2½ hrs, several daily, US$9, **Don Otto**. To **Bahía Blanca**, 4 hrs, many daily, US$21-30.

Puerto Madryn and around → *Phone code: 0280. Population 74,000.*

Puerto Madryn is a seaside town 250 km south of San Antonio Oeste. It stands on the wide bay of Golfo Nuevo, the perfect base for the Península Valdés and its extraordinary array of wildlife, just 70 km east. It was the site of the first Welsh landing in 1865 and is named after the Welsh home of the colonist, Jones Parry. Popular for skin diving and the nature reserves, the town's main industries are a huge aluminium plant and fish processing plants. You can often spot whales directly from the coast at the long beach of **Playa El Doradillo**, 16 km northeast (October to December). **EcoCentro** ① *Julio Verne 3784, T445 7470, www.ecocentro.org.ar, daily 1500-1900 (usually closed Tue and Mon Apr, Jun, closed May; open longer in summer, but check website as times change), US$10.* An inspired interactive sea life information centre, art gallery, reading room and café, it is perched on a cliff at the south end of town, with fantastic views of the whole bay. **Museo de Ciencias Naturales y Oceanográfico** ① *Domecq García y J Menéndez, Mon-Fri 0900-1200, 1500-1900, Sat 1430-1900, US$2,* is an informative museum which has displays of local flora and fauna. The **tourist office** ① *Av Roca 223, T445 3504, www.madryn.gov.ar/turismo, Mon-Fri 0700-2300, Sat-Sun 0830-2300,* is extremely helpful.

Around Puerto Madryn

With elephant seal and sea lion colonies at the base of chalky cliffs, breeding grounds for Southern right whales in the sheltered Golfo Nuevo and the Golfo San José, and guanacos, rheas, patagonian hares and armadillos everywhere on land, the area around Puerto Madryn, especially the Península Valdés, is a spectacular region for wildlife. Whales can be seen from June to mid-December, particularly interesting with their young September to October. The sea lion breeding season runs from late December to late January, but visiting is good up to late April. Bull elephant seals begin to claim their territory in the first half of August and the breeding season is late September/early October. Orcas can be seen attacking seals at Punta Norte in February/March. Conservation officials can be found at the main viewpoints, informative but only Spanish spoken. The **EcoCentro** in Puerto Madryn, studies the marine ecosystems. **Punta Loma** ① *0800-1200, 1430-1930; US$6, children US$3 (free with Península Valdés ticket), information and video, many companies offer tours.* This is a sea lion reserve 15 km southeast of Puerto Madryn, best visited at low tide; sea lions can even be seen in Puerto Madryn harbour. See also Puerto Deseado, page 32, and Punta Tombo, page 28.

Península Valdés

ⓘ *Entry US$17 for foreigners, children US$8.50; administration T445 0489, www.peninsulavaldes.org.ar.*

The Península Valdés, near Puerto Madryn, in Chubut province, has an amazing array of wildlife: marine mammals including Southern right whales, penguins and guanacos. There are other penguin colonies on the coast, a fine palaeontological museum in Trelew and villages where Welsh settlers set up home. Several estancias offer excellent hospitality for those who wish to get to know the vastness of this land. The best way to see the wildlife is by car. See Puerto Madryn for car hire. Take your time, roads are all unpaved except the road from Puerto Madryn to Puerto Pirámide. In summer there are several shops, but take sun protection and drinking water.

Puerto Madryn

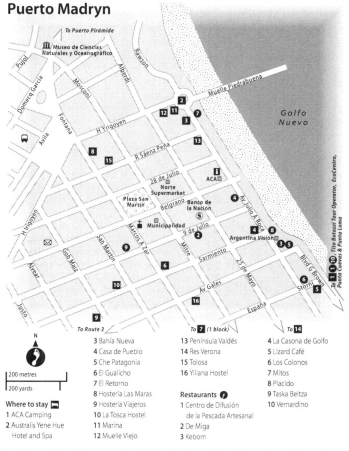

N

200 metres
200 yards

Where to stay 🛏
1 ACA Camping
2 Australis Yene Hue
  Hotel and Spa
3 Bahía Nueva
4 Casa de Pueblo
5 Che Patagonia
6 El Gualicho
7 El Retorno
8 Hostería Las Maras
9 Hostería Viajeros
10 La Tosca Hostel
11 Marina
12 Muelle Viejo
13 Península Valdés
14 Res Verona
15 Tolosa
16 Yiliana Hostel

Restaurants 🍴
1 Centro de Difusión
  de la Pescada Artesanal
2 De Miga
3 Kebom
4 La Casona de Golfo
5 Lizard Café
6 Los Colonos
7 Mitos
8 Placido
9 Taska Beltza
10 Vernardino

The Golfos Nuevo and San José are separated by the Istmo Carlos Ameghino, which leads to Península Valdés, a bleak, but beautiful treeless splay of land. In depressions in the heart of the peninsula are large salt flats; Salina Grande is 42 m below sea level. At the entrance to the peninsula, on the isthmus, there is an interesting Visitors' Centre with wonderful whale skeleton. Five kilometres from the entrance, Isla de los Pájaros can be seen in Golfo San José, though its seabirds can only be viewed through fixed telescopes (at 400 m distance); best time is September to April. The main tourist centre of the Peninsula is **Puerto Pirámide** (*Population: 430*), 107 km east of Puerto Madryn, where boat trips leave to see the whales in season (sailings controlled by Prefectura – Naval Police, according to weather). There is accommodation and eating places here (tourist information, T449 5084, www.puertopiramides.gov.ar).

Punta Norte (176 km) at the north end of the Valdés Peninsula, isn't usually included in tours, but has elephant seals and penguins (September-March) below its high, white cliffs, best seen at low tide, also, occasionally, orcas. There are several reasonably priced restaurants. At **Caleta Valdés**, 45 km south of Punta Norte, you can see huge colonies of elephant seals at close quarters, and there are three marked walks. At **Punta Delgada** (at the south of the peninsula) elephant seals and other wildlife can be seen. The beach on the entire coast is out of bounds; this is strictly enforced.

Puerto Madryn and around listings

For hotel and restaurant price codes and other relevant information, see pages 10-12.

🛏 Where to stay

Puerto Madryn *p21, map p22*
Book ahead in summer, and whale season.
$$$$ Australis Yene Hue Hotel and Spa,
Roca 33, T447 1214, www.australiset.com.ar.
Luxury hotel on the beachfront with a small spa, modern rooms, and nice buffet breakfast. Ask for a room with a view.
$$$$-$$$ Hostería Las Maras, Marcos A Zar 64, T445 3215, www.hosterialas maras.com.ar. Nice modern place under new management, well decorated rooms with large beds and cable TV, a/c, cheaper with fan, Wi-Fi, parking.
$$$$-$$$ Península Valdés, Av Roca 155, T447 1292, www.hotelpeninsula.com.ar. Luxurious sea front hotel with great views. Spa, sauna, gym.
$$$ Bahía Nueva, Av Roca 67, T445 1677, www.bahianueva.com.ar. One of the best sea-front hotels, quite small but comfortable rooms, professional staff, cheaper in low season.

$$$ Marina, Av Roca 7, T445 4915, teokou@ infovia.com.ar. Great value little seafront apartments for up to 5 people, book ahead.
$$ Casa de Pueblo, Av Roca 475, T447 2500, www.madryncasadepueblo.com.ar. Reputed to be the first brothel in town, now a charming seafront chalet hotel with homely atmosphere, good value.
$$ Hostería Viajeros, Gob Maiz 545, T44 56457, www.hostelviajeros.com. With breakfast, rooms for 2, 3 and 4 people, big kitchen/dining room, lawn, TV, helpful.
$$ Muelle Viejo, H Yrigoyen 38, T447 1284, www.muelleviejo.com. Ask for the comfortable modernized rooms in this funny old place. Rooms for 4 are excellent value, kitchen facilities.
$$ Tolosa, Roque Sáenz Peña 253, T447 1850 www.hoteltolosa.com.ar. Extremely comfortable, modern, great breakfasts. Disabled access. Recommended.
$$-$ Res Verona, 25 de Mayo 874, T445 1509, hotel_verona@hotmail.com. With breakfast, also has 3 apartments, excellent value.

$ pp Che Patagonia, Alfonsina Storni 16, T445 5783, www.chepatagoniahostel.com.ar. Good view of the beach (and whales in season), helpful owners, use of kitchen, mixed and single dorms, doubles with shared bath (**$$**), with breakfast, lockers, Wi-Fi, bicycle hire and many other services. A good choice.

$ pp El Gualicho, Marcos A Zar 480, T445 4163, www.elgualicho.com.ar. Best budget option, some double rooms, HI discounts, nicely designed, recently expanded, enthusiastic owner, English-speaking staff, heating, free pick up from bus terminal, Wi-Fi, parrilla, garden, bikes for hire, runs tours with good guides and value. Highly recommended.

$ El Retorno, Bartomolmé Mitre 798, T445 6044, www.elretornohostel.com.ar. 3 blocks from beach, hot water, lockers, cosy common area, rents bikes, free bus terminal pick-up. Double rooms available (**$$**).

$ pp La Tosca Hostel, Sarmiento 437, Chubut, T445 6133, www.latoscahostel.com. Dorms have bathrooms, free pick-up from bus station if you call them, helpful. Also has small but cosy doubles (**$$**).

$ pp Yiliana Hostel, Av Gales 268, T447 5956, www.yilianahostel.com.ar. Family run, dorms and private rooms (**$$** with bath), kitchen, good breakfast, nice patio area, hot showers, laundry arranged, Wi-Fi, bike hire.

Camping ACA, Blvd Brown 3860, 4 km south of town at Punta Cuevas, T445 2952. Open Sep-Apr, hot showers, café, shop, also duplexes for 4-6, no kitchen facilities, shady trees, close to the sea. Closed out of season. Península Valdés p184

Puerto Pirámide

$$$$ Las Restingas, 1a Bajada al Mar, T449 5101, www.lasrestingas.com. Exclusive, sea views, very comfortable, with sophisticated regional restaurant. Good deals available in low season.

$$$ ACA Motel, T449 5004, aca@piramides.net. Welcoming, handy for the beach, with good seafood restaurant (you might spot whales from its terrace), camping. Jan-Feb reserved for ACA members only. There is also an ACA service station (daily) with good café and shop.

$$$ Cabañas en el Mar, T449 5049, www.piramides.net. Comfortable, well-equipped 2- to 6-bed *cabañas* with sea view.

$$$ Del Nómade, Av de las Ballenas s/n, T449 5044, www.ecohosteria.com.ar. Hostería ecológica, uses solar power and water recycling, buffet breakfast, heating, internet, Wi-Fi, café, specializes in wildlife watching, nature and underwater photography, kayaking, adventure sports, courses offered.

$$$ The Paradise, 2a Bajada al Mar, T449 5030, www.hosteriaparadise.com.ar. Large comfortable rooms, suites with jacuzzis, fine seafood restaurant.

$$ La Nube del Angel, 2a Bajada al Mar, T449 5070, soniacuestas@yahoo.com.ar. Open all year, lovely owners, small *cabañas* for 2 -6 people, quiet, 5 mins' walk from the beach.

Camping Municipal campsite by the black-sand beach, T449 5084, hot showers in evening, good, get there early to secure a place. Do not camp on the beach: people have been swept away by the incoming tide.

Estancias

Several, including:

$$$$ Faro Punta Delgada, Punta Delgada, T445 8444, www.puntadelgada.com. Next to a lighthouse, amazing setting, half and full board, excellent food, very helpful. Recommended; book in advance, no credit cards.

$$$$ Rincón Chico, near Punta Delgada, T154 688303 (T447 1733 in Puerto Madryn), www.rinconchico.com. A working sheep farm with luxurious accommodation, 8 rooms, walking and cycling circuits, half and full board available. Recommended.

$$$ La Elvira, Caleta Valdés, near Punta Cantor, T154 698709 (office in Puerto Madryn

T447 4248), www.laelvira.com. Traditional Patagonian dishes and comfortable accommodation (B&B, half and full board available).
$$$ San Lorenzo, on RP3, 20 km southwest of Punta Norte, T445 1427 (contact through **Argentina Visión** in Puerto Madryn, see Tour operators). Great for day excursions to a beautiful stretch of coast to see penguins, fossils, birdwatching and horse treks.

🔊 Restaurants

Puerto Madryn *p21, map p22*
Excellent seafood restaurants mostly charging similar prices, but quality varies. There are also less-touristy takeaways.
$$$ Placido, Av Roca 506, T445 5991, www.placido.com.ar. On the beach, stylish, intimate, excellent service, seafood and vegetarian options, also cheaper pasta dishes.
$$$ Taska Beltza, 9 de Julio 345, T154 668085. Excellent food, chef 'El Negro' cooks superb paella, with Basque influence – book ahead, closed Mon. Highly recommended.
$$ Centro de Difusión de la Pescada Artesanal, Brown, 7th roundabout, no sign, T154 538085. Authentic *cantina*, where the fishermen's families cook meals with their catch, very popular, go early.
$$ Los Colonos, Av Roca y A Storni, T445 8486. Built into the wooden hull of a boat, cosy, *parrilla*, seafood and pastas. Ideal for families, with soft play area.
$$ Vernardino, Blvd Brown 860, T447 4289, www.vernardinoclubdemar.com.ar. One of the nicest restaurants on the beach, serving great seafood and pastas. Good choice for lunch.
$ La Casona de Golfo, Av Roca 349, T445 5027. Good value *tenedor libre parrilla*, seafood, and *helados libre* (as much ice cream as you can eat). Great for families.

Cafés

De Miga, 9 de Julio 160. Cosy local favourite with affordably priced sandwiches and pizzas.
Kebom, Av Roca 542. Popular ice cream place with big soft play area for kids.

Lizard Café, Av Roca y Av Galés, on the seafront. Lively funky place with friendly people. Good for plentiful pizzas or for late-night drinks.
Mitos, 28 de Julio 80. Stylish café with good atmosphere, televised football too. Recommended.

🔺 What to do

Puerto Madryn *p21, map p22*

Diving

Puerto Madryn is a diving centre, with several shipwrecked boats in the Golfo Nuevo. A 1st dive (*bautismo*) for beginners costs about US$66 pp.
Aquatours, Av Roca 550, T445 1954, www.aquatours.com.ar. A variety of options, including PADI courses, good value.
Lobo Larsen, Roca 885, loc 2, T447 0277, www.lobolarsen.com. Friendly company that specializes in diving with the sea lion colony at Punta Lomas.
Puerto Madryn Buceo, Blvd Brown, 3rd roundabout in Balneario Nativo Sur, T154 513997, www.madrynbuceo.com. Courses of all kinds from beginners' dives to a week-long PADI course, around US$190, or US$66 for a day excursion.
Scuba Duba, Blvd Brown 893, T445 2699/445 2633, www.scubaduba.com.ar. Professional and good fun, diving with sealions at Punta Loma, pick-up from hotel, offer a hot drink and warm clothes after the dive, good equipment, instructor Javier A Crespi is very responsible.

Mountain bike hire

From US$10. At **El Gualicho**, see Where to Stay, or **Vernardino**, see Restaurants, above.

Tours

Many agencies do similar 7- and 9-hr tours to the Península Valdés, about US$57 pp, plus US$17 entrance to the Peninsula. They include the interpretation centre, Puerto

Pirámides (the whales boat trip is US$60 extra), Punta Delgada and Caleta Valdés. Shop around to find out how long you'll spend at each place, how big the group is, and if your guide speaks English. On all excursions take binoculars. Most tour companies stay about 1 hr on location. Tours to see the penguins at Punta Tombo and Welsh villages are better from Trelew. Tours do not run after heavy rain in the low season. Recommended for Península Valdés:

Alora Viaggio, Av Roca 27, T445 5106, www.aloraviaggio.com. Helpful company, also has an office at the bus terminal (T445 6563).

Argentina Visión, Av Roca 536, T445 1427, www.argentinavision.com. Also 4WD adventure trips and **estancia** accommodation, English and French spoken.

Chaltén Travel, Av Roca 115 (terminal 25 de Mayo 125), T445 4906, www.chaltentravel.com. Runs a tourist bus service to Perito Moreno on Ruta 40, every other day, for conections north to Bariloche and south to El Chaltén and El Calafate.

Cuyun Co, Av Roca 165, T445 1845, www.cuyunco.com.ar. Offers a friendly, personal service and a huge range of conventional and more imaginative tours: guided walks with biologists, 4WD expeditions, and can arrange estancia accommodation. Bilingual guides. Recommended.

Tito Botazzi, Blvd Brown y Martín Fierro, T447 4110, www.titobottazzi.com, and at Puerto Pirámide (T449 5050). Particularly recommended for small groups and well-informed bilingual guides; very popular for whale watching.

Península Valdés: Puerto Pirámide *p22*
Hydrosport, Primera Bajada,al Mar, T449 5065, hysport@infovia.com.ar. Rents scuba equipment and boats, and organizes land and sea wildlife tours to see whales and dolphins.

Whales Argentina, 1a Bajada al Mar, T449 5015. Recommended for whale watching.

⊖ Transport

Puerto Madryn *p21, map p22*
Air Airport 8 km west; taxi US$12. LADE to **Buenos Aires**, **Bahía Blanca**, **Viedma**, **Trelew**, **Comodoro Rivadavia** and other Patagonian airports. Andes (T445 2355) also flies to Buenos Aires Mon, Wed, Fri. More flights to **Bariloche**, Buenos Aires, and El Calafate from Trelew. Buses to Trelew stop at entrance to airport if asked. Direct bus to Trelew airport, Puma, US$5, leaves 1½ hrs before flight and takes arriving passengers to Puerto Madryn.

Bus Terminal at Av Avila, entre Necochea e Independencia, T445 1789, expanded, with new facilities. To **Buenos Aires**, 18 hrs, several companies, US$110-138. To **Bahía Blanca**, 9½ hrs with **Don Otto** and others, US$56-74. To **Comodoro Rivadavia**, 6 hrs, US$31-38 with **Don Otto** and **Transportadora Patagónica**. To **Río Gallegos**, 18 hrs; US$104-138, 4 companies. To **Trelew**, 1 hr, every hr, US$5 with 28 de Julio, Mar y Valle.

Car hire Expensive, US$60-75 per day, and note large excess for turning car over. Drive slowly on unpaved *ripio* roads; best to hire 4WD! **Budget**, Roca 353, T154 530723, for good value. Madryn, Roca 624, T445 2355. **Localiza** has an office (see Car hire in Planning your trip). **Sigma**, T447 1379, or 154 699465 (24 hrs), www.sigmarentacar.com. Will deliver car to your hotel. **Wild Skies**, Morgan 2274, p 1, Depto 6 B Sur, T154 676233, www.wildskies.com.ar. Efficient service, English spoken, recommended.

Taxi There are taxis outside the bus terminal, T445 2966/447 4177, and on the main plaza.

Península Valdés *p22*
Bus 28 de Julio bus company from Puerto Madryn to Puerto Pirámide, daily at 1000. returns 1800, US$5 each way, 1½ hrs.

Puerto Madryn *p22, map p22*
Airline offices Aerolíneas Argentinas, Foca
427, T445 1998. LADE, Roca 119, T445 1256.

Banks Lots of ATMs at banks. **Medical
services** For emergencies call 107 or
451240. Late-night pharmacy at on
Belgrano y 25 de Mayo.

Trelew and the Chubut Valley → *Phone code: 0280. Population: 90,000.*

Pronounced 'Trel-ay-oo', Trelew is a busy town, with an excellent museum and a shady
plaza, which hosts a small handicraft market at weekends. Visit mid-October to see the
Eisteddfod (Welsh festival of arts). Evidence of Welsh settlement remains only in a few
brick buildings: the 1889 **Capilla Tabernacl**, on Belgrano, between San Martín and 25 de
Mayo, and the **Salón San David**, a 1913 Welsh meeting hall. On the road to Rawson, 3 km
south, is one of the oldest standing Welsh chapels, **Capilla Moriah**, from 1880, with a
simple interior and graves of many original settlers in the cemetery. **Museo
Paleontológico Egidio Feruglio** ⓘ *Fontana 140, T442 0012, www.mef.org.ar. Sep-Mar
daily 0900-2000, otherwise Mon-Fri 1000-1800, Sat-Sun 1000-2000, US$8, full disabled
access and guides for the blind*, is an excellent museum, which presents the origins of life

Trelew

Where to stay
1 Galicia
2 Libertador
3 Rayentray
4 Rivadavia
5 Touring Club

Restaurants
1 Café de mi Ciudad
2 Delikatesse
3 El Quijote
4 El Viejo Molinc
5 La Bodeguita

100 metres
100 yards

and dynamically poised dinosaur skeletons. It has good information in Spanish and free tours in English, German and Italian; also a café and shop. Also has information about Parque Paleontológico Bryn-Gwyn, 8 km from Gaiman (see below). **Museo Regional Pueblo de Luis** ① *Fontana y Lewis Jones 9100, T442 4062, Mon-Fri 0800-2000, Sat-Sun 1400-2000, US$2*. In the old 1889 railway station, it has displays on indigenous societies, failed Spanish attempts at settlement and on Welsh colonization. The **Museo Municipal de Artes Visuales** ① *MMAV, Mitre 350, T443 3774*, is in an attractive wooden building, with exhibitions of local artists. **Tourist office** ① *Mitre 387, T442 0139, www.trelew.gov.ar, Mon-Fri 0800-2000, Sat-Sun 0900-2100, map available*, is on the plaza; also at the airport and bus station. See also **Entretur**, www.trelewpatagonia.gov.ar.

Gaiman and around → *District population: 12,947.*

A small pretty place with old brick houses retaining the Welsh pioneer feel, Gaiman hosts the annual Eisteddfod (Welsh festival of arts) in October. It's renowned for delicious, and excessive Welsh teas and its fascinating tiny museum, **Museo Histórico Regional Galés** ① *Sarmiento y 28 de Julio, T449 1007, US$1, Tue-Sun 1500-1900*, revealing the spartan lives of the idealistic Welsh pioneers. **Geoparque Bryn Gwyn** ① *8 km south of town, T443 2100, www.mef.org.ar, open daily 0900-1900, closed 25 Dec and 1 Jan, US$3, getting there: taxi from Gaiman US$4.50*. Fossil beds 40 million years old are shown on a good guided tour; there is a visitor centre offering try-outs in paleontology fieldwork. **El Desafío** ① *Brown 52, 2 blocks west of plaza, US$2*, is a quaint, if weatherbeaten, theme park comprising dinosaurs made of rubbish. **Tourist office** ① *Belgrano 574, T449 1571, www.gaiman.gov.ar, Mon-Sat 0900-2000, Sun 1100-1800*.

Dolavon, founded in 1919, is a quiet settlement, with a few buildings reminiscent of the Welsh past. The main street, Avenida Roca, runs parallel to the irrigation canal built by the settlers, where willow trees now trail into the water, and there's a Welsh chapel, **Capilla Carmel** at one end. The old **flour mill** ① *Maipú y Roca, T449 2290, Mon-Sun 1100-1900, US$3.50*, dates from 1927 and can be visited. There's **Autoservicio Belgrano** at the far end of San Martin, for food supplies, one tea room, **El Molienda** ① *Maipú 61, US$10*, but nowhere to stay. The municipal campsite, two blocks north of the river, is free, with good facilities.

In the irrigated valley between Dolavon and Gaiman, you'll see more Welsh chapels tucked away among fringes of tall *alamo* (poplar) trees and silver birches (best if you're in your own transport). The **San David chapel** (1917) is a beautifully preserved brick construction, with an elegant bell tower, and sturdy oak-studded door, in a quiet spot surrounded by birches.

Paved Ruta 25 runs from Dolavon west to the upper Chubut Valley, passing near the **Florentino Ameghino dam**, a leafy spot for a picnic. From Ameghino to Tecka on Ruta 40 (south of Trevelin) is one of the most beautiful routes across Patagonia to the Andes, lots of wildlife to see. It goes through **Las Plumas** (mind the bridge if driving), **Los Altares**, which has an ACA motel (**$$**, dep_6076@aca.org.ar), camping, fuel and some shops, and **Paso de Indios**.

South of Trelew

Punta Tombo ① *Park entrance US$8. Tours from Trelew and Puerto Madryn, US$57; 45 mins at the site, café and toilets, usually include a stop at Gaiman. Access from Ruta 1, a ripio road*

Keeping up with the Joneses

On 28 July 1865, 153 Welsh immigrants landed at Puerto Madryn, then a deserted beach deep in *indígena* country. After three weeks they pushed, on foot, across the parched pampa and into the Chubut river valley, where there is flat cultivable land along the riverside for a distance of 80 km upstream. Here, maintained in part by the Argentine government, they settled, but it was three years before they realized the land was barren unless watered. They drew water from the river, which is higher than the surrounding flats, and built a fine system of irrigation canals. The colony, reinforced later by immigrants from Wales and from the US, prospered, but in 1899 a great flood drowned the valley and some of the immigrants left for Canada. The last Welsh contingent arrived in 1911. The object of the colony had been to create a 'Little Wales beyond Wales', and for four generations they kept the Welsh language alive. The language is, however, dying out in the fifth generation. There is an offshoot of the colony of Chubut at Trevelin, at the foot of the Andes nearly 650 km to the west, settled in 1838. It is interesting that this distant land gave to the Welsh language one of its most endearing classics: *Dringo'r Andes* (Climbing the Andes), written by one of the early women settlers.

between Trelew and Camarones. Best visited Sep-Mar. This nature reserve is 125 km south of Trelew, open from September, when huge numbers of Magellanic penguins come here to breed, the largest single penguin colony on the South American subcontinent. Chicks can be seen from mid-November; they take to the water January to February. It's fascinating to see these creatures up close, but to avoid tourist crowds, go in the afternoon. You'll see guanacos, hares and rheas on the way. Another large **penguin colony** ① *all year, US$5* – with lots of other marine life, including whales and orcas – is at Cabo Dos Bahías, easily reached from the town of **Camarones** 275 km north of Comodoro Rivadavia. The Guarda Fauna is 25 km from town.

Some 90 km south of Camarones along the coast is **Bahía Bustamante**, a settlement of seaweed harvesters and sheep ranchers on Golfo San Jorge (180 km north of Comodoro Rivadavia). It is now an award-winning resort with full-board and self-catering accommodation (www.bahia bustamante.com, Wi-Fi, electricity dusk to 2300) and its main attractions are the coastal and steppe landscapes of the Patagonia Austral national park, observing birds, marine and land mammals, hiking and cycling. Horse riding and kayaking are extra. Guides are on hand.

Trelew and the Chubut Valley listings

For hotel and restaurant price codes and other relevant information, see pages 10-12.

🛏 Where to stay

Trelew p27, map p27
$$$ Galicia, 9 de Julio 214, T443 3802, www.hotelgalicia.com.ar. Central, grand entrance, comfortable rooms, excellent value. Recommended.
$$$ La Casona del Río, Chacra 105, Capitán Murga, T443 8343, www.lacasonadelrio.com.ar. Feb-Jul, 5 km from town, pick-up arranged, attractive, family-run B&B with heating, TV, meals available, bicycles,

massage, laundry, tennis and bowls, English spoken.

$$$ Libertador, Rivadavia 31, T442 0220, www.hotellibertadortw.com. Modern hotel, highly recommended for service and comfortable bedrooms and breakfast is included.

$$$ Rayentray, San Martín y Belgrano, T443 4702, www.cadenarayentray.com.ar. Large, modernized, comfortable rooms, professional staff, breakfast included, pool.

$$ Rivadavia, Rivadavia 55, T443 4472, hotelriv@infovia.com.ar. Simple, comfortable rooms with TV, breakfast extra, the cheapest recommendable place.

$$ Touring Club, Fontana 240, T443 3997, www.touringpatagonia.com.ar. Gorgeous 1920s bar, faded elegance, simple rooms, great value, breakfast extra. Open from breakfast to the small hours for sandwiches and drinks. Recommended.

Gaiman *p28*

$$ Hostería Ty'r Haul, Sarmiento 121, T449 1880, www.hosteriatyrhaul.com.ar. Central, in a historic building, rooms are comfortable and well-lit. Recommended.

$$ Posada Los Mimbres, Chacra 211, 6 km west of Gaiman, T449 1299, www.posadalos mimbres.com.ar. Rooms in the old farmhouse or in modern building, good food, very relaxing.

$$ Plas y Coed, Yrigoyen 320, T449 1133, www.plasycoed.com.ar. Marta Rees' delightful tea shop has double and twin rooms in an annex next door, with bath and TV, includes breakfast. Highly recommended.

$$ Ty Gwyn, 9 de Julio 111, T449 1009, tygwyn@cpsarg.com. Neat, comfortable, with TV, above the tea rooms, excellent value.

Camping Los Doce Nogales is an attractive site south of the river at Chacra 202, close to **Ty Te Caerdydd** tea room, T154 518030, with showers. **Municipal site** of the Bomberos (fire brigade), US$2 pp.

Trelew *p27, map p27*

$$ La Bodeguita, Belgrano 374, T443 7777. Delicious pastas and pizzas, with interesting art on the walls, lively atmosphere. Recommended.

$$ El Quijote, 25 de May 90, T443 4564. Recommended *parrilla*, popular with locals.

$$ El Viejo Molino, Gales 250, T442 8019. Open 1130-0030 (closed Mon), best in town, in renovated 1886 flour mill, for Patagonian lamb, pastas, good value set menu with wine included.

$ Delikatesse, Belgrano y San Martin. Best pizzas in town, cheery place, popular with families.

$ Supermercado Anónima, Av Belgrano, 1 block north of Av Colombia, has a good food hall.

$ Supermercado Norte, Soberanía y Belgrano. Cheap takeaway food.

Cafés

Café de mi Ciudad, Belgrano 394. Smart café serving great coffee; read the papers here.

Gaiman *p28*

El Angel, Rivadavia 241. Stylish small restaurant serving excellent food.

La Colonia, on the main street. A good-quality *panadería*.

Siop Bara, Tello y 9 de Julio, sells cakes and ice creams.

Welsh teas

Served from about 1500, US$16, by several tea rooms.

Plas Y Coed (see Where to stay, above). The best, and oldest; Marta Rees is a wonderful raconteur and fabulous cook.

Ty Cymraeg, A Mathews 74. Lovely spot with room for big groups. Sells good cakes.

Ty Gwyn, 9 de Julio 111. Large tea room, more modern than some, welcoming; generous teas.

Ty Nain, Irigoyen 283. The prettiest house and full of history, owned by the charming Mirna Jones (her grandmother was the first woman to be born in Gaiman).

⛰ What to do

Trelew p27, map p27
Agencies run tours to Punta Tombo, US$40, Chubut Valley (half-day), US$50 both as full day US$70. Tours to Península Valdés are best done from Puerto Madryn.
Nieve Mar, Ital a 98, T443 4114, www.nieve martours.com.ar. Punta Tombo and Valdés, bilingual guides (reserve ahead), organized and efficient.
Patagonia Grandes Espacios, Belgrano 338, T443 5161, infopge@speedy.com.ar. Good excursions to Punta Tombo and Gaiman, but also palaeontological trips, staying in *chacras*, whale watching. Recommended.

⊖ Transport

Trelew p27, map p27
Air AR have flights to/from **Buenos Aires**, **Bariloche**, **El Calafate** and **Ushuaia**. LADE flies to Patagonian airports and Buenos Aires once a week. Airport 5 km north of centre; taxis about US$5-6. Local buses to/from Puerto Madryn stop at the airport entrance if asked, turning is 10 mins' walk, US$5; **AR** runs special bus service to connect with its flights.
Bus The terminal is on the east side of Plaza Centenario, T442 0121. **Local**: Mar y Valle and **28 de Julio** both go frequently to

Gaiman, 30 mins; US$2.50, and **Dolavon** 1 hr, US$2.50, to **Puerto Madryn**, 1hr, US$5. To **Puerto Pirámides**, 2½ hrs, US$8, daily, Mar y Valle.
Long distance: Buenos Aires, 19-20 hrs; US$132-172, several companies go daily; to **Comodoro Rivadavia**, 5 hrs, US$28-33, many companies, to **Río Gallegos**, 17 hrs; US$99-131 (with connections to El Calafate, Puerto Natales, Punta Arenas), many companies. To **Esquel**, 9-10 hrs; US$43-56, several companies.
 Bus companies Andesmar, T443 3535; Tramat, T443 5162; El Pingüino, T442 7400; El Cóndor, T443 3748; **28 de Julio/Mar y Valle**, T443 2429; Que Bus, T442 2760; El Ñandú, T442 7499.
Car hire Expensive. Airport desks are staffed only at flight arrival times and cars are snapped up quickly. All have offices in town.

South of Trelew: Camarones p28
Bus Don Otto buses from **Trelew**, Mon and Fri, 2½ hrs, returns same day 1600. There are buses to **Reserva Natural Cabo Dos Bahías** Mon, Wed, Fri 0800 from **Trelew**, El Nañdú, US$8, 2½ hrs, returns same day 1600.

❶ Directory

Trelew p27, map p27
Airline offices Aerolíneas Argentinas, 25 de Mayo 33, T0810-222 86527. **LADE**, Terminal de Omnibus. offices 12 /13, T443 5740. **Banks** Mon-Fri 0830-1300.

Comodoro Rivadavia and inland → *Phone code: 0297. District population: 182,630.*

The largest city in the province of Chubut, 375 km south of Trelew, oil was discovered here in 1907. It looks rather unkempt, reflecting changing fortunes in the oil industry, the history of which is described ① *3 km north, San Lorenzo 250, T455 9558, Tue-Fri 0900-2000, Sat-Sun 1500-2000, getting there: taxi US$4.* at the **Museo del Petroleo** There's a beach at Rada Tilly, 8 km south (buses every 30 minutes); walk along beach at low tide to see sea lions. **Tourist office** ① *Rivadavia 430 y Pellegrini, T445 2376, www.comodoro turismo.gob.ar. Mon-Fri 0900-1400, English spoken; also in bus terminal, daily 0800-2100, very helpful, English spoken.*

Sarmiento ➔ *Phone code: 0297. Population: 10,000.*

If you're keen to explore the petrified forests south of Sarmiento and the Cueva de las Manos near Perito Moreno, take the road to Chile running west from Comodoro Rivadavia. It's 156 km to Colonia Sarmiento (known as Sarmiento), a quiet relaxed place, sitting just south of two large lakes, Musters and Colhué Huapi. This is the best base for seeing the 70 million-year old **petrified forests** of fallen araucaria trees. Most accessible is the **Bosque Petrificado José Ormachea** ① *32 km south of Sarmiento on a ripio road, warden T489 8047, US$5.* Less easy to reach is the bleaker **Víctor Szlapelis petrified forest**, some 40 km further southwest along the same road (follow signposts, road from Sarmiento in good condition). From December to March a combi service runs twice daily: contact Sarmiento tourist office. Taxi Sarmiento to forests, US$20 (three passengers), including one-hour wait. Contact Sr Juan José Valero, the park ranger, for guided tours, Uruguay 43, T0297-489 8407 (see also the Monumento Natural Bosques Petrificados). **Tourist office** ① *Pietrobelli 388, T489 8220, www.coloniasarmiento.gov.ar,* is helpful, has a map of town and arranges taxi to the forests.

Comodoro Rivadavia to Río Gallegos

Caleta Olivia (*Population: 40,000*) lies on the Bahía San Jorge, 74 km south of Comodoro Rivadávia, with hotels (one opposite bus station, good) and a municipal campsite near beach (tourist information Güemes y San Martín, T485 0988). A convenient place to break long bus journeys; see the sound sculptures, **Ciudad Sonora** ① *at Pico Truncado (a few simple hotels, campsite, tourist information T499 2202), daily bus service, 58 km southwest,* where the wind sings through marble and metal structures.

In a bizarre lunar landscape surrounding the Laguna Grande, **Monumento Natural Bosques Petrificados** is the country's largest area of petrified trees. The araucarias, 140 million years old, lie in a desert which was once, astonishingly, a forest. There is a museum and a well-documented 1-km trail that passes the most impressive specimens. No charge but donations accepted; please do not remove 'souvenirs'. Tours from Puerto Deseado with Los Vikingos (address on page 34). Access is by Ruta 49 which branches off 91 km south of Fitz Roy. There are no facilities amnd the nearest **campsite** is at Estancia La Paloma, on Ruta 49, 24 km before the entrance, T0297-444 3503.

Puerto Deseado (*Phone code: 0297; Population: 10,200*) is a pleasant fishing port on the estuary of the Río Deseado, which drains, strangely, into the Lago Buenos Aires in the west. It's a stunning stretch of coastline and the estuary is a wonderful nature reserve, with Magellanic penguins, cormorants, and breeding grounds of the beautiful Commerson's dolphin. **Cabo Blanco**, 72 km north, is the site of the largest fur seal colony in Patagonia, breeding season December to January. **Tourist office** ① *vagón histórico, San Martín 1525, T487 0220, www.puertodeseado.tur.ar.*

The quiet **Puerto San Julián** (*Phone code: 02962; Population: 7150*) is the best place for breaking the 778 km run from Comodoro Rivadavia to Río Gallegos. It has a fascinating history, little of which is visible today. The first mass in Argentina was held here in 1520 after Magellan had executed a member of his mutinous crew. Francis Drake also put in here in 1578, to behead Thomas Doughty, after amiably dining with him. There is much wildlife in the area: red and grey foxes, guanacos, wildcats in the mountains, rheas and an impressive array of marine life in the coastal Reserva San Julián. Recommended zodiac boat trip run by **Excursiones Pinocho** ① *T454600, www.pinochoexcursiones.com.ar,* to see

Magellanic penguins (September-March), cormorants and Commerson's dolphins (best in December). Ceramics are made at the **Escuela de Cerámica**; good handicraft centre at Moreno y San Martín. There is a regional museum at the end of San Martin on the waterfront. **Tourist office** ① *Blvd de Av San Martín al 500, T454396, www.sanjulian.gov.ar and in the bus station.*

Piedrabuena (*Population: 4900*) on Ruta 3 is 125 km south of San Julián on the Río Santa Cruz. On Isla Pavón, south of town on Ruta 3 at the bridge over Río Santa Cruz, is a tourist complex, with popular wooded campsite and wildlife park, T497498, liable to get crowded in good weather. **Hostería Municipal Isla Pavón**, is a four-star catering for anglers of steelhead trout. National trout festival in March; **tourist office** ① *Av G Ibáñez 157 (bus station), T02962-155 73065.* See Transport, page 53, for Las Lengas bus Piedrabuena–El Chaltén bus service. Santa Cruz (turn off 9 km south of Piedrabuena) has the **Museo Regional Carlos Borgialli**, with a range of local exhibits. There is a tourist information centre at Av Piedra Buena y San Martin. T02962-498700. Municipal campsite. Some 24 km further south, a dirt road branches 22 km to **Parque Nacional Monte León** ① *office at Belgrano y 9 de Julio, Puerto de Santa Cruz, T02962-489184, monteleon@apn.gov.ar,* which includes the Isla Monte León, an important breeding area for cormorants and terns, where there is also a penguin colony and sea lions. There are impressive rock formations and wide isolated beaches at low tide. The **Hostería Estancia Monte León** ① *Ruta 3, Km 2399, T011-4621 4780 (Buenos Aires), www.monteleon-patagonia.com,* is a good base for visiting the park (open November to April, four tasteful rooms, **$$$$**, library, living room and small museum).

Comodoro Rivadavia and inland listings

◉ Where to stay

Comodoro Rivadavia *p31*
$$$ Lucania Palazzo, Moreno 676, T449 9300, www.lucania-palazzo.com. Most luxurious business hotel, superb rooms, sea views, good value, huge American breakfast, sauna and gym included. Recommended.
$$ Azul, Sarmiento 724, T446 7539. Breakfast extra, quiet old place with lovely bright rooms, kind, great views from the *confitería*.
$$ Comodoro 9 de Julio 770, T447 7324, www.comodorohotel.com.ar. Buffet breakfast included, pay extra for larger rooms.
$$ Hospedaje Cari Hue, Belgrano 563, T447 2946, www.hospedajecarihue. com.ar. Sweet rooms, with separate bathrooms, very nice owners, breakfast extra. The best budget choice.

$$ Rua Marina, Belgrano 738, T446 8777, ruamarinapatagonia@yahoo.com.ar. With TV and breakfast, another good choice, owners are backpacker-friendly.

Sarmiento *p32*
$$ Chacra Labrador 10 km from Sarmiento, T0297-489 3329, agna@cocpsar.com.ar. Excellent small estancia, breakfast included, other meals extra and available for non-residents, English and Dutch spoken, runs tours to petrified forests at good prices, will collect guests from Sarmiento (same price as taxi).
$ Colón, Perito Moreno 650, T489 4212. One of the better cheap places in town.
$ Hostería Los Lagos, Roca y Alberdi, T489 3046. Good, heating, restaurant.
Camping Club Deportivo Sarmiento, 25 de Mayo y Ruta 20, T489 3101. **Rio Senguer**, Ruta Provincial 24, 1 km from centre, T489 8482.

Comodoro Rivadavia
to Río Gallegos *p32*
Puerto Deseado
$$ Isla Chaffers, San Martín y Mariano Moreno, T487 2246. Modern, central.
$$ Los Acantilados, Pueyrredón y España, T487 2167. Beautifully located, good breakfast.

Puerto San Julián
$$$ Bahía, San Martín 1075, T453144, www.hotelbahiasanjulian.com.ar. Modern, comfortable, good value. Recommended.
$$$ Estancia La María, 150 km northwest of Puerto San Julián, offers transport, lodging, meals, visits to caves with paintings of human hands, guanacos, etc 4000-12,000 years old, less visited than Cueva de las Manos. Contact Fernando Behm in San Julián, Saavedra 1163, T452328.
$$ Municipal Costanera, 25 de Mayo y Urquiza, T452300, www.costanerahotel.com. Very nice, well run, good value, no restaurant.
$$ Sada, San Martín 1112, T452013, www.hotelsada.com.ar. Fine, hot water, on busy main road, poor breakfast.
Camping Good municipal campsite. Magallanes 650 y M Moreno, T452806. US$2 pp plus US$1 for the use of shower, repeatedly recommended, all facilities.

🍽 Restaurants

Comodoro Rivadavia *p32*
$$ Cayo Coco, Rivadavia 102. Bistro with excellent pizzas, good service.
$$ Dionisius, 9 de Julio y Rivadavia. Elegant *parrilla*, set menu US$8.
$$ Peperoni, Rivadavia 481. Cheerful, modern, pastas.
$ La Barca, Belgrano 935. Good *tenedor libre*.
Café El Sol, Av Rivadavia y 25 de Mayo. Good café to hang out in.

Comodoro Rivadavia
to Río Gallegos *p32*
Puerto Deseado
$$ Puerto Cristal, España 1698, T487 0387. Panoramic views of the port, a great place for Patagonian lamb, *parrilla* and seafood.
Puerto San Julián
$$ La Rural, Ameghino y Vieytes. Good, but not before 2100. Also bars and tea rooms.
$$ Sportsman, Mitre y 25 de Mayo. Excellent value.

⛰ What to do

Comodoro Rivadavia
to Río Gallegos *p32*
Puerto Deseado
Darwin Expediciones, España 2601, T156 247554, www.darwin-expeditions.com. Excursions by boat to Ría Deseado reserve and trips to the Monumento Natural Bosques Petrificados.
Los Vikingos, Estrada 1275, T156 245141/487 0020, www.losvikingos.com.ar. Excursions by boat to Ría Deseado reserve and Reserva Provincial Isla Pingüino, bilingual guides, customized tours.

⊖ Transport

Comodoro Rivadavia *p32*
Air Airport, 13 km north. Bus No 6 from bus terminal, hourly (45 mins), US$0.75. Taxi to airport, US$6. To **Buenos Aires**, AR/Austral. LADE flies to all Patagonian destinations once or twice a week, plus **Bariloche**, **El Bolsón** and **Esquel**.
Bus Terminal in centre at Pellegrini 730, T446 7305; has luggage store, *confitería*, toilets, excellent tourist information office 0800-2100, some kiosks. In summer buses usually arrive full; book ahead. Services to **Buenos Aires** 2 daily, 28 hrs, US$135-167. To **Bariloche**, 14½ hrs, US$69-76, Don Otto, T447 0450, **Tramat**. To **Esquel** (paved road) 8 hrs direct with **ETAP**, T447 4841, and Don Otto, US$41-46. To **Río Gallegos**, daily, 10-12 hrs, US$74-86. To **Puerto Madryn**,

US$31-38, and **Trelew**, 3 daily, 4 hrs, US$28-33, several companies. To/from **Sarmiento** and **Caleta Olivia**, see below. To **Puerto Deseado**, Sportman, 2 a day, US$32. To **Coyhaique** (Chile), 12 hrs, **Giobbi** twice a week.

Sarmiento *p32*
Bus 3 daily to/from **Comodoro Rivadavia**, US$12, 2½ hrs. To **Chile** via **Río Mayo**, 0200, twice weekly; seats are scarce in Río Mayo. From Sarmiento you can reach **Esquel** (448 km north along Rutas 20 and 40); overnight buses on Sun stop at Río Mayo, take food for journey.

Comodoro Rivadavia to Río Gallegos *p32*
Caleta Olivia
Bus To **Río Gallegos**, Andesmar, Sportman (overnight) and **El Pingüino**, US$68-78, 9½ hrs. Many buses to/from **Comodoro Rivadavia**, 1 hr, US$9-12, and 2 daily to **Puerto Deseado**, 2½-3 hrs, US$23,

Sportman. To **Perito Moreno** and **Los Antiguos**, 5-6 hrs, US$31-37, **Sportman**, 2 a day.

Puerto Deseado
Air LADE (Don Bosco 1519, T487 2674) flies weekly to **Comodoro Rivadavia**, **El Calafate**, **Río Gallegos** and **Ushuaia**.

Puerto San Julián
Bus Many companies to both **Comodoro Rivadavia**, US$38-44, and **Río Gallegos**, 6 hrs, US$35-40.

ⓘ Directory

Comodoro Rivadavia *p32*
Airline offices Aerolíneas Argentinas, 9 de Julio 870, T444 0050. LADE, Rivadavia 360, T447 0585. **Banks** Many ATMs and major banks along San Martín. Change money at **Thaler**, Mitre 943, Mon-Fri 0900-1300, or at weekends **ETAP** in bus terminal. **Consulates** Chile, Almte Brown 456, entrepiso. of 3, T446 24 4.

Río Gallegos and around → *Phone code: 02966. Population: 75,000.*

The capital of Santa Cruz Province, 232 km south of Piedrabuena, on the estuary of the Río Gallegos, this pleasant open town was founded in 1885 as a centre for the trade in wool and sheepskins, and boasts a few smart shops and some excellent restaurants. The delightful Plaza San Martín, two blocks south of the main street, Avenida Roca, has an interesting collection of trees, many planted by the early pioneers, and a tiny corrugated iron cathedral, with a wood-panelled ceiling in the chancel and stained glass windows. The small **Museo de los Pioneros** ⓘ *Elcano y Alberdi, daily 1000-1900, free*, is worth a visit. Interesting tour given by the English-speaking owner, a descendent of the Scottish pioneers; great photos of the first sheep-farming settlers, who came here in 1884 from the Malvinas/Falkland Islands. **Museo de Arte Eduardo Minichelli** ⓘ *Maipú 13, Mon-Fri 0800-1900, Sat-Sun and holidays 1400-1800 (closed Jan/Feb)*, has work by local artists. **Museo Regional Padre Manuel José Molina** ⓘ *in the Complejo Cultural Santa Cruz, Av Ramón y Cajal 51, Mon-Fri 1000-1800, Sat 1500-2000*, has rather dull rocks and fossils and a couple of dusty dinosaur skeletons. **Museo Malvinas Argentinas** ⓘ *Pasteur 74. Mon and Thu 0800-1300, Tue and Fri 1300-1730, 3rd Sun of month 1530-1830*. More stimulating, it aims to inform visitors, with historical and geographical reasons, why the Malvinas are Argentine. The **provincial tourist office** ⓘ *Roca 863, T422702, http://santacruz patagonia.gob.ar, Mon-Fri 0900-1800*. At Roca y San Martín is the **Carretón Municipal**, an information caravan open till 2100. Helpful, English spoken, has list of estancias, and will phone round hotels for you. At the airport, an information desk operates in high season. Small desk at bus terminal, T442159, open till 2030 daily.

Cabo Vírgenes ① *134 km south of Río Gallegos, US$5*, is where a nature reserve protects the second largest colony of Magellanic penguins in Patagonia. There's an informative self-guided walk to see nests among the *calafate* and *mata verde* bushes. Good to visit from November, when chicks are born, to January. Great views from Cabo Vírgenes lighthouse. *Confitería* close by with snacks and souvenirs. Access from *ripio* Ruta 1, 3½ hours. Tours with tour operators listed below cost US$40. About 13 km north of Cabo Vírgenes is **Estancia Monte Dinero** ① *T428922, www.montedinero.com.ar*, where the English-speaking Fenton family offers accommodation (**$$$** per person), food and excursions (US$90 for a day visit); excellent.

Río Gallegos

Where to stay
1 Apart Hotel Austral
2 Comercio
3 Covadonga
4 Nevada
5 Oviedo
6 París
7 Punta Arenas
8 Santa Cruz
9 Sehuen
10 Sleepers Inn

Restaurants
1 Chino
2 El Club Británico & Café Central
3 El Horreo
4 Laguanacazul
5 Los Long
6 Puesto Molino
7 RoCo

200 metres
200 yards

Río Gallegos and around listings

For hotel and restaurant price codes and other relevant information, see pages 10-12.

🛏 Where to stay

Río Gallegos *p35, map p36*
$$$ Santa Cruz, Roca 701, T420601, http://usuarios.advance.com.ar/htlscruz/index.htm. Good value, spacious rooms with good beds, full buffet breakfast included. Recommended.
$$ Apart Hotel Austral, Roca 1505, T434314, apartaustral@infovia.com.ar. Modern, with bright, sunny rooms, good value, basic kitchen facilities, breakfast US$1.70 extra.
$$ Comercio, Roca 1302, T422458, hotelcomercio@informacionrgl.com.ar. Good value, including breakfast nice design, comfortable, cheap *confitería*.
$$ Covadonga, Roca 1244, T420190, hotelcovadongargl@hotmail.com. Small rooms with TV, attractive old building, breakfast extra.
$$ Nevada, Zapiola 480, T435790. Good budget option, nice simple rooms, cable TV, no breakfast.
$$ París, Roca 1040, T420111. Simple rooms, shared bath, good value, with breakfast.
$$ Punta Arenas, F Sphur 55, T427743. Rooms with shared bath (**$**). Smart, rooms in new wing cost more. **Something Café** attached.
$$ Sehuen, Rawson 160, T425683, www.hotelsehuen.com. Good, cosy, helpful, with breakfast.
$ Oviedo, Libertad 746, T420118. A cheaper budget option, breakfast extra, laundry facilities, café, parking.
$ pp Sleepers Inn, F Sphur 78, T444037, sleepersinn@gmail.com. Simple, clean rooms with one colourful wall, shared bath, warm water, TV on from early till late echoes down corridor. Breakfast is rather DIY and can't use kitchen.

Camping Camping ATSA, Ruta 3, en route to bus terminal, T422310, atsa-polid@hotmail.com. Club Pescazaike, Paraje Guer Aike, Ruta 3, 30 km west, T423442, info@pescazaike.com.ar, also *quincho* and restaurant, and Chacra Daniel, Paraje Río Chico, 3.5 km from town, T423970, ofaustral@ciudad.com.ar, *parrilla* and facilities.

🍴 Restaurants

Río Gallegos *p35, map p36*
$$ El Club Británico, Roca 935, T427320. Good value, excellent steaks, "magic".
$$ El Horreo, Roca 863, next door to Puesto Molino. Delicious lamb dishes and good salads.
$$ Laguanacazul, Sarmiento y Gob Lista, T444114, near the river, looking across Plaza de la República. Patagonian dishes.
$$ Puesto Molino, Roca 862, opposite the tourist office. Inspired by estancia life, excellent pizzas and *parrilla* (US$15 for 2).
$$ RoCo, Roca 1157. Large, smart restaurant, popular, with a varied menu of meat, fish, pasta and other dishes.
$$-$ Los Long, Sarsfield 90. Restaurant and *salón de té*.
$ Chino, 9 de Julio 29. Varied *tenedor libre*.
Café Central, Roca 900 block, next to El Club Británico. Smart and popular.

⛰ What to do

Río Gallegos *p35, map p36*
Macatobiano Turismo, Roca 998, T422466, macatobiano@macatobiano.com. Air tickets and tours to Pingüinero Cabo Vírgenes (see above), all day trip US$40, ½-day trip to Laguna Azul, a beautiful lake in a volcanic crater, US$20, and to Estancia Monte León, as well as tickets to El Calafate and Ushuaia. Recommended.

Río Gallegos *p35, map p36*

Air Airport 10 km from centre. Taxi (*remise*) to/from town US$6-8, see below). Regular flights to/from **Buenos Aires**, **Ushuaia** and **Río Grande** direct, with **AR. LADE** flies to many Patagonian destinations between **Buenos Aires** and **Ushuaia**, including **El Calafate** and **Comodoro Rivadavia**, but not daily. Book as far in advance as possible.

Bus Terminal, T442159, at corner of Ruta 3 and Av Eva Perón, 3 km from centre (small, so can get crowded, left luggage, *confitería*, toilets, kiosk, ATM); taxi to centre US$3.50, bus Nos 1 and 12 from posted stops around town. For all long-distance trips, turn up with ticket 30 mins before departure. Take passport when buying ticket; for buses to Chile some companies give out immigration and customs forms. To **El Calafate**, 4-5 hrs, US$23-27, **Sportman**, and **Taqsa** (T442194, and at airport, www.taqsa.com.ar), US$35 **Marga** *cama* service. To **Comodoro Rivadavia**, Andesmar, **Don Otto/ Transportadora Patagónica**, Sportman, El Pingüino (T442169, also has an office at Estrada 173, where tickets can be bought) and others, 10-12 hrs, US$74-86. For **Bariloche**, **Marga**, daily, 24 hrs, US$144, otherwise change in **Comodoro Rivadavia**.

To **Buenos Aires**, 36 hrs, several daily with El Pingüino, TAC, Andesmar, US$185-234. To **Río Grande** US$79, 9 hrs, Marga, and to **Ushuaia** US$102.

To Chile: **Puerto Natales**, El Pingüino and Bus Sur, 2-3 weekly each, 4½ hrs, US$18. To **Punta Arenas**, El Pingüino, 1300 daily, 5½ hrs, US$20. By car make sure your car papers are in order (go first to tourist office for necessary documents, then to the customs office at the port, at the end of San Martín, very uncomplicated). For road details, see Tierra del Fuego sections in Argentina and Chile.

Car hire Localiza, Sarmiento 245, T436717. Cristina, Libertad 123, T425709. **Hertz** at the airport. Essential to book rental in advance in season.

Taxi Taxi ranks plentiful, rates controlled, *remise* slightly cheaper. Note: *Remise* meters show metres travelled, refer to card for price; taxi meters show cost in pesos.

Río Gallegos *p35, map p36*

Airline offices Aerolíneas Argentinas, San Martín 545, T422020. **LADE**, Fagnano 53, T422316. **Banks** Change TCs here if going to El Calafate, where it is even more difficult. 24-hr ATMs for all major international credit and debit cards all over town. **Cambio El Pingüino**, Zapiola 469, and **Thaler**, San Martín 484. Both will change Chilean pesos as well as US$. **Consulates** Chile, Mariano Moreno 148, T422364. Mon-Fri 0900-1300, 1400-1730.

Ruta 40 to the glaciers

Río Mayo (*Phone code: 02903*; tourist office Avenida Ejército Argentino s/n, T420400, riomayoturistico@yahoo.com.ar; fuel and hotels **$$-$**) is reached by Ruta 22 (paved) which branches southwest 74 km west of Sarmiento. Every November, it holds the **Fiesta Nacional de la Esquila** (national sheep-shearing competition). From Río Mayo, a road continues west 140 km to the Chilean border at Coyhaique Alto for Coyhaique in Chile. **South of Río Mayo** Ruta 40 is unpaved as far as Perito Moreno (124 km, high-clearance advised). There is no public transport and very few other vehicles even in mid-summer. At Km 31 on this road a turning leads west to Lago Blanco, to Chile via Paso Huemules and Balmaceda (border open 0800-2000).

Perito Moreno (*Phone code: 02963; Population: 6000; Altitude: 400 m*), not to be confused with the famous glacier of the same name near El Calafate, nor with nearby Parque Nacional Perito Moreno, is a provincial town with some interesting historical houses and plenty of character, 25 km east of Lago Buenos Aires, the second largest lake in South America. Southwest is Parque Laguna, with varied birdlife and fishing. The town calls itself the 'archaeological capital of Santa Cruz' because of the **Cueva de las Manos** (see below). To see that you'll probably stop off here for at least one night, but if staying longer consider going the extra 56 km west to Los Antiguos (see below), especially if heading for Chile Chico. Two ATMs; traveller's cheques and US$, euros and Chilean pesos can be changed at **Banco Santa Cruz** ① *Av San Martín 1385, T432028.* **Tourist office** ① *Av San Martín y Gendarmería Nacional, T432732, low season 0800-2000, high season 0700-2300,* can advise on tours. Also has information on Patagonian estancias, in English.

Most of Ruta 40 is reinforced but unpaved south of Perito Moreno, but paving is complete for 50 km south of the town and around Bajo Caracoles. 124 km south, a marked road runs 46 km northeast to the famous **Cueva de las Manos** ① *US$13 for foreigners, half-price for locals, under 12 free, compulsory guided tours with rangers who give information 0900-1900.* In a beautiful volcanic canyon is an intriguing series of galleries containing an exceptional assemblage of cave art, executed between 13,000 and 9500 years ago; paintings of human hands and animals in red, orange, black, white and green. It was declared a World Heritage Site in 1999. The best time to visit is early morning or evening. Road difficult after rain. Tour from Perito Moreno (eg with **Zoyen**, Avenida San Martín y Perón) cost US$45

After hours of spectacular emptiness, even tiny **Bajo Caracoles** (*Population: 100*) is a relief: a few houses with an expensive grocery store selling uninspiring empanadas and very expensive fuel. From here Ruta 41 goes 99 km northwest to **Paso Roballos**, continuing to Cochrane in Chile.

Parque Nacional Perito Moreno

① *Free. Park office in Gobernador Gregores, Av San Martín 409, T02962-491477. Accessible only by own transport, Nov-Mar.*
South of Bajo Caracoles, 101 km, is a crossroads. Ruta 40 heads southeast while the turning northwest goes to remote Parque Nacional Perito Moreno (free), at the end of a 90-km *ripio* track. There is trekking and abundant wildlife among the large, interconnected system of lakes below glaciated peaks, though much of the park is dedicated to scientific study only. Lago Belgrano, the biggest lake, is a vivid turquoise, its surrounding mountains streaked with a mass of differing colours. Ammonite fossils can be found. The Park ranger, 10 km beyond the park entrance, has maps and information on walks and wild ife, none in English. Camping is free: no facilities, no fires. There is no public transport into the park.

From the Parque Moreno junction to Tres Lagos, Ruta 40 improves considerably. East of the junction (7 km) is **Hotel Las Horquetas** (closed) and 15 km beyond is **Tamel Aike** village (police station, water). After another 34 km Ruta 40 turns sharply southwest, but if you need fuel before Tres Lagos, you must make a 72 km detour to **Gobernador Gregores** (always carry spare). **Estancia La Siberia**, between Ruta 40 and Lago Cardiel some 90 km from the turning, is a lunch stop on the El Calafate–Bariloche bus route, but also has rooms (**$$**, open October-April, no phone). At **Tres Lagos** a road turns off northwest to

Lago San Martín. From Tres Lagos Ruta 40 deteriorates again and remains very rugged until the turnoff to the Fitz Roy sector of Parque Nacional Los Glaciares. 21 km beyond is the bridge over Río La Leona, with delightful **Hotel La Leona** whose café serves good cakes. Near here are petrified tree trunks 30 m long, protected in a natural reserve.

Border with Chile: Los Antiguos From Perito Moreno Ruta 43 (paved) runs south of Lago Buenos Aires to Los Antiguos, an oasis set on the lake, in the middle of a desert, 2 km from the Chilean border (*Phone code: 02963*). Blessed by a lovely climate and famous for its cherries and great views, Los Antiguos is an increasingly popular tourist town. It is developing fast, with new hotels, restaurants, bus terminal, internet and other services, ideal for a couple of days' rest and for stocking up on the basics before journeying on. **Tourist office** ① *Av 11 de Julio 446, T491261, Dec-Easter 0800-2400, 0800-2000 rest of year, http://losantiguos.tur.ar.*

Ruta 40 to the glaciers listings

For hotel and restaurant price codes and other relevant information, see pages 10-12.

🛏 Where to stay

Río Mayo *p38*
$$$$ Estancia Don José, 2.5 km west of Río Mayo, T420015 or 0297-156 249155, www.guenguel. com.ar. Excellent estancia, with superb food, 2 rooms and 1 cabin. The family business involves sustainable production of guanaco fibre.

Perito Moreno *p39*
$$ Americano, San Martín 1327, T432538. With breakfast, has a decent restaurant.
$$ El Austral, San Martín 1381, T432605, hotelaustral@speedy.com.ar. Similar to others on the main street, but clean.
$$ Belgrano, San Martín 1001, T432019. This hotel is often booked by Ruta 40 long-distance bus companies, basic, not always clean, 1 key fits all rooms, helpful owner, breakfast extra, excellent restaurant.
$ Alojamiento Dona María, 9 de Julio 1544, T432452. Basic but well kept.
$ pp **Santa Cruz**, Belgrano 1565. Simple rooms.

Camping Municipal site 2 km at Laguna de los Cisnes, T432072. Also 2 *cabaña* places.

Estancias 2 estancias on RN40: 28 km south:
$$$$ pp **Telken**, sheep station of the Nauta family, T02963-432079, telkenpatagonia@ argentina.com or jarinauta@yahoo.com.ar. Comfortable rooms, all meals available shared with family, English and Dutch spoken, horse treks and excursions (Cueva de las Manos US$80). Highly recommended.
$$$ Hostería Cueva de Las Manos, 20 km from the cave at Estancia Las Toldos, 60 km south, 7 km off the road to Bajo Caracoles, T02963-432856 (Buenos Aires 4901 0436), www.estanciasdesantacruz.com. Open 1 Nov-5 Apr, closed Christmas and New Year, runs tours to the caves, horse riding, meals extra and expensive.
$ Estancia Turística Casa de Piedra, 75 km south of Perito Moreno on Ruta 40, in Perito Moreno ask for Sr Sabella, Av Perón 941, T02963-432199. Price is for rooms, camping, hot showers, home-made bread, use of kitchen, excursions to Cueva de las Manos and volcanoes by car or horse.

Bajo Caracoles *p39*
$$ Hotel Bajo Caracoles, T490100. Old-fashioned but hospitable, meals.

Parque Nacional Perito Moreno *p39*
Nearest accommodation is **$$$** full board
Estancia La Oriental, T02962-452196,
elada@uvc.com.ar. Splendid setting,
with comfortable rooms. Nov-Mar,
with horse riding, trekking. See www.cielos
patagonicos.com or www.estanciasdesanta
cruz.com. for other estancias in Santa Cruz
Menelik near PN Perito Moreno, and **El
Cóndor**, on the southern shore of Lago
San Martín, 135 km from Tres Lagos.

Tres Lagos
$ Restaurant Ahoniken, Av San Martín,
has rooms.
Camping At Estancia La Lucia, US$2.50,
water, barbecue, "a little, green paradise";
supermarket, fuel.

Border with Chile: Los Antiguos *p40*
$$$ Antigua Patagonia, Ruta 43, T491033,
www.antiguapatagonia.com.ar. Luxurious
rooms with beautiful views, excellent
restaurant. Tours to Cueva de las Manos
and nearby Monte Cevallos.
$$$-$ Mora, Av Costanera, T154 207472.
Rooms range from dorms to 1st class with
private bath. Laundry, hairdresser, as well as
disabled access restaurant, phramacy and
communal kitchen.
$ pp Albergue Padilla, San Martín 44 (just
off main street), T491140. Comfortable dorms,
doubles (**$$**); *quincho* and garden. Also
camping. El Chaltén travel tickets.
$ pp Albergue y Bungalows Sol de Mayo,
Av 11 de Julio, Chacra 133 'A', T491232.
Another budget option. Basic rooms with
shared bath, central.
Camping An outstanding **Camping
Municipal**, 2 km from centre on Ruta
Provincial 43, T491265, with hot showers,
US$4 pp, also has cabins for 4 (no linen).

⊙ Restaurants

Border with Chile: Los Antiguos *p40*
Confitería y Restaurante El Tío, Av 11 de
Julio 508.
Viva El Viento, 11 de Julio 477, T491109,
www.vivaelviento.com. Dutch-owned, good
atmosphere, very good food and coffee, open
0900-0100, also has Wi-Fi internet, lots of
information, boats on the lake arranged,
horse riding, trips to Cueva de Las Manos.
Recommended.

⊙ Transport

Río Mayo *p38*
Bus To **Sarmiento** and **Coyhaique** from
bus office in the centre. Mon-Fri at 0300
Giobbi buses take Ruta 40 north from Río
Mayo direct to **Esquel**.

Parque Nacional Perito Moreno *p39*
Road distances: Bariloche 823 km, El Chaltén
582 km, El Calafate 619 km. It is nearly
impossible to hitchhike between Perito
Moreno and El Calafate. Hardly any traffic
and few services.
Bus Terminal on edge of town next to petrol
station, T432072, open only when buses
arrive or depart. If crossing from Chile at Los
Antiguos, 2 buses daily in summer, 1 hr,
US$3.35, **La Unión**, T432133. To **El Chaltén**
and **El Calafate**, **Chaltén Travel**, see next
paragraph, at 1000. Chaltén Travel also runs a
tourist service at 0630 from **Hotel Belgrano**
every other day to **Puerto Madryn**.
Car Several mechanics on C Rivadavia and
Av San Martín, good for repairs. **Taxi** Parada
El Turista, Av San Martín y Rivadavia, T432592.

Border with Chile: Los Antiguos *p40*
Bus Bus terminal on Av Tehuelches with
large café/restaurant, free Wi-Fi. Most bus
companies will store the luggage. Minibuses
from Chile arrive at this terminal. To
Comodoro Rivadavia, take **Sportman**
(at Terminal, T0297-15-405 3769) to **Perito**

Moreno, US$8-10, and on to **Caleta Olivia**, US$37. To **El Chaltén** (10 hrs) and **El Calafate** (12 hrs), via Perito Moreno, every other (even) day at 0800, US$70, also north to **Bariloche**, every even day, US$70, **Chaltén Travel** (open only in high season, at Hotel Belgrano, www.chalten travel.com), mid-Nov-Apr, also **Marga** all year round at 1600 via Perito Moreno. To **Chile**, La Unión to **Chile Chico**, 8 km west, US$4, 45 mins including border

crossing (for routes from Chile Chico to Coyhaique, see page 96).

Border with Chile: Los Antiguos *p40*
Banks ATM on Av 11 de Julio. **Medical services** Hospital and medical emergency: Patagonia, Argentina 68, T491303. **Pharmacy:** Rossi Abatedaga, Av 11 Julio 231, T491204.

Parque Nacional Los Glaciares

This park, the second largest in Argentina, extends over 724,000 ha. It is a UNESCO World Heritage Site. 40% of it is covered by ice fields (*hielos continentales*) from which 13 major glaciers descend into two great lakes, Lago Argentino and, further north, Lago Viedma, linked by the Río La Leona, flowing south from Lago Viedma. The only accessible areas of the park are the southern area around Lago Argentino, accessible from El Calafate, and the northern area around Cerro El Chaltén (Fitz Roy). Access to the central area is difficult and there are no tourist facilities.

Arriving at Parque Nacional Los Glaciares
Access to the southern part of the park is 50 km west of El Calafate, US$23 for non-Argentines. **National Park Office** ① *Av del Libertador 1302, Calafate, T491005, www.losglaciares.com, helpful, English spoken; in El Chaltén across the bridge at the entrance to the town, T493004, Jan-Feb 0700-2200, low season: 0900-1600.* An informative talk about the national park and its paths is given to all incoming bus passengers. Both hand out helpful trekking maps of the area, with paths and campsites marked, distances and walking times. Note that the hotel, restaurant and transport situation in this region changes greatly from year to year.

El Calafate and around → *Phone code: 02902. Population: 8000.*
This town sits on the south shore of **Lago Argentino** and exists almost entirely as a tourist centre for the Parque Nacional los Glaciares, 50 km away. In both El Calafate and El Chaltén most of the inhabitants came from Buenos Aires and other provincial cities. With the recent decline in tourism as a result of global recession, many people have returned north and the local population has fallen. The town has been known to get packed out in January and February, but it is empty and quiet all winter. It's neither cheap nor beautiful, but it is spotless and tidy and Lago Argentino's turquoise waters are stunning. The shallow part at Bahía Redonda is good for birdwatching in the evenings. **Tourist office** ① *in the bus station, T491476, open 0800-2000 (May-Sep 0830-1430), and Rosales y Av del Libertador, T491090, open 0800-2000, www.elcalafate.gov.ar.* Helpful staff speak several languages. **Provincial tourist office** ① *1 de Mayo 50, T492353. See also www.calafate.com.*
For the main excursions to the glaciers, see below.

At **Punta Gualicho** (or Walichu) on the shores of Lago Argentino 7 km east of town, there are cave paintings (badly deteriorated); six-hour horse ride (US$40 pp). A recommended 15-minute walk is from the Intendencia del Parque, following Calle Bustillo up the road towards the lake through a quiet residential area to **Laguna Nímez** ① *US$1, guides at the entrance in summer (likely to be closed in low season, though still a nice area away from busy centre)*, a bird reserve (fenced in), with flamingos, ducks, black-necked swans and abundant birdlife. **Centro de Interpretación Histórica** ① *Av Brown y Bonarelli, US$3*, has a very informative anthropological and historical exhibition about the region, with pictures and bilingual texts, also a very relaxing café/library. There are several estancias within reach, offering a day on a working farm, *asado al palo*, horse riding and accommodation. **Estancia Alice 'El Galpón del Glaciar'** ① *T497503, Buenos Aires T011-5217 6719, www.elgalpondelglaciar.com.ar.* **Estancia Nibepo Aike** ① *on Brazo Sur of Lago Argentino in the National Park, 55 km southwest (book at Av Libertador 1215 p 1A, T02902-492797, Buenos Aires T011-5272 0341, www.nibepoaike.com.ar),* beautiful

El Calafate

To **2 8** , Punta Gualicho, Laguna Nímez &
Centro de Interpretación Histórica

N

200 metres
200 yards

Where to stay ▭
1 Albergue y Hostal Lago
  Argentino
2 Alto Verde
3 América del Sur

4 Arie
5 Cabañas Nevis
6 Calafate Hostel & Hostería
7 Camping AMSA
8 Casa de Grillos
9 Cerro Cristal
10 El Quijote
11 Hostel Buenos Aires
12 Hostel del Glaciar
  'Libertador'
13 Hostel del Glaciar
  'Pioneros'

14 I Keu Ken Hostel
15 Kau Yatún
16 Kosten Aike
17 Los Alamos
18 Marcopolo Calafate
19 Michelangelo
20 Patagonia Rebelde
21 Sir Thomas
22 Vientos del Sur

Restaurants ⑦
1 Borges y Alvarez
2 Casablanca
3 El Puesto
4 Heladería Aquarela
5 La Cocina
6 La Tablita
7 La Vaca Atada
8 Mi Viejo & Rick's Café
9 Pura Vida
10 Viva la Pepa

setting in a more remote area, traditional 'estancia' style with original furniture, largely self-sustainable, delightful meals served, trekking, riding and other rural pursuits. **Cerro Frías** ⓘ *25 km west, T492808, www.cerrofrias.com*, excursion includes one meal and an ascent of Cerro Frías (1030 m) for great views; options are by horse, on 4WD vehicles or on foot, US$59 (US$45 without lunch). See also **Helsingfors**, in Where to stay, below, or visit www.estanciasdesantacruz.com.

Glaciar Perito Moreno

At the western end of Lago Argentino (80 km from El Calafate) the major attraction is the Glaciar Perito Moreno, one of the few glaciers in the world that is both moving and maintaining in size, despite global warming. It descends to the surface of the water over a 5-km frontage and a height of about 60 m. Several times in the past, it advanced across the lake, cutting the Brazo Rico off from the Canal de los Témpanos; then the pressure of water in the Brazo Rico broke through the ice and reopened the channel. This spectacular rupture last occurred in March 2012. The glacier can be seen close up from a series of walkways descending from the car park. Weather may be rough. The vivid blue hues of the ice floes, with the dull roar as pieces break off and float away as icebergs from the snout, are spectacular, especially at sunset. ▸▸ *See also Transport, page 52.*

Glaciar Upsala

At the northwest end of Lago Argentino, 60 km long and 4 km wide, Upsala Glacier is a stunning expanse of untouched beauty. The glacier itself, unlike its cousin Perito Moreno, is suffering badly from global warming. When large parts break from the main mass of ice access by lake may be blocked. Normally it can be reached by motorboat from Punta Bandera, 50 km west of El Calafate, on a trip that also goes to Lago Onelli and Spegazzini glaciers. Small Lago Onelli is quiet and very beautiful, beech trees on one side, and ice-covered mountains on the other. The lake is full of icebergs of every size and sculpted shape.

El Chaltén and around → *Phone code: 02962.*

This small tourist town lies 217 km northwest of El Calafate in the north of the park (road paved), at the foot of the jagged peaks of the spectacular Fitz Roy massif, which soars steeply from the Patagonian steppe, its sides too steep for snow to stick. Chaltén is the Tehuelche name meaning the 'smoking mountain', and occasionally at sunrise the mountains are briefly lit up bright red for a few seconds, a phenomenon known as the 'sunrise of fire', or '*amanecer de fuego*'. The town is windy, with an Alpine feel. It's a neat place, but incredibly expensive. Nevertheless you should not let the acute commercialism detract from the fact that it offers amazing views of the nearby peaks, is the base for some of the country's finest trekking and has some very good restaurants and places to sleep. If you haven't got a tent, you can easily rent all you'll need. **Tourist office** ⓘ *Güemes 21, T493371, www.elchalten.com, excellent site with accommodation listed, Mon-Fri 0900-2000, Sat-Sun 1300-2000.*

The **Lago del Desierto**, 37 km north of El Chaltén, is surrounded by forests, a stunning virgin landscape. A short walk to a mirador at the end of the road gives fine views. Excursions from El Chaltén by **Chaltén Travel** daily in summer, and from **Restaurant Las Lengas** (see Restaurants, below), US$40 for six hours, who also runs daily transfers to connect with boats, 0830, 1200, 1500, US$30, two-hour waiting time. Campsite at the southern end of Lago del Desierto (usually no food, although there is a kiosk that advertises *choripán*), and *refugios* at its northern end. There is also the new, secluded **Aguas Arriba Lodge** ⓘ *T0: 1-4326 0280, www.aguasarribalodge.com*, reached only by boat. To get to Villa O'Higgins (Chile), the southernmost town on the Carretera Austral, take the Las Lengas transfer, or JR minibus to Lago del Desierto, then a 45-minute boat trip goes to the northern end (US$24.50), or walk up a path along the east shores 4½ hours to reach the northern end. From there you can trek or go on horseback (19 km, seven hours with guide, US$32) to Puerto Candelario Mancilla on Lago O'Higgins. A 4WD service runs from the Chilean border to Candelario Mancilla, 14 km: US$30, call Hans Silva in Villa O'Higgins T+56-67-431821 to reserve, same number for horses. Overnight at Estancia Candelario Mancilla. Next day, take a boat from Candelario Mancilla to Bahía Bahamóndez (three hours, US$86), then a bus to Villa O'Higgins, 7 km, US$4. The border is closed from May to November (check at www.villachiggins.com for dates, tours and boat availability and see Chile chapter, **Villa O'Higgins**, for more details).

Also daily boat trips on Lago Viedma to pass Glaciar Viedma, with ice trekking optional in the day-long tour. The estancia **Hostería El Pi ar** (see Where to stay) is a base for trekking up Río Blanco or Río Eléctrico, or try the multi-activity adventure circuit. **Las Lengas** has buses daily at 0830, 1200, 1500 to El Pilar, US$11.50, and to Río Eléctrico, US$14, for several of the hikes above and below. Highly recommended.

Trekking and climbing

Trekking The two most popular walks are to 1) **Laguna Torre** (three hours each way). After one to 1½ hours you'll come to Mirador Laguna Torre with great view of Cerro Torre and Fitz Roy, and 1¼ hours more to busy Camping De Agostini near the lake, where you have fantastic views. 2) **Laguna de Los Tres** (four hours each way). Walk 1¾ hours up to Camping Capri, great views of Fitz Roy, then another hour to Camping Poincenot. Just beyond it is Camping Río Blanco (only for climbers, registration at the National Park office required). From Río Blanco you can walk another hour, very steep, to Laguna de los Tres where you'll get a spectacular view (not a good walk if it's cloudy). You can connect the two paths by taking one that takes about two hours and branches off south, northwest of Laguna Capri, passes by Lagunas Madre e Hija and reaches the path to Laguna Torre, west of the Mirador. This may be too long for a day. From El Chaltén to Laguna Torre along this route takes about seven hours. 3) **Loma del Pliegue Tumbado** (four hours each way). To a viewpoint where you can see both cordons and Lago Viedma: marked path from Park Ranger's office, a good day walk, best in clear weather. 4) **Laguna Toro** (seven hours each way). For more experienced trekkers, to wild glacial lake across the ice cap. 5) **Up Río Blanco to Piedra del Fraile** (seven hours each way, two hours each way from the road to Lago del Desierto). A beautiful walk out of the National Park to campsite with facilities, and Refugio Piedra del Fraile, neither is free. Recommended. The best day walks are **Laguna Capri**, Mirador Laguna Torre, both of which have great views after an hour or so. A one-hour hike is to Chorillo del Salto, a small but pristine waterfall; take the road to Lago del Desierto for about 30 minutes, then follow the marked path. No guide is necessary.

Most paths are very clear and well worn, but a map is essential, even on short walks: the park information centre gives helpful maps of treks, as do the tourist office and hotels. If you wish to buy maps, the best are by **Zagier and Urruty**, www.patagoniashop.net, 1:50,000 (US$6-12), updated quite regularly and available in shops in El Calafate and El Chaltén.

Climbing Base camp for Fitz Roy (3405 m) is Campamento Río Blanco (see above). Other peaks include Cerro Torre (3102 m), Torre Egger (2900 m), Cerro Solo (2121 m), Poincenot (3002 m), Guillaumet (2579 m), Saint-Exupery (2558 m), Aguja Bífida (2394 m) and Cordón Adela (2938 m): most of these are for very experienced climbers. Generally the best time is mid February to end March; November and December are very windy; January is fair; winter is extremely cold, but weather is unpredictable and it all depends on the specific route being climbed. Permits for climbing are available at the national park information office. Guides are available in El Chaltén.

El Calafate to Chile

If travelling from El Calafate to Torres del Paine by car or bike, you'll cross this bleak area of steppe. About 40 km before reaching the border there are small lagoons and salt flats with flamingos (between El Calafate and Punta Arenas it is also possible to see guanacos and condors). From Calafate you can take the paved combination of Ruta 11, RN 40 and RN 5 to La Esperanza (165 km), where there's fuel, a campsite and a large but expensive *confitería* (lodging **$$** with bath). From La Esperanza, Ruta 7 heads west (not completely paved) along the valley of the Río Coyle. A shorter route (closed in winter) missing La Esperanza, turns off at El Cerrito and joins Ruta 7 at **Estancia Tapi Aike**. Ruta 7 continues to the border crossing from Cancha Carrera to Cerro Castillo, meeting the good road between Torres del Paine (20 km north) and Puerto Natales (63 km south). For bus services along this route see under El Calafate.

Río Turbio → *Phone code: 02902. Population: 6600.*

A charmless place, 267 km west of Río Gallegos, 30 km from Puerto Natales (Chile), you're most likely to visit en route to or from Torres del Paine in Chile. The site of Argentina's largest coalfield hasn't recovered from the depression hitting the industry in the 1990s. It has a cargo railway, connecting it with Punta Loyola; Mina 1 is where the first mine was opened. There is a ski centre: **Valdelén** has six pistes and is ideal for beginners, also scope for cross-country skiing between early June and late September. **Tourist information** ⓘ *Plazoleta Castillo, T421950.*

Border with Chile

1) Paso Mina Uno/Dorotea is 5 km south of Río Turbio. Open all year, 0900-2400. On the Chilean side this runs south to join the main Puerto Natales–Punta Arenas road. **2) Paso Casas Viejas/Laurita** is 33 km south of Río Turbio via 28 de Noviembre. Open all year, 0900-0100. On the Chilean side this runs west to join the main Puerto Natales–Punta Arenas road. **3) Paso Río Don Guillermo** (or **Cancha Carrera**) is 48 km north of Río Turbio, this is the most convenient crossing for Parque Nacional Torres del Paine. Open all year, 0900-2300. Argentine customs are fast and friendly. On the Chilean side the road continues 7 km to the border post at Cerro Castillo, where it joins the road from Puerto Natales to Torres del Paine. All crossings may have different hours in winter; see www.gendarmeria.gov.ar.

Parque Nacional Los Glaciares listings

For hotel and restaurant price codes and other relevant information, see pages 10-12.

🛏 Where to stay

Parque Nacional Los Glaciares *p42*
$$$$ Estancia Helsingfors, 73 km north-west of La Leona, on Lago Viedma, in BsAs: T011-4315 1222, www.helsingfors.com.ar. Fabulous place in splendid position on Lago Viedma, stylish rooms, welcoming lounge delicious food (full board), and excursions directly to glaciers and to Laguna Azul, by horse or trekking, plus boat trips. Open Oct-Apr.
$$$$ Los Notros, 70 km west of Calafate on the road to the Moreno glacier, T499510 (in BA: T011-4813 7285), www.losnotros.com. Exclusive retreat with wonderful views of the glacier, spacious rooms, all-inclusive packages.
Camping AMSA, Olavarría 65 (50 m off the main road, turning south at the fire station) T492247. Hot water, open in summer, US$6 pp. **El Huala**, 42 km from El Calafate, on the road to Lago Roca. Free with basic facilities, open all year round. **Lago Roca**, 50 km from El Calafate, T499500, beautifully situated, US$6 pp, bike hire, fishing licences, restaurant/*confitería*, open Oct-Apr. (**Ferretería Chuar**, 1 block from bus terminal, sells camping gas.)

El Calafate *p42, map p43*
Prepare to pay more for accommodation here than elsewhere in Argentina. El Calafate is very popular in Jan-Feb, so book all transport and accommodation in advance. Best months to visit are Oct, Nov and Mar, Apr when it is less crowded and less overpriced. Many hotels open only from Sep/Oct to Apr/May.
$$$$ El Quijote, Gob Gregores 1155, T491017, www.quijotehotel.com.ar. A very good hotel, spacious, well-designed with traditional touches, tasteful rooms with TV, restaurant **Sancho**, English and Italian spoken.

$$$$ Kau Yatún, Estancia 25 de Mayo (10 blocks from centre, east of arroyo Calafate), T491059, www.kauyatun.com. Renovated main house of a former estancia, well-kept grounds, 2 excellent restaurants, only half board or all inclusive packages that include excursions in the National Park.
$$$$ Kosten Aike, Gob Moyano 1243, T492424, www.kostenaike.com.ar. Relaxed yet stylish, elegant spacious rooms, jacuzzi, gym, excellent restaurant, **Ariskaiken** (open to non-residents), cosy bar, garden, English spoken. Recommended.
$$$$ Los Alamos, Gob Moyano y Bustillo, T491144, www.posacalosalamos.com. Cheaper in low season. Very comfortable, charming rooms, good service, lovely gardens and without doubt the best restaurant in town, **La Posta**.
$$$ Alto Verde, Zupic 138, T491326, www.welcomeargentina.com/altoverde. Top quality, **$$** in low season, spotless, spacious, helpful, breakfast included, also with apartments for 4.
$$$ Cabañas Nevis, Av del Libertador 1696, T493180, www.cabanasnevis.com.ar. Owner Mr Patterson offers very nice cabins for 5 and 8 (price quoted is for 5), some with lake view, great value. Recommended.
$$$ Casa de Grillos, Pasaje Las Bardurrias, T491160, www.casadegrillos.com.ar. Welcoming B&B in the calm green area, next to Nímez nature reserve. It has all the comfort and charm of a family house, **$$** low season.
$$$ Michelangelo, Espora y Gob Moyano, T491045, www.michelangelohotel.com.ar. Lovely, quiet, welcoming, TV, breakfast included, restaurant. Recommended.
$$$ Patagonia Rebelde, José Haro 442, T494495, www.patagonia rebelde.com. Charming new building in traditional Patagonian style, like an old inn with rustic decor, good comfort with well-heated bedrooms and comfy sitting-rooms.

$$$ Vientos del Sur, up the hill at Río Santa Cruz 2317, T493563, www.vientosdelsur.com. Very hospitable, calm, comfortable, TV, good views, kind family attention.

$$$-$$ Ariel, Av Libertador 1693, T493131, www.hotelariel.com.ar. Modern, functional, well maintained, TV, with breakfast.

$$ Cerro Cristal, Gob Gregores 989, T491088, www.cerrocristalhotel.com.ar. Comfortable, quiet, free Wi-Fi internet and TV, breakfast included, very good value in low season.

$$ Hostel Buenos Aires, Buenos Aires 296, 200 m from terminal, T491147, www.glaciares calafate.com. Quiet, kind owner, helpful, comfortable with doubles breakfast, cheaper without bath, good hot showers, Wi-Fi, laundry service, luggage store, bikes for hire.

$$ Sir Thomas, Espora 257, T492220, www.sirthomas.com.ar. Modern, comfortable wood-lined rooms, breakfast extra.

$$-$ pp Albergue y Hostal Lago Argentino, Campaña del Desierto 1050-61 (near bus terminal), T491423, www.interpatagonia.com/lagoargentino. **$** pp shared dorms with kitchen facilities, too few showers when full, nice atmosphere, good flats and **$$** doubles with breakfast on a neat garden.

$$-$ pp Marcopolo Calafate, C 405, T493899, www.hostel-inn.com. Part of Hostelling International. **$** pp in dorms. Laundry facilities, breakfast included, free Wi-Fi, various activities and tours on offer.

$ pp América del Sur, Puerto Deseado 153, T493525, www.americahostel.com.ar. Panoramic views from this comfortable, relaxed hostel, welcoming, well-heated rooms, with breakfast (dorms for 4, **$$** doubles with views, one room adapted for wheelchair users), chill-out area, fireplace, internet access, Wi-Fi, kitchen facilities. Warmly recommended, but can be noisy.

$ pp Calafate Hostel, Gob Moyano 1226, 400 m from bus terminal, T492450, www.calafatehostels.com. A huge log cabin with good rooms: dorms with or without

bath, breakfast extra, **$$** doubles with bath and breakfast. Also has Hostería at corner with 25 de Mayo, T491256, in **$$** range. Kitchen facilities, internet access, lively sitting area. Book a month ahead for Jan-Feb and call ahead for free shuttle from airport, HI discounts, helpful travel agency, **Chaltén Travel** (see below).

$ pp Hostel del Glaciar 'Libertador', Av del Libertador 587 (next to the bridge), T491792, www.glaciar.com. HI discounts, open year round. Smaller and pricier than 'Pioneros', rooms are good and well-heated, all with own bath (**$** pp dorms for 4 and **$$$-$$** doubles), breakfast extra, cooking facilities, internet access, Wi-Fi. Free transfer from bus terminal. Owners run **Patagonia Backpackers** (see below under What to do).

$ pp Hostel del Glaciar 'Pioneros', Los Pioneros 251, T491243, www.glaciar.com. Discount for HI members, open mid Sep to mid Apr. Accommodation for all budgets: standard **$$** doubles (also for 3 and 4) with bath, superior **$$** doubles with bath, shared dorms up to 4 beds, **$** pp. Many languages spoken, lots of bathrooms, internet access, Wi-Fi, kitchen facilities, no breakfast, free shuttle from bus terminal. Very popular, so book well in advance and double-check. **Punto de Encuentro** restaurant with some vegetarian options. Owners run **Patagonia Backpackers** (see What to do, below).

$ pp i Keu Ken Hostel, F M Pontoriero 171, T495175, www.patagoniaikeuken.com.ar. On a hill, very helpful, flexible staff, with breakfast, hot water, heating, luggage store, good.

Camping

AMSA, Olavarría 65 (50 m off the main road, turning south at the fire station), T492247. Only open in summer. US$6 pp, hot water, security.

There are 2 campsites in the park en route to Lago Roca: **El Huala**, 42 km from El Calafate, free with basic facilities and open all year round; and **Lago Roca**, 50 km from El Calafate, T499500, beautiful setting, with hot water, public phone, restaurant and bike hire, US$6 pp.

El Chaltén p44

In high season places are full: you must book ahead. Most places close in low season.

$$$$ Hostería El Puma, Lionel Terray 212, T493095, www.hosteriaelpuma.com.ar. A little apart, splendid views, lounge with log fire, tasteful stylish furnishings, comfortable, transfers and big American breakfast included. Can also arrange tours through their excellent agency **Fitz Roy Expeditions**, see below. Recommended.

$$$$ Los Cerros, Av San Martín, Santa Cruz, T493182, www.loscerrosdelchalten.com. Stylish and sophisticated, but expensive, in a stunning setting with mountain views, heated swimming pool. Half-board and all-inclusive packages with excursions available.

$$$$-$$$ Senderos, Perito Moreno s/n, T493336, www.senderoshosteria.com.ar. 4 types of room and suite in a new, wood-framed structure, comfortable, warm, can arrange excursions, excellent restaurant, Wi-Fi in public areas.

$$$ El Pilar, R23, Km 17, T493002, www.hosteria elpilar.com.ar. Country house in a spectacular setting at the meeting of Ríos Blanco and de las Vueltas, with clear views of Fitz Roy. A chance to sample the simple life with access to less-visited northern part of the park. Simple comfortable rooms, great food, very special.

$$$ Hostería Posada Lunajuim, Trevisán s/n, T493047, www.interpatagonia.com/lunajuim/. Stylish yet relaxed, comfortable (duvets on the beds), lounge with wood fire, with full American breakfast. Recommended.

$$ Hospedaje La Base, Lago del Desierto s/n, T493031. Good rooms for 2, 3 and 4, all with bath, tiny kitchen, self service breakfast included, great video lounge. Recommended.

$$ Nothofagus, Hensen s/n, T493087, www.nothofagusbb.com.ar. Cosy bed and breakfast, simple rooms, cheaper without bath and in low season. good value Recommended.

$$-$ Ahonikenk Chaltén, Av Martin M de Güemes 23, T493070, ahonikenkchalten23@yahoo.com.ar. Nice simple rooms, some dorms, restaurant/pizzería attached, good pastas.

$ pp Albergue Patagonia, Av San Martín 392, T493019, www.patagoniahostel.com.ar. HI-affiliated, cheaper for members, small and cosy with rooms for 2 with own bath (**$$**) or for 2 (**$$**), 4, 5 or 6 with shared bath, kitchen, video room, bike hire, laundry, luggage store and lockers, restaurant, very welcoming. Helpful information on Chaltén, also run excursions to Lago del Desierto. Closed Jun-Sep.

$ pp Albergue Rancho Grande, San Martín s/n, T493005, chaltenrancho@yahoo.com.ar. HI-affiliated, in a great position at the end of town with good open views and attractive restaurant and lounge, accommodates huge numbers of trekkers in rooms for 4, with shared bath, breakfast extra. Also **$$** doubles, breakfast extra. Helpful, internet, English spoken. Recommended. Reservations in **Calafate Hostel/Chaltén Travel**, Calafate.

$ pp Cóndor de los Andes, Av Río de las Vueltas y Halvorsen, T493101, www.condordelosandes.com. Nice little rooms for up to 6 with bath, sheets included, breakfast extra, also doubles with bath (**$$**), laundry service, library, kitchen, quiet, HI affiliated.

Camping del Lago, Lago del Desierto 135, T493010, centrally located with hot showers. Several others. A gas/alcohol stove is essential for camping as open fires are prohibited in campsites in of the national park. Take plenty of warm clothes and a good sleeping bag. It is possible to rent equipment in El Chaltén, ask at park office or Rancho Grande.

In the national park Poincenot, Capri, **Laguna Toro, Laguna Torre**. None has services, all river water is drinkable. Pack up all rubbish and take it back to town, do not wash within 70 m of rivers. **Camping Los Troncos/Piedra del Fraile** on Río Eléctrico is beyond park boundary, privately owned, has facilities.

Río Turbio *p46*
$$ De La Frontera, 4 km from Río Turbio, Paraje Mina 1, T421979. The most recommendable. Also has a hostel.
$ Hostería Capipe, Dufour, 9 km from town, T482935, www.hosteriacapipe.com.ar. Simple, with internet, restaurant.

🍴 Restaurants

El Calafate *p42, map p43*
$$ El Puesto, Gob Moyano y 9 de Julio, T491620. Tasty thin-crust pizzas in a cosy old house. Pricier regional meals and takeaway. Recommended.
$$ La Cocina, Av del Libertador 1245. Good pizza and pasta, and a large variety of pancakes.
$$ La Tablita, Cnel Rosales 28 (near the bridge). Typical *parrilla*, generous portions and quality beef.
$$ La Vaca Atada, Av del Libertador 1176. Good home-made pastas and more elaborate and expensive dishes based on trout and king crab.
$$ Mi Viejo, Av del Libertador 1111. Popular *parrilla*, US$6 for grilled lamb.
$$ Pura Vida, Av Libertador 1876, near C 17. Comfortable sofas, home-made Argentine food, vegetarian options, lovely atmosphere, lake view (reserve table). Recommended.
$$ Rick's Café, Av del Libertador 1091. Lively *parrilla* with good atmosphere.
$$ Viva la Pepa, Emilio Amado 833. Closed Wed. A mainly vegetarian café with great sandwiches and crêpes filled with special toppings.

Cafés
Borges y Alvarez, Av del Libertador 1015 (**Galería de los Gnomos**). A lively café/book-shop, open till 0100, good place to hang out.
Casablanca, 25 de Mayo y Av del Libertador. Jolly place for omelettes, hamburgers, vegetarian, US$7 for steak and chips.

Heladería Aquarela, Av del Libertador 1177. The best ice cream – try the *calafate*.

El Chaltén *p44*
$$ Estepa, Cerro Solo y Antonio Rojo. Small, intimate place with good, varied meals, friendly staff.
$$ Fuegia, San Martín s/n. Pastas, trout, meat and vegetarian dishes. Dinner only, recommended.
$$ Josh Aike, Lago de Desierto 105. Excellent *confitería*, home-made food, beautiful building. Recommended.
$$ Pangea, Lago del Desierto y San Martín. Open for lunch and dinner, drinks and coffee, calm, good music, varied menu. Recommended.
$$ Patagonicus, Güemes y Madsen. Lovely warm place with salads, pastas *caseras* and fabulous pizzas for 2, US$3-8, open midday to midnight. Recommended.
$$ Ruca Mahuida, Lionel Terray s/n. Widely regarded as the best restaurant with imaginative and well-prepared food.
$$ Zaffarancho (behind Rancho Grande), bar-restaurant, good range and reasonably priced.
$ Las Lengas, Viedma 95, opposite tourist office, T493023, laslengaselchalten@yahoo. com.ar. Cheaper than most. Plentiful meals, basic pastas and meat dishes. US$3 for meal of the day. Lots of information. See Lago del Desierto, above, and Transport, below, for owner's minibus services.
$ Domo Blanco, Costanera y De Agostini, and Güemes y Río de las Vueltas. Delicious ice cream.

🎵 Bars and clubs

El Chaltén *p44*
Cervecería Bodegón El Chaltén, San Martín 564, T493109, http://elchalten.com/cerveceria/. Brews its own excellent beer, also local dishes and pizzas, coffee and cakes, English spoken. Recommended.

O Shopping

El Calafate *p42, map p43*
La Anónima. Supermarket on Av del Libertador y Perito Moreno.

El Chaltén *p44*
Several outdoor shops. Also supermarkets, all expensive, and little fresh food available: **El Gringuito**, Av Antonio Rojo, has the best choice. Fuel is available next to the bridge.

▲ What to do

El Calafate *p42, map p43*
Most agencies charge the same rates and run similar excursions. Note that in winter boat trips can be limited by bad weather, even cancelled

Chaltén Travel, Av del Libertador 1174, T492212 (in Bs As T011-4326 7282), also Av Güemes 7, T493092, El Chaltén, www.chaltentravel.com. Huge range of tours (has a monopoly on some): glaciers, estancias, trekking, and bus to El Chaltén. Sell tickets along the Ruta 40 to Perito Moreno, Los Antiguos, US$70, and Bariloche, US$150, departures 0800 on odd-numbered days (0830 from El Chaltén) mid-Nov-Apr, overnight in Perito Moreno (cheaper to book your own accommodation), 36 hrs, English spoken.

Fernández Campbell, at Solo Patagonia, Av del Libertador 867, T491155, www.fernandezcampbell.com. This company runs most boat excursions on Lago Argentino, from 1-hr trips to the north side of Perito Moreno Glacier, US$12.25, to the much longer circuits for viewing Upsala, Onelli and Spegazzini glaciers, US$72.

Hielo y Aventura, Av del Libertador 935, T492205, www.hieloyaventura.com. Minitrekking includes walk through forests and 2-hr trek on Moreno glacier (crampons included). Also half-day boat excursion to Brazo Sur for a view of stunning glaciers, including Moreno. Recommended.

Lago San Martín. Av del Libertador 1215, p 1, T492858, www.lagosanmartin.com. Operates with **Estancias Turísticas** de Santa Cruz, specializing in arranging estancia visits, helpful.

Mar Patag, 9 de Julio 57, of 4, T492118, www.cruceros marpatag.com (in BsAs T4314 4567). Exclusive 2-day boat excursion to Upsala, Spegazzini and Moreno glaciers, US$350 pp, full board.

Mil Outdoor Adventure, Av del Libertador 1029, T491437, www.miloutdoor.com. Excursions in 4WD to panoramic views, 3-6 hrs.

Mundo Austral, Av del Libertador 1114, T492365, mundoaustral@cotecal.com.ar. For all bus travel and cheaper trips to the glaciers, helpful bilingual guides.

Patagonia Backpackers, at Hosteles del Glaciar, T491243, www.patagonia-backpackers.com. Alternative Glacier tour, entertaining, informative, includes walking, US$45. Recommended constantly. Also Supertrekking en Chaltén, Oct-Apr, 2-day hiking trip, featuring the best treks in the Fitz Roy massif, including camping and ice trekking. Highly recommended. Also sells tickets for **Navimag** ferries (Puerto Natales–Puerto Montt).

El Chaltén *p44*
For **trekking on horseback** with guides: **Rodolfo Guerra**, T493020 (also hires animals to carry equipment, but can be poorly planned); **El Relincho**, T493007.

In summer **Restaurant Las Lengas**, see above, runs a regular minibus to Lago del Desierto passing by some starting points for treks and by **Hostería El Pilar**, see above.

Casa De Guías, Av Costanera Sur s/n, T493118, www.casadeguias.com.ar. Experienced climbers who lead groups to nearby peaks, to the Campo de Hielo Continental and easier treks.

Fitz Roy Expediciones, San Martín 56, T436424, www.fitzroyexpediciones.com.ar. Organizes trekking and adventure trips including on the Campo de Hielo Continental, ice climbing schools, and fabulous longer trips. Climbers must be fit, but no technical experience required; equipment provided. Email with lots of notice to reserve. Highly recommended.

Patagonia Aventura, T493110, www.patagonia-aventura.com.ar. Has various ice trekking and other tours to Lago and Glaciar Viedma, also to Lago del Desierto.

● Transport

El Calafate *p42, map p43*
Air Airport, T491230, 23 km east of town, **Transpatagonia Expeditions**, T493766, runs service from town to meet flights, US$7 open return. Taxi (T491655/491745), US$10.
AR/Austral flies daily to/from **Buenos Aires**. Many more flights in summer to **Bariloche**, **Ushuaia** and **Trelew** (office at 9 de Julio 57, T492814). LADE flies to **Ushuaia**, **Comodoro Rivadavia**, **Río Gallegos**, **Esquel** and other Patagonian airports (office at J Mermoz 160, T491262).
Bus Terminal on Roca 1004, 1 block up stairs from Av del Libertador. Some bus companies will store luggage for a fee. To **Perito Moreno** glacier, see below. To **Río Gallegos** daily with 4-5 hrs, US$23-27, **Sportman** (T02966-15 464841), **Taqsa** (T491843) and **Marga** (US$35). To **El Chaltén** daily with Taqsa, **Chaltén Travel** (T492212, at 0800, 1300, 1830), **Los Glaciares**, **Cal-Tur** (T491842), 4-5 hrs, US$14-18. To **Bariloche**, see above for **Chaltén Travel**'s buses via Los Antiguos and Perito Moreno. **Marga/Taqsa** runs a daily bus to **Bariloche** via Los Antiguos at 1600, 36 hrs, US$110-122. To **Ushuaia** take bus to Río Gallegos for connections.
  Direct bus services to Chile (Take passport when booking bus tickets to Chile.) To **Puerto Natales**, daily in summer with **Cootra** (T491444), via Río Turbio, 7 hrs, or with **Turismo Zaahj** (T491631), Wed, Fri, Sun, 5 hrs, US$20 (advance booking recommended, tedious customs check at

border). **Note** Argentine pesos cannot be exchanged in Torres del Paine.
Car hire Average price under US$100 per day for small car with insurance but usually only 200 free km. **Cristina**, Av del Libertador 1711, T491674, crisrenta@rnet.com.ar.
Localiza, Av del Libertador 687, T491398, localiza calafate@hotmail.com. **ON Rent a Car**, Av del Libertador 1831, T493788 or T02966-156 29985, onrentacar@cotecal. com.ar. All vehicles have a permit for crossing to Chile, included in the fee, but cars are poor.
Bikes for hire, US$17 per day.

Glaciar Perito Moreno *p44*
Boat A 45-min catamaran trip departs from near the entrance to the walkways and gets closer to the glacier's face, US$12.25; can be arranged independently through **Fernández Campbell** (see above) or is offered with the regular excursions. Another boat trip and a mini-trekking on the glacier are organized by **Hielo y Aventura** (see What to do, above).
Bus From **El Calafate** with Taqsa, **Interlagos**, US$20 return; also guided excursions. Many agencies in El Calafate also run minibus tours (park entry not included). Out-of-season trips to the glacier may be difficult to arrange. **Taxis** about US$75 for 4 passengers round trip including wait of 3-4 hrs at the glacier. A reliable driver is **Rubén**, T498707. There is small taxi stand outside the bus terminal.

El Chaltén *p44*
Bus Tax of US$1.15 is charged at the terminal. In summer, buses fill quickly: book ahead. Fewer services off season. Daily buses to **El Calafate**, 4-5 hrs (most stop at El Calafate airtport), US$14-18 one way, companies given above, El Chaltén phone numbers: **Chaltén Travel**, see below, **Cal Tur**, T493079. See page 26 for **Chaltén Travel** to Los Antiguos and Bariloche; **Chaltén Travel**, Av del Libertador 1174, T492212 (in Buenos Aires T011-4326 7282),

also Av Güemes 7, T493092, El Chaltén, www.chaltentravel.com. Huge range of tours (has a monopoly on some): glaciers, estancias, trekking, and bus to El Chaltén. Sell tickets along the Ruta 40 to Perito Moreno, Los Antiguos, US$70, and Bariloche, US$150, departures 0800 on odd-numbered days (0830 from El Chaltén) mid-Nov to Apr, overnight in Perito Moreno (cheaper to book your own accommodation), 36 hrs, English spoken. To **Piedrabuena** on Ruta 3, for connections to Los Antiguos, Puerto Madryn, etc, **Las Lengas** (see Restaurants, above, www.transportelaslengas.com.ar), 0500, return 1300, daily, US$37. **Las Lengas** also run to El Calafate airport at 0630, 1030, 1300 daily, return 1330, 1530, 1930, US$28, reserve in advance.

Taxi Servicio de Remís El Chaltén, Av San Martén 430, T493042, reliable.

Río Turbio *p46*
Bus To **Puerto Natales**, 2 hrs, US$5, hourly with **Cootra** (Tte del Castillo 01, T421448, cootra@oyikil.com.ar), and other companies. To **El Calafate**, Cootra, 4 hrs, US$14.
Río Gallegos, 5 hrs, US$14-27 (**El Pingüino**; **Taqsa/Marga**, T421422).

❶ Directory

El Calafate *p42, map p43*
Banks Best to take cash as high commission is charged on exchange, but there are ATMs at airport and banks. **Thaler,** Av del Libertador 963, loc 2, changes money and TCs.

El Chaltén *p44*
Banks 24-hr ATM next to the gas station at the entrance to town. Credit cards are accepted in all major hotels and restaurants.

Tierra del Fuego

The island at the extreme south of South America is divided between Argentina and Chile, with the tail end of the Andes cordillera providing dramatic mountain scenery along the southern fringe of both countries. There are lakes and forests, mostly still wild and undeveloped, offering good trekking in summer and downhill or cross-country skiing in winter. Until a century ago, the island was inhabited by four ethnic groups, Selk'nam (or Ona), Alacaluf (Kaweskar), Haush (Manekenk) and Yámana (Yahgan). They were removed by settlers who occupied their land to introduce sheep and many died from disease. Their descendants (except for the extinct Haush) are very few in number and live on the islands. Many of the sheep-farming estancias which replaced the indigenous people can be visited. Ushuaia, the island's main city, is an attractive base for exploring the southwest's small national park, and for boat trips along the Beagle channel to Harberton, a fascinating pioneer estancia. There's good trout and salmon fishing, and a tremendous variety of birdlife in summer. Autumn colours are spectacular in March and April.

Arriving in Tierra del Fuego

Getting there There are no road/ferry crossings between the Argentine mainland and Argentine Tierra del Fuego. You have to go through Chilean territory. (Accommodation is sparse and planes and buses fill up quickly from November to March. Essential to book ahead.) From Río Gallegos, Ruta 3 reaches the Chilean border at Monte Aymond (67 km; open 24 hours summer, 0900-2300 April-October), passing Laguna Azul. For bus passengers the border crossing is easy, although you have about a 30-minute wait at each border post as luggage is checked and documents are stamped (it's two more hours to Punta Arenas). Hire cars need a document for permission to cross the border. Thirty kilometres into Chile is **Kamiri Aike**, with a dock 16 km east at **Punta Delgada** for the 20-minute Magellan Strait ferry-crossing over the Primera Angostura (First Narrows) to **Bahía Azul**. At Punta Delgada is Hostería El Faro for food and drinks. Three boats work continuously, 0700-0100 (0830-2345 April-October), US$29 per vehicle, foot passengers US$3.45, www.tabsa.cl. The road is paved to Cerro Sombrero, from where *ripio* (unsurfaced) roads run southeast to Chilean San Sebastián (130-140 km from ferry, depending on route taken). Chilean San Sebastián is just a few houses with **Hostería La Frontera** 500 m from the border. It's 15 km east, across the border (24 hours), to Argentine San Sebastián, not much bigger, with a seven-room ACA *hostería* (**$$**, T02964-425542; service station open 0700-2300). From here the road is paved to Río Grande (see below) and Ushuaia.

The other ferry crossing is **Punta Arenas–Porvenir**. RN255 from Kamiri Aike goes southwest 116 km to the intersection with the Punta Arenas-Puerto Natales road, from where it is 53 km to Punta Arenas. The ferry dock is 5 km north of Punta Arenas centre, at Tres Puentes. The ferry crosses to Bahía Chilota, 5 km west of Porvenir Tuesday-Sunday (subject to tides, **Transportadora Austral Broom**, www.tabsa.cl, publishes timetable a month in advance), two hours 20 minutes, US$72 per vehicle, foot passengers US$11.50. From Porvenir a 234 km *ripio* road runs east to Río Grande (six hours, no public transport) via San Sebastián. **Note** Fruit and meat may not be taken onto the island, nor between Argentina and Chile. ➸ *See also Transport, page 57. For details of transport and hotels on Chilean territory, see pages 121-124.*

Río Grande and around → *Phone code: 02964. Population: 53,000.*

Río Grande is a sprawling modern town in windy, dust-laden sheep-grazing and oil-bearing plains. (The oil is refined at San Sebastián in the smallest and most southerly refinery in the world.) Government tax incentives to companies in the 1970s led to a rapid growth in population. Although incentives were withdrawn, it continues to expand, most recently into mobile phone and white goods assembly. The city was founded by Fagnano's Salesian mission in 1893; you can visit the original building **La Candelaria** ① *11 km north, T421642, Mon-Sat 1000-1230, 1500-1900, US$2, afternoon teas, US$3, getting there: taxi US$7 with wait.* The museum has displays of indigenous artefacts and natural history. Río Grande's **Museo Virginia Choquintel** ① *Alberdi 555, T430647, Mon-Fri 0900-1700, Sat 1500-1900,* is also recommended for its history of the Selk'nam, the pioneers, missions and oil. Next door is a handicraft shop called **Kren** ('sun' in Selk'nam), which sells good local products. Nearby estancias can be visited, notably **María Behety** (15 km), with a vast sheep-shearing shed, but the area's main claim to fame is sport-fishing, especially for trout. **Local festivals**: Sheep shearing in January. Rural exhibition and handicrafts second week of February. Shepherd's day, with impressive sheepdog display first week of March. **Tourist office** ① *Rosales 350, on the plaza, T431324, www.riogrande.gov.ar, Mon-Fri 0900-1700. Provincial office: Av Belgrano 319, T422887.*

Tolhuin
About 20 km south of Río Grande, trees begin to appear on the steppe while the road, Ruta 3, runs parallel to the seashore. On Sunday people drive out to the woods for picnics, go fishing or look for shellfish on the mudflats. The road is mostly very good as it approaches the mountains to the south. Tolhuin, 'la corazón de la isla' at the eastern tip of Lago Fagnano, is 1¼ hours from Río Grande. The small town is caters for horse riders, anglers, mountain bikers and trekkers. There are cabins, hostels and campsites. On Sunday it is crammed full of day-trippers. The **Panificadora La Unión** in the centre is renowned for its breads, pastries and chocolate and is an obligatory stop. Líder and Montiel minibuses break the Río Grande-Ushuaia journey here. **Tourist office** ① *Av de los Shelknam 80, T02901-492125, tolhuinturismo@tierradelfuego.org.ar.*

The road leaves Lago Fagnano and passes lenga forest destroyed by fire in 1978 before climbing into healthier forests. After small Lago Verde and fjord-like Lago Escondido, the road crosses the cordillera at Paso Garibaldi. It then descends to the Cerro Castor winter sports complex and the Tierra Mayor recreation area (see Ushuaia, What to do, page 65). There is a police control just as you enter the Ushuaia city limits; passports may be checked.

Río Grande and around listings

For hotel and restaurant price codes and other relevant information, see pages 10-12.

⊙ Where to stay

Río Grande *p55*
Book ahead, as there are few decent choices. Several estancias offer full board and some, mainly on the northern rivers, have expensive fishing lodges, others offer horse riding. See www.tierradelfuego.org.ar and www.estanciasfueguinas.com.
$$$$ pp Estancia Viamonte, 40 km southeast on the coast, T430861, www.estanciaviamonte. com. For an authentic experience of Tierra del Fuego, built in 1902 by pioneer Lucas Bridges, writer of *Uttermost Part of the Earth*, to protect the Selk'nam/Ona people, this working estancia has simple and beautifully furnished rooms in a spacious cottage. Price is for full board and all activities: riding and trekking; cheaper for dinner, bed and breakfast only. Delicious meals. Book a week ahead.
$$$ Posada de los Sauces, Elcano 839, T430868, posadadelossauces@speedy.com.ar. Best by far, with breakfast, beautifully decorated, comfortable, good restaurant (trout recommended), cosy bar, very helpful staff.
$$ Argentino, San Martín 64, T422546, hotelargentino@yahoo.com. Room with bath, **$** pp without bath, camping, oldest hotel in city, breakfast included, Wi-Fi, internet, kitchen, parking, book exchange, library, helpful owner.
$$ Isla del Mar, Güemes 963, T422883. Pink building on river front, has seen better days, breakfast is included and staff are very friendly.

$$ Villa, Av San Martín 281, T424998, hotelvillarg@hotmail.com. Central, modern, restaurant/*confitería*, internet, TV, parking, discount given for cash.

Camping
Refugio Camping Club Náutico, T420536, nauticorg@speedy.com.ar, Rita and Carlos Hansen. Very helpful.

Tolhuin *p55*
$$$ Cabañas Khami, on Lago Fagnano, 8 km from Tolhuin, T422296, www.cabanas khami.com.ar. Well-equipped, rustic cabins, good value with linen. Price given for 6 people, 3-night weekend rates available.

❶ Restaurants

Río Grande *p55*
$$ El Rincón de Julio, next to Posada de los Sauces, Elcano 800 block. For excellent *parrilla*.
$$ La Nueva Colonial, Av Belgrano y Lasserre. Delicious pasta, warm family atmosphere.
$$ La Rueda, Islas Malvinas 998. Excellent *parrilla*, has another branch on O'Higgins 200 block.
$ La Nueva Piamontesa, Av Belgrano y Mackinlay, T426332. Cheap set menus and take away.

Cafés
El Roca (sic), Espora entre Av San Martín y Rosales, ½ block from Plaza. *Confitería* and bar in historic premises (the original cinema), good and popular.
Tío Willy, Alberdi entre Espora y 9 de Julio. Serves *cerveza artesanal* (microbrewery).

Río Grande p55

Air Airport 4 km west of town, T420600.
Taxi US$2. To **Buenos Aires, AR** daily,
3½ hrs direct. LADE flies to **Río Gallegos**.
Bus To **Punta Arenas**, Chile, via Punta
Delgada, 7-9 hrs, Pacheco (Av Perito Moreno
635, T425611) and Tecni Austral (Moyano
516, T430610), US$30. To **Río Gallegos**,
Tecni Austral, Mon-Sat, 8 hrs; Marga/Taqsa
(Mackinley 545, T434316), daily, 0815, US$79,
connection to El Calafate and Comodoro
Rivadavia. To **Ushuaia**, 3½-4 hrs, **Montiel**
(25 de Mayo 712, T420997) and **Líder** (Perito
Moreno 635, T420003, www.lidertdf.com.ar),
US$23. Both use small buses, frequent
departures. They stop en route at **Tolhuin**,
US$15. Also Tecni Austral, about 1600 (bus
has come from Punta Arenas), **Marga**
and Pacheco.
Car hire Europcar, Av Belgrano 423,
T430365. **Localiza**, San Martín 642, T430191.

Río Grande p55

Airline offices Aerolíneas Argentinas,
San Martín 607, T424467, Mon-Fri 0900-1230,
1500-1900, Sat 0930-1200. LADE, Lasserre
445, T422968. **Banks** ATMs: several banks
on San Martín by junction with Av 9 de Julio.
Link ATM at YPF station at river end of
Belgrano. Thaler cambio, Espora 631, open
Mon-Fri 1000-1500. **Consulates** Chile,
Belgrano 369, T430523, Mon-Fri 0830-1330.
Supermarkets Norte, San Martín y
Piedrabuena, good selection; also La
Anónima on San Martín near Belgrano.

Ushuaia and around → Phone code: 02901. Population: 45,000.

Situated 212 km southwest of Río Grande, the most southerly town in Argentina and
growing fast, Ushuaia is beautifully positioned on the northern shore of the Beagle
Channel, named after the ship in which Darwin sailed here in 1832. Its streets climb
steeply towards snow-covered Cerro Martial and there are fine views to neighbouring
peaks and over the Beagle Channel to the jagged peaks of Isla Navarino (Chile). Tourist
offices at the **Muelle Turístico** ① T437666, 0800-1800; San Martín 674, esq Fadul, T424550,
www.turismoushuaia.com, Mon-Fri 0800-2200, Sat-Sun 0900-2000. 'Best in Argentina',
helpful English-speaking staff, who find accommodation in summer. Information
available in English, French and German. There is a tourist desk at the airport. **Oficina
Antártica** ① Muelle Turistico, T423340, antartida@tierradelfuego.org.ar, Mon-Fri
0900-1900, has information on Antarctica and a small library with navigational charts.
Provincial tourist office ① Maipú 505, T423340, info@tierradelfuego.org.ar.

Best time to visit March to April is a good time because of the autumn colours and the
most stable weather. November, spring, has the strongest winds (not good for sailing to
Antarctica). Most visitors arrive in January. Summer temperatures average at about 15ºC,
but exceed 20º more frequently than in the past. Likewise, there has been a reduction in
snowfall in winter (average temperature 0ºC). Lots of Brazilians come to ski, so there is a
mini high season in July and August. European skiers also come to train in the northern
hemisphere summer.

Places in Ushuaia

First settled in 1884 by missionary Thomas Bridges, whose son Lucas became a great defender of the indigenous peoples here, Ushuaia's fascinating history is still visible in its old buildings and at Estancia Harberton, 85 km west (see below). A penal colony for many years, the old prison, **Presidio** ① *Yaganes y Gob Paz, at the back of the Naval Base, Mon-Sun 0900-2000, US$12 for foreigners, ticket valid 48 hrs, tours in Spanish 1130, 1830, English 1400* houses the small **Museo Marítimo**, with models and artefacts from seafaring days, and, in the cells of most of the huge five wings, the **Museo Penitenciario**, which details the history of the prison and of the pioneers who came to the area. There are also temporary exhibitions, a shop and a café. Highly recommended. **Museo del Fin del Mundo** ① *Maipú y Rivadavia, T421863, www.tierradel fuego.org.ar/museo, daily 0900-2000 (Mon-Sat 1200-1900 May-Oct), US$5, guided tours 1100, 1400, 1700, fewer in winter.* In the 1912 bank building, it small displays on indigenous peoples, missionaries and first settlers, as well as nearly all the birds of Tierra del Fuego (stuffed). Recommended. The building also contains an excellent library with helpful staff. **Museo Yámana** ① *Rivadavia 56, T422874, www.tierradelfuego.org.ar/mundoyamana, daily 1000-2000 high season, 1200-1900 low season, US$3.50.* Scale models depicting the geological evolution of the island and the everyday life of Yamana people, texts in English, also recommended. The **Antigua Casa de Gobierno** ① *Maipú 465, Mon-Fri 1000-1200, weekends 1500-2000, free,* is another building open to the public with an exhibition on the history of the city and temporary exhibitions. **Local events**: second half of April, Classical Music Festival (www.festivaldeushuaia.com); winter solstice, the longest night with a torch-light

Ushuaia

Where to stay 🛏
1 Albergue Cruz del Sur
2 Antarctica
3 Canal Beagle

4 Cap Polonio
5 Familia Velásquez
6 Freestyle
7 Galeazzi-Basily
8 Hostal Malvinas

9 Hostería Posada
   Fin del Mundo
10 La Casa de Tere
11 Lennox
12 Los Cormoranes

13 Mil810
14 Nahuel
15 Paisaje del Beagle
16 Tzion
17 Yakush

procession and fireworks, 20-21 June; August, annual sled dog race and Marcha Blanca, a ski trek from Lago Escondido to Tierra Mayor valley.

Cerro Martial, about 7 km behind the town, offers fine views down the Beagle Channel and to the north. Take a chairlift (*aerosilla*), daily first up 1000, last up 1645, last down 1730, US$8.50, tariffs change in winter, closed for repair for a time in April. To reach the chairlift, follow Magallanes out of town, allow 1½ hours. Several companies run minibus services from the corner of Maipú and Fadul, frequent departures daily in summer, US$4. Taxis charge US$7 to the base, from where you can walk down all the way back. There are several marked trails, leaflet given out at the lower platform, including to a viewpoint and to **Glaciar Martial** itself, from 600 m to 1 km. Splendid tea shop at the Cumbres de Martial *cabañas* at the base; basic *refugio* with no electricity up at the Cerro. Also by the lower platform is the **Canopy** ⓘ *US$30, US$20 for a shorter run, T02901-155 10307, www.canopyushuaia.com.ar*, a series of zip lines and bridges in the trees, eleven stretches in all. All visitors are accompanied by staff, safe, good fun. The café at the entrance, **Refugio de Montaña**, serves hot chocolate and coffee, cakes, pizzas and has a warm stove.

The **Estancia Harberton** ⓘ *T422742, www.estanciaharberton.com, US$7, daily 15 Oct-15 Apr, except 25 Dec, 1 Jan and Easter, museum: US$3.30*, the oldest on the island and run by descendants of British missionary, Thomas Bridges, whose family protected the indigenous peoples here, is 85 km from Ushuaia on Ruta J. It's a beautiful place, offering guided walks through protected forest and delicious teas, US$6.60, or lunch, US$30 (reserve ahead), in the Mánakatush casa de té overlooking the bay. The impressive **Museo Acatushún** ⓘ *www.aca tushun.org*, has skeletons of South American sea

Restaurants 🍴
1 137 Pizzas & Pastas
2 Bodegón Fueguino
3 Café Bar Banana
4 Café de la Esquina
5 Café Tante Sara
6 Chicho's
7 Cositas Ricas
8 El Bambú
9 El Turco
10 Kaupé
11 La Estancia
12 Laguna Negra
13 Martinica
14 Moustacchio
15 Panadería Petit Ideal
16 Parrilla La Rueda
17 Ramos Generales
18 Sandwchería Kami
19 Tía Elvira
20 Volver

mammals and birds, the result of 25 years' scientific investigation in Tierra del Fuego, with excellent tours in English. You can camp free, with permission from the owners, or stay in cottages. Access is from a good unpaved road which branches off Ruta 3, 40 km east of Ushuaia and runs 45 km through forest before the open country around Harberton; marvellous views, about two hours (no petrol outside of Ushuaia and Tolhuin). The road passes Laguna Victoria, where there is a good chance of seeing condors, and the turning to Puerto Almansa fishing port.

Short boat excursions from Ushuaia are highly recommended, though the Beagle Channel can be very rough. These can be booked through most agencies. They leave from the **Muelle Turístico**, where all operators have ticket booths and representatives (**Tolkeyen** and **Rumbo Sur** also have offices on San Martín). All passengers must pay US$1.65 port tax; this is not included in tickets. Operators offer slight variations on a basic theme of trips to Isla de los Lobos, Isla de los Pájaros, Les Eclaireurs lighthouse and Harberton. See under What to do below for details of these and of longer sea trips.

Tren del Fin del Mundo ① *T431600, www.trendelfindelmundo.com.ar, 4-5 departures daily, US$36 tourist, US$55 1st class return, US$71 premium and US$117 special, cheaper in winter, plus US$20 park entrance and cost of transport to the station, tickets at station, the port, or travel agencies, sit on left outbound for the best views*, is the world's southernmost steam train, running new locomotives and carriages on track first laid by prisoners to carry wood to Ushuaia. A totally touristy experience with commentary in English and Spanish (written material in other languages), 50-minute ride from the Fin del Mundo station, 8 km west of Ushuaia, into Tierra del Fuego National Park (one way of starting a hike). There is one stop at Estación Macarena, 15 minutes, for a view of the river and a walk up to Macarena waterfall. In 1st class you can buy food and drinks at the station *confitería* to eat at your table. At the same entrance as the train station is Ushuaia's nine-hole golf course.

Parque Nacional Tierra del Fuego
① *US$20. Tierra del Fuego National Park Office, San Martín 1395, Ushuaia, T421315, tierradelfuego@ apn.gov.ar, Mon-Fri 0900-1600. Tourist office and National Park office have details and a map of park, with walks. For buses see Transport, page 67.*
Covering 63,000 ha of mountains, lakes, rivers and deep valleys, this small but beautiful park stretches west to the Chilean border and north to Lago Fagnano, though large areas are closed to tourists. Public access is allowed from the park entrance 12 km west of Ushuaia, where you'll be given the basic map with marked walks. **1) Senda Costera**, 8 km, three hours each way. Along the shore from Ensenada. From Lago Roca, continue along to Río Lapataia, crossing the broad green river, where there are more short paths to follow. From Ensenada a boat goes to Isla Redonda, a provincial Reserva Natural, first at 1000, last back at 1700, US$23 return, US$30 to Isla Redonda and on to Lapataia. There are four trails on island, two hours, a *refugio* for sleeping, hot water, and a post office, open end-October to beginning of April. **2) Senda Hito XXIV**, along the northeast shore of Lago Roca to the Chilean frontier, 3.5 km, 90 minutes one way, lots of birdlife. **3) Cerro Guanaco** (1106 m), 4 km, four hours one way. Challenging hike up through forest to splendid views. **4) Senda Pampa Alta**, 4.9 km via a mirador (look out), or 3.7 km via the road, to Río Pipo. The main campsite is in a good spot at Lago Roca: see below for details of this and other sites. It's best to go in the early morning or afternoon to avoid the tour buses. You'll see geese, the torrent duck, Magellanic woodpeckers and austral parakeets. There are no legal crossing points to

Chile. Helpful *guardaparque* (ranger) at Lago Roca. Remember that the weather can be cold, damp and unpredictable, even in summer; winter days are short.

Ushuaia and around listings

For hotel and restaurant price codes and other relevant information, see pages 10-12.

⊙ Where to stay

Ushuaia *p57, map p53*
The tourist office has a comprehensive list of all officially registered accommodation and will help with rooms in private homes, campsites, etc. An excellent choice is to stay with Ushuaia families on a B&B basis. The range of lodging is growing at all budget levels, from the very chic, to *cabañas*, to the basic B&B, in the centre and the suburbs. There are too many to list here. Despite the expansion, you must book in advance in high season.

Cabañas and places outside town
All are recommended.
$$$$ Cabañas del Beagle, Las Aljabas 375, T432785/155 11323, www.cabaniasdel beagle.com. 3 rustic-style cabins 1.3 km above the city, fully equipped with kitchen, hydromassage, fireplace, heating, phone, self-service breakfast, very comfortable, personal attention.
$$$$ Cumbres del Martial, Luis F Martial 3560, 7 km from town, T424779, www.cumbresdel martial.com.ar. At the foot of the aerosilla to Glaciar Martial, 4 *cabañas* and 6 rooms, beautifully set in the woods, charming, very comfortable, cabins have whirlpool baths. Small spa (massage extra) with saunas. The tea room is open all year, restaurant from Dec.
$$$$ Finisterris Lodge Relax, Monte Susana, Ladera Este, 7 km from city, T156 12121, Buenos Aires 011-5917 8288, www.finisterris.com. In 17 ha of forest, 5-star luxury in individual cabins, with top-of-the-

range fittings, hydromassage and private spa (massage arranged, extra), rustic style but spacious, 'home-from-home' atmosphere, 24-hr attention from owner, given mobile phone on arrival. Meals can be ordered in, or private chef and sommelier can be booked for you.
$$$$ Las Hayas, Luis Martial 1650 (road to Glaciar Martial), T430710, www.lashayas.com.ar. 4 standards of room, all very good with TV, safe, 3 types of view, channel, mountains or forest. 2 restaurants: Martial for lunch and dinner, Drake for breakfast. Everything is included in room price except massages and hairdresser. A fine hotel. Just beyond is the same family company's.
$$$$ Los Acebos, Luis F Martial 1911, T011-4393 4750, www.losacebos.com.ar. All rooms with channel view, safe, Wi-Fi, free internet, games room, **Rêve d'Orange** restaurant independent of hotel. Very comfy, as expected, but less characterful than Las Hayas.
$$$$ Los Cauquenes, at Bahía Cauquen, C Reinamora 3462, T441300, www.los cauquenes.com. High quality 5-star hotel overlooking Beagle Channel, price varies according to size and view, spa, very tastefully decorated, prize-winning restaurant with US$13 lunch menu, regional food on dinner menu.
$$$$ Los Yámanas, Costa de los Yámanas 2850 western suburbs, T445960, www.hotelyamanas.com.ar. In the same group as Canoero tour operator, all rooms with Channel view, spacious, well-decorated with DirectTV, Wi-Fi, hydromassage, fitness centre, spa and conference centre outside in wooded grounds, shuttle to town. Very pleasant.

$$$$ Tierra de Leyendas, Tierra de Vientos 2448, T443565, www.tierradeleyendas.com.ar. In the western suburbs. Five very comfortable rooms with views of the Beagle Channel, or the mountains at the back, 1 room with jacuzzi, all others with shower, excellent restaurant serving regional specialties, open only for guests for breakfast and dinner. Free internet, no cable TV, but DVDs, living room with games, library, deck overlooking Río Pipo's outflow. Only for non smokers. Recommended and award-winning.

$$$ pp Estancia Harberton, T422742, www.estanciaharberton.com. 2 restored buildings on the estancia (see above), very simple rooms, wonderful views, heating. Price includes breakfast, walking tour and entry to museum; 2 rooms with bath, 1 room with 2 beds, shared bath, 1 room with bunks, shared bath. Kitchenette for tea and coffee. Lunch and dinner US$30 pp without drinks. Open mid-Oct-mid-Apr, no credit cards.

In town
$$$$ Canal Beagle, Maipú y 25 de Mayo, T432303, www.hotelcanalbeagle.com.ar. ACA hotel (**$$$** Apr-Oct; discounts for members), comfortable and well-attended, with a small pool, gym, sauna, clear views over the channel from some rooms (others see the container dock), good restaurant.

$$$$ Lennox, San Martín 776, T436430, www.lennoxhotel.com.ar. Boutique hotel on the main street, with breakfast, services include internet, hydromassage, TV, frigobar, restaurant and *confitería* on 4th floor.

$$$$ Mil810, 25 de Mayo 245, T437710, www.hotel1810.com. City hotel with 30 standard rooms, one with disabled access, no restaurant but breakfast and *confitería*, all rooms with flat-screen TV, minibar, safe, quite small but cosy, calm colours, good views, business centre and multiple use room where you can hang out while waiting for flight.

$$$ Cap Polonio, San Martín 746, T422140, www.hotelcappolonio.com.ar. Smart, central, modern, comfortable, TV, free internet, Wi-Fi, popular restaurant/café **Marcopolo**.

$$$ Paisaje del Beagle, Gob Paz 1347, T421214, www.paisajedelbeagle.com. Family-run, quiet, with a cosy dining area for good breakfast (included), free internet, laundry service. Recommended.

$$ Galeazzi-Basily, Gdor Valdez 323, T423213, www.avesdelsur.com.ar. Among the best, beautiful family home, incredible welcome, in pleasant area 5 blocks from centre, breakfast included, shared bath, free internet. Also excellent *cabañas* (**$$$**) in the garden. Recommended.

$$ Hostal Malvinas, Gob Deloqui 615, T422626, www.hostalmalvinas.net. Comfortable but small rooms, small breakfast, free tea and coffee.

$$ Hostería Posada Fin del Mundo, Gob Valdez 281, T437345, www.posadafin delmundo.com.ar. Family atmosphere, comfortable rooms, good value, has character.

$$ pp La Casa de Tere, Rivadavia 620, T422312, www.lacasadetere.com.ar. Shared bath, with breakfast, home-made bread and cake, use of kitchen, some rooms get lots of sun, singles, doubles and triples, hot water, helpful owner.

$$ Nahuel, 25 de Mayo 440, T423068, byb_nahuel@ yahoo.com.ar. Charming Sra Navarrete has a comfortable B&B with channel views from the upper rooms and the terrace, good value, but noisy street.

$$ Tzion, Gob Valdez 468, T432290, tzion_byb@ hotmail.com. B & B with 3 rooms, 1 with bath, high above town, 10 mins' walk from centre, nice family atmosphere (contact Daniel Pirruccio at Tolkar Turismo), cheaper low season, laundry service, English and French spoken.

$$-$ Familia Velásquez, Juana Fadul 361, T421719, almayo@arnet.com.ar. Welcoming, cosy house of a pioneer, with basic rooms, breakfast, cooking and laundry facilities, good.

$ pp Albergue Cruz del Sur, Deloqui 242, T434099, xdelsur@yahoo.com. In a new location and under new management, cosy, kitchen facilities and free tea, coffee and *mate*, book in advance, free internet.

$ pp Antárctica, Antártida Argentina 270, T435774, www.antarcticahostel.com. Central, welcoming, spacious chill-out room, excellent 24-hr bar, dorms for 6 and large doubles, breakfast, free internet/Wi-Fi and kitchen facilities, bike rental. Recommended.

$ pp Freestyle, Gob Paz 866, T432874, www.ushuaiafreestyle.com. Very busy but good, central hostel, with laundry (US$3), TV room, DVDs and pool table. Also has doubles with bath (**$$$-$$**), TV and kitchenette, at the Alto Andino hotel, which is built in front.

$ pp Los Cormoranes, Kamshen 788 y Alem, T423459, www.loscormoranes.com. Large hostel, with good views, cosy rooms, with lockers, OK bathrooms and a well-equipped kitchen. Doubles (**$$**) available. They can book tours. HI member discount.

$ pp Yakush, Piedrabuena 118 y San Martín, T435807, www.hostelyakush.com.ar. Very well run, central with spacious dorms, also doubles (**$$** with bath, cheaper without), with breakfast, free internet, book exchange and library, light kitchen and dining room and a steep garden with views. Recommended.

Camping In town: La Pista del Andino, Leandro N Alem 2873, T435890, www.lapistadelandino.com.ar. Set in the Club Andino ski premises in a woodland area, it has wonderful views over the channel. Electricity, hot showers, tea room and grocery store, US$11 per pitch, very helpful. Recommended.

Parque Nacional Tierra del Fuego *p60*
Camping

Camping Lago Roca, T433313, 21 km from Ushuaia, by forested shore of Lago Roca, a beautiful site with good facilities, reached by bus Jan-Feb. It has a backpackers' *refugio*,

toilets, showers 1800-2030, restaurant and *confitería*, expensive small shop; camping US$4, equipment for hire with deposit, eg US$100 for tent, 40 for sleeping bag.

There are also camping agreste sites with no facilities at **Río Pipo**, 16 km from Ushuaia, **Laguna Verde**, 20 km, near Lapataia, and **Bahía Ensenada**.

❽ Restaurants

Ushuaia *p57, map p58*
Lots of restaurants along San Martín and Maipú. Most open at lunchtime and again from 1900 at the earliest. Several cafés are open all the time. Ask around for currently available seafood, especially *centolla* (king crab) and *cholga* (giant mussels). Much cheaper if prepare your own meal; **Pesquera del Beagle**, Maipú 227 (closed 1600-1800 on Sun, 1300-1600 Mon), sells *centollón* (US$15 per kg ready to eat) and *centolla* (US$11 per kg; US$22.50 per kg ready to eat, just add lemon). Note *centolla* may not be fished Nov-Dec. Beer drinkers should try the handcrafted brews of the **Cape Horn** brewery, Pilsen, Pale Ale and Stout.

$$$ Bodegón Fueguino, San Martín 859. Tapas, home-made pastas and good roast lamb with varied sauces in a renovated 1896 *casa de pioneros*, open 1200-1500, 2000-2400, closed Mon.

$$$ Kaupé, Roca 470 y Magallanes. T437396. Best restaurant in town, king crab, meat.

$$$ Tía Elvira, Maipú 349. Excellent seafood, open Mon-Sat 1200-1500, 1900-2300.

$$$ Volver, Maipú 37. Delicious seafood and fish in atmospheric 1898 house, with ancient newspaper all over the walls. Recommended.

$$$-$$ La Estancia, San Martín 253. A cheery and good value *parrilla*. Packed in high season. All-you-can-eat for US$13.

$$$-$$ Moustacchio, 2 branches 2 doors apart, San Martín 272 and at Gdor Godoy. Long-established, good for seafood and meat, all-you-can-eat branch US$13.

$$$-$$ Parrilla La Rueda, San Martín y Rivadavia. Good *tenedor libre* (US$14 with dessert) for beef, lamb and great salads. Recommended for freshness.

$$ 137 Pizzas and Pastas, San Martín 137. Tasty filling versions of exactly what the name says, plus *empanadas*, elegant decor.

$$ Chicho's, Rivadavia 72, T423469. Bright, cheerful place just off the main street, friendly staff, kitchen open to view. Fish, meat and chicken dishes, pastas, wide range of *entradas*.

$$ El Turco, San Martín 1410. A very popular place, serving generous *milanesas*, pastas, pizzas, seafood and meat.

$$-$ Martinica, San Martín entre Antártida Argentina y Yaganes. Cheap, small, busy, sit at the bar facing the *parrilla* and point to your favourite beef cut. Takeaway (T432134) and good meals of the day, also pizzas and *empanadas*. Open 1130-1500, 2030-2400.

Cafés

El Bambú, Piedrabuena 276. Purely vegetarian and the only such place in town, take-away only, home-made food, delicious and good value.

Café Bar Banana, San Martín 273, T424021. Quite small, always busy, with a pool table at the back, offers good fast food, such as burgers, small pizzas, puddings, breakfasts and an all-day *menú* for US$7.50.

Café Chocolates, San Martín 783. Good *submarinos* (hot chocolate) and home-made chocolate, also good value.

Café de la Esquina, San Martín y 25 de Mayo. Lots of lunch choices, daily specials, sandwiches, *tortas*, *picadas*, *lomitos*, café and bar. Open for 15 years, used by locals and tourists.

Café Tante Sara, San Martin y Fadul. Opposite the tourist office, is very good, smart, good coffee, tasty sandwiches, always busy. Also has Cositas Ricas at San Martín 185, a smart *confitería* and *chocolatería*, selling breads, sandwiches, chocolates, *empanadas* and snacks, coffee, lots of choice.

Laguna Negra, San Martín 513. Mainly a shop selling chocolate and other fine produce, catering to the cruise ship passengers, but has a good little café at the back for hot chocolate and coffee. Also at Libertador 1250, El Calafate. Sells postcards and stamps, too.

Panadería Petit Ideal, next to **Bar Ideal**, San Martín 393, which is a **$$$** restaurant serving seafood and meat dishes in an old building at the corner of Roca. Good selection.

Ramos Generales, Maipú 749, T424317, www.ramosgeneralesushuaia.com. An old warehouse, with wooden floor and shelves and a collection of historic objects and dusty ledgers. Sells breads, pastries, wines and drinks, also cold cuts, sandwiches, salads, ice cream and coffee. Also has a dish of the day or soup for lunch, breakfasts till 1300, teas 1300-2000. Not cheap but atmospheric. Recommended.

Sandwichería Kami, San Martín 54, open 0800-2130. Friendly, simple sandwich shop, selling rolls, baguettes and *pan de miga*.

○ Shopping

Ushuaia *p57, map p58*
Ushuaia's tax free status doesn't produce as many bargains as you might hope. Lots of souvenir shops on San Martín and several offering good quality leather and silver ware. In comparison, the **Pasaje de Artesanías**, by the Muelle Turístico, sells local arts and crafts.

Atlántico Sur, San Martín 627, is the (not especially cheap) duty free shop.

Boutique del Libro, San Martín y Piedrabuena and 25 de Mayo 62. A good range of books on Patagonia and Antarctica, also DVDs, English titles and guidebooks.

La Anónima, Gob Paz y Rivadavia and San Martín y Onas. Large supermarket.

Norte, 12 de Octubre y Karukinka. Supermarket, takeaway, fresh food, and fast-food diner.

Ushuaia p57, map p58

Boat trips and cruises

All short boat trips leave from the Muelle Turístico. Take your time to choose the size and style of boat you want. Representatives from the offices are polite and helpful. All have a morning and afternoon sailing and include Isla de los Lobos, Isla de los Pájaros and Les Eclaireurs lighthouse, with guides and some form of refreshment. Note that weather conditions may affect sailings, prices can change and that port tax is not included.

Barracuda, T437233, www.motonave barracuda.com.ar. On a lovely old motor yacht, the first tourist boat in Ushuaia, US$32; their other boat, Lanín, includes Isla Bridges, US$36.

Canoero, T433893, www.catamaranes canoero.com.ar. Catamarans for 60-100 passengers, 2½-hr trips to the 3 main sites and Isla Bridges, US$36. They also have a 5-hr trip almost daily to the Pingüinera on Isla Martillo near Estancia Harberton (Oct-Mar only), boats stay for 1 hr, but you cannot land on Martillo. Passengers can return to Ushuaia by bus: US$65 without stops on bus ride, US$76 with stops.

Patagonia Adventure Explorer, T154 65842, www.patagoniaadvent.com.ar. Has a sailing boat and motor boats for the standard trip, plus Isla Bridges: US$50 sailing, US$40 motoring. Good guides.

Pira-Tour, T435557, www.piratour.com.ar. Runs 2-3 buses a day to Harberton. from where a boat goes to the Pingüinera on Isla Martillo: 15 people allowed to land (maximum 45 per day – the only company licensed to do this). US$85 for a morning tour, including lunch at Harberton and entry to Acatushún museum; US$70 for afternoon tour.

Tres Marías, T421987, www.tresmarias web.com. The only company licensed to visit Isla H, which has archaeological sites,

cormorants, other birds and plants. Also has sailing boat, no more than 10 passengers; specialist guide, café on board, US$40 on Tres Marías, US$50 on sailing boat. Also **Rumbo Sur** and **Tolkeyen**; see Tours, below.

Sea trips

Ushuaia is the starting point, or the last stop, en route to Antarctica for several cruises from Oct-Mar that usually sail for 9 to 21 days along the western shores of the Antarctic peninsula and the South Shetland Islands. Other trips include stops at Falkland/Malvinas archipelago and at South Georgia. Go to Oficina Antártica for advice (see page 57). Agencies sell 'last minute tickets', but the price is entirely dependent on demand (available 1 week before sailing). Coordinator for trips is **Turismo Ushuaia**, Gob Paz 865, T436003, www.ushuaiaturismoevt.com.ar, which operates with IAATO members only. See the website for prices for the upcoming season. Port tax is US$15 per passenger and an exit tax of US$10 is also charged.

To Chile Cruceros Australis, www.australis. com, operates two luxury cruise ships between Ushuaia and **Punta Arenas**, with a visit to Cabo de Hornos, frequently recommended. Full deta ls are given under Punta Arenas, Tour operators. Check-in at **Comapa** (see below). **Antarctic Shipping** offer daily landings in the Antarctic. See under Shipping, Punta Arenas, Chile, for full details.

Fernández Campbell have a 1½-hr crossing to **Puerto Williams**, Fri, Sat, Sun 1000, return 1500, US$125 for foreigners, tickets sold at **Zenit Explorer**, Juana Fadul 126, Ushuaia, T433232, and **Naviera RFC** in Puerto Williams.

Ushuaia Boating, Gob Paz 233. T436193 (or at the Muelle Turístico), www.ushuaia boating.com.ar. Operates all year round a channel crossing to Puerto Navarino (Isla Navarino), 20-90 mins depending on weather, and then bus to Puerto Williams, 1 hr, US$120 one way, not including taxes. At **Muelle**

AFASYN, near the old airport, T435805, ask about possible crossings with a club member to Puerto Williams, about 4 hrs, or if any foreign sailing boat is going to Cabo de Hornos or Antarctica. From Puerto Williams a ferry goes once a week to Punta Arenas.

Fishing
Trout season is Nov-mid Apr, licences US$15 per day (an extra fee is charged for some rivers and lakes). **Asociación de Caza y Pesca** at Maipú 822, T423168, cazapescush@infovia.com.ar, open Mon, Wed, Fri 1700-2100, sells licences, with list on door of other places that sell it.

Hiking and climbing
Club Andino, Fadul 50, T422335, www.clubandinoushuaia.com.ar. For advice, Mon-Fri 1000-1200, 1400-2030. Sells maps and trekking guidebooks; free guided walks once in a month in summer; also offers classes, eg yoga, dancing, karate, and has excercise bikes. The winter sports resorts along Ruta 3 (see below) are an excellent base for summer trekking and many arrange excursions.
Nunatak, 25 de Mayo 296, T430329, www.nunatakadventure.com. Organizes treks, canoeing, mountain biking and 4WD trips to Lagos Escondido and Fagnano.

Horse riding
Centro Hípico, Ruta 3, Km 3021, T155 69099, www.centrohipicoushuaia.com.ar. Rides through woods, on Monte Susana, along coast and through river, 2 hrs, US$40; 4-hr ride with light lunch, US$80; 7-hr ride with asado, US$105. Gentle horses, well cared for, all guides have first-aid training. Very friendly and helpful. All rides include transfer from town and insurance. Hats provided for children; works with disabled children. They can arrange long-distance rides of several days, eg on Península Mitre.

Winter sports
Ushuaia is becoming popular as a winter resort with 11 centres for skiing, snow-boarding and husky sledging. The Cerro Castor complex, Ruta 3, Km 27, T499301, www.cerrocastor.com, is the only centre for Alpine skiing, with 24 km of pistes, a vertical drop of 800 m and powder snow. Attractive centre with complete equipment rental, also for snowboarding and snowshoeing. The other centres along Ruta 3 at 18-36 km east of Ushuaia offer excellent cross country skiing (and alternative activities in summer). **Tierra Mayor**, 20 km from town, T437454, www.tierramayor.com, is the largest and recommended. In a beautiful wide valley between steep-sided mountains, offering half and full day excursions on sledges with huskies, as well as cross country skiing and snowshoeing. Equipment hire and restaurant. **Kawi Shiken** at Las Cotorras, Ruta 3, Km 26, T444152, 155 19497, www.tierradelfuego.org.ar/hugoflores, specializes in sled dogs, with 100 Alaskan and Siberian huskies: 2 km ride on snow US$25, 2-hr trips with meal US$60. In summer offers 2-km rides in a dog cart, US$15.

Tours
Lots of companies offer imaginative adventure tourism expeditions. All agencies charge the same fees for excursions; ask tourist office for a complete list: Tierra del Fuego National Park, 4 hrs, US$35 (entry fee US$16 extra); Lagos Escondido and Fagnano, 7 hrs, US$48 without lunch. With 3 or 4 people it might be worth hiring a *remise* taxi.
All Patagonia, Juana Fadul 40, T433622, www.allpatagonia.com. Trekking, ice climbing, and tours; trips to Cabo de Hornos and Antarctica.
Canal, 9 de Julio 118, loc 1, T437395, www.canalfun.com. Huge range of activities, trekking, canoeing, riding, 4WD excursions. Recommended.

Comapa, San Martín 409, T430727, www.comapa.tur.ar. Conventional tours and adventure tourism, bus tickets to Punta Arenas and Puerto Natales, trips to Antarctica, agents for Cruceros Australis and for Navimag ferries for Puerto Natales–Puerto Montt (10% ISIC discount for Navimag tickets). Hertz also at this office.

Compañía de Guías de Patagonia, San Martín 628, T437753, 154 93288, www.compania deguias.com.ar. The best agency for walking guides, expeditions for all levels, rock and ice climbing (training provided), also diving, sailing, riding, 7-day crossing of Tierra del Fuego on foot and conventional tours. Recommended.

Límite Vertical, T156 00868, www.limite verticaltdf.com.ar. 4WD adventures off-road to the shores of Lagos Escondido and Fagnano, taking logging trails and *ripio* roads, seeing beaver damage in the forests, etc. Lunch is an asado at an old saw mill; similar tours by other companies stop for lunch on shore of Fagnano. Good fun.

Rumbo Sur, San Martín 350, T422275, www.rumbosur.com.ar Flights, buses, conventional tours on land and sea, including to Harberton, plus Antarctic expeditions, mid-Nov to mid-Mar, English spoken

Tolkar, Roca 157, T431412, www.tolkar turismo.com.ar. Flights, bus tickets to Argentina and Chile, conventional and adventure tourism, canoeing and mountain biking to Lago Fagnano.

Tolkeyen, San Martín 1267, T437073, www.tolkeyenpatagonia.com. Bus and flight tickets, catamaran trips (50-300 passengers), including to Harberton (Mon, Wed, Fri, US$66) and Parque Nacional, large company.

Travel Lab, San Martín 1444, T436555, www.travellab.com.ar. Conventional and unconventional tours, mountain biking, trekking etc, English and French spoken, helpful

Turismo de Campo, Fuegia Basket 414, T437351, www.turismodecampo.com. Adventure tourism, English/French speaking guides, boat and trekking trips in the National Park, birdwatching, sailing and trips to Antarctica.

Transport

Ushuaia *p57, map p58*

Air Airport 4 km from town. Book ahead in summer; flights fill up fast. In winter flights often delayed. Taxi to airport US$4.60 (no bus). Schedules tend to change from season to season. Airport tourist information only at flight times, T423970. To **Buenos Aires** (Aeroparque or Ezeiza), 3½ hrs, **El Calafate**, 1 hr, and **Río Gallegos**, 1 hr. with AR/Austral and **LADE** (longer flights) also to **Río Grande**, 1 hr, several a week (but check with agents). In summer **LAN** flies to **Punta Arenas** twice a week. The **Aeroclub de Ushuaia** flies Mon, Wed, Fri to **Puerto Williams**, US$100 one way from the downtown airport.

Bus Urban buses from west to east across town, most stops along Maipú, US$0.50. Tourist office provides a list of minibus companies that run daily from town (stops along Maipú) to nearby attractions.

To the national park: in summer buses and minibuses leave from the bus stop on Maipu at the bottom of Fadul. **Pasarella**, 9 a day from 0800, last back 1900, US$12 return, US$13.50 to Lapataia: **Eben Ezer**, 8 a day from 0830, last back 2000. From same bus stop, many other *colectivos* go to the Tren del Fin del Mundo, Lago Escondido, Lago Fagnano and Glaciar Martial, leave when full. For **Harberton**, check the notice boards at the station at Maipú y Fadul. The only regular bus is run by **Pira-Tur**, see What to do, above.

Passport needed when booking international bus tickets. Buses always booked up Nov-Mar; buy your ticket to leave as soon as you arrive. To **Río Grande**, 3½-4 hrs, combis **Líder** (Gob Paz 921,

T436421), and **Montiel** (Deloqui 110, T421366), US$23. Also buses en route to Río Gallegos and Punta Arenas.

To **Río Gallegos**, **Tecni Austral**, 0530, 11½ hrs, US$102 (through Tolkar), and **Marga/Taqsa**, Godoy 41, daily at 0600. To **Punta Arenas**, US$46-60, **Tecni Austral**, 0530, 11-12 hrs (through Tolkar); **Pacheco**, 0800 Mon, Wed, Fri, 12-13 hrs (San Martín 1267, T430727), connect with **Bus Sur** for **Puerto Natales**, and others.

Car hire Most companies charge from about US$50 per day, including insurance and 200 km per day, special promotions available. **Localiza**, Sarmiento 81, T437780, localizaush@speedy. com.ar. Cars can be hired in Ushuaia to be driven through Chile and then left in any Localiza office in Argentina, but you must buy a one-off customs document for US$50, to use as many times as you like to cross borders. Must reserve well in advance and pay a drop-off fee. **Europcar**, Maipú 857, T430786. Hertz, San Martín 245. **Budget**, Godoy 45. Note that hiring a car in Tierra del Fuego is 21% cheaper than anywhere else in the current tax régime.

Taxi Cheaper than *remises*, T422007, T440225. Taxi stand by the Muelle Turístico. **Remises Carlitos**, San Martín y Don Bosco, T422222; **Bahía Hermosa**, T422233.

Directory

Ushuaia *p57, map p58*

Airline offices Aerolíneas Argentinas, Maipú 823, T436342, Mon-Fri 0930-1700, Sat 0930-1200, airport office opens daily 0800-2000. **LADE**, San Martín 542, shop 5B, T421123. Open Mon-Fri 0800-2000, Sat-Sun 0900-1600. **Banks** Banks open 1000-1500 in summer. ATMs are plentiful all along San Martín, using credit cards is easiest (but Sat, Sun and holidays machines can be empty), changing TCs is difficult and expensive. **Agencia de Cambio Thaler**, San Martín 209, T421911, www.cambio-thaler.com, open Mon-Fri 1000-1500, 1700-200, Sat 1000-1300, 1700-2000, Sun 1700-2000.

Consulates Chile, Jainén 50, T430909, Mon-Fri 0900-1300. **Useful addresses** Dirección Nacional de Migraciones, Fuegia Basket 87. **Biblioteca Popular Sarmiento**, San Martín 1589, T423103. Mon-Fri 0830-2000, Sat 1000-1300, library with a good range of books about the area.

Contents

Chilean Patagonia

Puerto Montt and around

Just 20 minutes south of Puerto Varas, and 1016 km south of Santiago, Puerto Montt is the gateway to the shipping lanes to the south, namely the island of Chiloé and the wilds of Patagonia. It's a rapidly growing, disordered modern city, developing in line with a boom in salmon fishing. Angelmó, a fishing port 2 km west, is most popular with visitors for its seafood restaurants and handicraft shops, but the city is not worth a visit of more than a day or two.

Puerto Montt → *Phone code: 065. Population: 160,000.*

Arriving in Puerto Montt

Tourist offices Puerto Montt: For information and town maps, there's a **municipal tourist office** ① *just southwest of the Plaza de Armas, T223027 (open till 1800 on Sat).* See www.puerto monttchile.cl for information on the web. For regional information **Sernatur** ① *Av Décima Región 480 (p 2), T256999, infoloslagos@sernatur.cl, 0830-1300, 1430-1730, Mon-Thu, 0830-1630 Fri,* is in the Intendencia Regional. **CONAF** ① *T486102, loslagos.oirs@conaf.cl,* is at Ochogavía 458, but cannot supply information on national parks. **Provincial office** ① *Urmeneta 977, p 5 (Edif Isla del Rey), T486400.*

Places in Puerto Montt

The capital of X Región (Los Lagos) was founded in 1853 as part of the German colonization of the area. Good views over the city and bay are offered from outside the Intendencia Regional on Avenida X Region. The port is used by fishing boats and coastal vessels, and is the departure point for vessels to Chaitén, Puerto Chacabuco, Laguna San Rafael and for the long haul south to Puerto Natales. A paved road runs 55 km southwest to Pargua, where there is a ferry service to Chiloé.

The **Iglesia de los Jesuitas** on Gallardo, dating from 1872, has a fine blue-domed ceiling; behind it on a hill is the campanario (clock tower). **Museo Regional Juan Pablo II** ① *Portales 997 near the bus terminal, daily 1030-1800, closed weekends off season, US$1,* documents local history and has a fine collection of historic photos of the city; also memorabilia of the Pope John Paul II's visit in 1988. The **Casa Pauly** ① *Rancagua 210* is one of the city's historic mansions, now in a poor state but which holds temporary exhibitions. Near the plaza, the **Casa del Arte Diego Rivera** ① *Varas y Quillota, www.corporacionculturalpuertomontt.cl* has a theatre and holds regular exhibitions. The fishing port of **Angelmó**, 2 km west, has become a tourist centre with seafood restaurants and handicraft shops (reached by Costanera bus along Portales and by *colectivos* Nos 2, 3 and 20 from the centre, US$0.30).

The wooded **Isla Tenglo**, reached by launch from Angelmó (US$1 each way), is a favourite place for picnics. Magnificent view from the summit. The island is famous for its *curantos*, served by restaurants in summer. Boat trips round the island from Angelmó last 30 minutes, US$5. **Parque Provincial Lahuen Ñadi** (US$3; you may have to call a cellphone number to enter) contains 200 ha of native forest including probably the most accessible ancient alerce forest in Chile. Take the main road to the airport, which leads off Ruta 5. After 5 km, turn right (north) and follow the signs. West of Puerto Montt the Río Maullín, which drains Lago Llanquihue, has some attractive waterfalls and good fishing (salmon). At the mouth of the river is the little fishing village of **Maullín**, founded in 1602.

To Argentina via Lago Todos Los Santos

This popular but ever more expensive route to Bariloche, involving ferries across Lago Todos Los Santos, Lago Frías and Lago Nahuel Huapi is outstandingly beautiful whatever the season, though the mountains are often obscured by rain and heavy cloud. The route is via Puerto Varas, Ensenada and Petrohué falls (20 minutes' stop) to Petrohué, where it connects with catamaran service across Lago Todos Los Santos to Peulla. Lunch stop in Peulla two hours (lunch not included in fare: Hotels Natura and Peulla are expensive). Chilean customs in Peulla, followed by a two-hour bus ride through the Paso Pérez Rosales to Argentine customs in Puerto Frías, 20-minute boat trip across Lago Frías to Puerto Alegre and 15-minute bus from Puerto Alegre to Puerto Blest, where there is a long wait (and poor food). From Puerto Blest it is a beautiful one hour catamaran trip along Lago Nahuel Huapi to Puerto Pañuelo (Llao Llao), from where there is a 30-minute bus journey to Bariloche (bus drops passengers at hotels, camping sites or in town centre). From 1 May to 30 August this trip is done over two days with overnight stay in Peulla at Hotel Peulla or Hotel Natura. (You may break the journey at any point and continue next day.) The route is operated by **Cruce Andino**, www.cruceandino.com. Fares are given under Transport, below.

Sea routes south of Puerto Montt

To Puerto Natales The dramatic 1460 km journey first goes through Seno Reloncaví and Canal Moraleda. From Bahía Anna Pink along the coast and then across the Golfo de Penas to Bahía Tarn it is a 12- to 17-hour sea crossing, usually rough. The journey continues through Canal Messier, Angostura Inglesa and the Concepción, Sarmiento and White channels. It takes just under four days. Navimag's vessel *Evangelistas*, a functional but comfortable 123-m-long freight and passenger roll-on roll-off ferry, makes the journey. It may call at Puerto Chacabuco en route south and north, and stops off Puerto Edén on Isla Wellington (one hour south of Angostura Inglesa). This is a fishing village with one hospedaje (20 beds), three shops, scant provisions, one off-licence, one café, and a *hospedaje* for up to 20 people (open intermittantly). Population is 180, including five *carabineros* and the few remaining Alacaluf. It is the drop-off point for exploring Isla Wellington, which is largely untouched, with stunning mountains. If stopping, take food; maps (not very accurate) available in Santiago. Passengers on the *Evangelistas* may disembark for 2½ hours on the third morning to walk around the village. Between November and March, the *Evangelistas* also visits the Pío XI, or Bruggen Glacier, the largest in South America, for an hour on the southward journey. Going north it stops at the Amalia or Brujo Glacier (depending on weather conditions) on the second evening. The service is not very reliable so always check that it is running.

Puerto Montt and around listings

For hotel and restaurant price codes and other relevant information, see pages 10-12.

● Where to stay

Puerto Montt *p70*

Accommodation is often much cheaper off season. Check with the tourist office.

$$$ Club Presidente, Av Portales 664, T251666, www.presidente.cl. 4-star, with breakfast, very comfortable, also suites, some rooms with view. Often full Mon-Fri with business travellers. Recommended.

$$$ Holiday Inn Express, Mall Paseo Costanera, T566000, www.holidayinn.cl. Good business standard. Spacious rooms with desks and great views, some with balcony. Slightly pokey bathrooms but still the best hotel in its category. Recommended.

$$$ Tren del Sur, Santa Teresa 643, T343939, www.trendelsur.cl. 'Boutique' *hostal* with pleasant public areas, objects recycled from the old railway, some rooms without windows, buffet breakfast, café, heating, Wi-Fi, helpful English-speaking owner.

$$$ Viento Sur, Huasco 143, T351212, www.hotelpuertosur.cl. Small business-oriented hotel in a quiet part of town. 4 floors, no lifts or views but good value and parking.

$$ Hospedaje Rocco, Pudeto 233, T272897, www.hospedajerocco.cl. **$** in dorms. Renovated, breakfast, real coffee, English spoken, laundry, quiet residential area, convenient for Navimag. Recommended.

$$ Hostal Central, Huasco 61, T263081, www.hostalcentralpuertomontt.cl. Small, neat rooms in an old wooden house, peaceful neighbourhood, no breakfast, kitchen facilities, midnight curfew. A couple of rooms with nice views. A good choice; do not confuse with the other **Hostal Central**.

$$ Hostal Pacífico, J J Mira 1088, T256229, www.hostalpacifico.cl. Breakfast included, cable TV, parking, comfortable, some rooms a bit cramped. Discounts for foreign tourists.

$$ Hostal Suizo, Independencia 231, T/F252640, rossyoelckers@yahoo.es. **$** pp in shared rooms, some rooms with bath. With small breakfast, painting and Spanish classes, German and Italian spoken, Spanish classes. Convenient for Navimag ferry.

$$ Vista al Mar, Vivar 1337, T255625, www.hospedajevistaalmar.unlugar.com. Impeccable small guesthouse, good breakfast, peaceful, great view from the double ensuite, Wi-Fi. Recommended.

$$ Vista Hermosa, Miramar 1486, T319600, http://hostalvistahermosa.cl/. With breakfast, simple, ask for front room for best views (10 mins' walk uphill from terminal), use of kitchen, Wi-Fi, also has a fully equipped cabin.

$$-$ Alda González, Gallardo 552, T253334. With or without bath, slightly careworn rooms in a big rickety wooden house, near the Plaza de Armas. With good breakfast, cooking facilities, popular, German and English spoken, very hospitable. Recommended.

$$-$ Casa Perla, Trigal 312, T262104, www.casaperla.com. Under US$12 pp in shared rooms. With breakfast, French, English spoken, helpful, use of kitchen, meals, Spanish classes offered off season, laundry, internet, pleasant garden, good meeting place. Recommended.

Camping **Camping Municipal** at Chinquihue, 10 km west (bus service),T257552, Oct-Apr, fully equipped with tables, seats, barbecue, toilets and showers; small shop, no kerosene. Others on this road: **Los Alamos**, Km 15, T264666.

● Restaurants

Puerto Montt *p70*

Local specialities include *picoroco al vapor*, a giant barnacle whose flesh looks and tastes like crab, and *curanto*.

In Angelmó, there are several dozen small, seafood restaurants in the old fishing port, past the fish market, very popular, lunches only except in Jan-Feb when they are open until late; ask for *té blanco* (white wine – they are not legally allowed to serve wine).

Other seafood restaurants in Chinquihue, west of Angelmó.

$$$ Club de Yates, Juna Soler s/n, Costanera east of centre, T284000. Excellent seafood, fine views from a pier.

$$$ Club Alemán, Varas 264, T297000. Old fashioned, good food and wine.

$$$-$$ Cotele, Juan Soler 1611, Pelluco. 4 km east, T278000. Closed Sun. Only serves beef, but serves it as well as anywhere in southern Chile. Reservations advised.

$$$-$$ Pazos, Pelluco, T252552. Serves the best *curanto* in the Puerto Montt area.

$$ Café Haussman, San Martín 185. German cakes, beer and *crudos*. Recommended.

$ Café Central, Rancagua 117. Spartan decor, generous portions (sandwiches and *pichangas* – savoury salad snack). Giant TV screen.

$ Café Real, Rancagua 137. For *empanadas*, *pichangas*, *congrío frito* and lunches.

Cafés
Asturias, Angelmó 2448. Often recommended.

○ Shopping

Puerto Montt p70
Woollen goods and Mapuche-designed rugs can be bought at roadside stalls in Angelmó and on Portales opposite the bus terminal.
Supermarkets Bigger, opposite bus terminal, open 0900-2200 daily. Also in the **Paseo del Mar** shopping mall. Talca y A Varas. **Paseo Costanera** is a newer, bigger mall on the seafront.

▲ What to do

Puerto Montt p70
Sailing 2 Yacht Clubs in Chinquihue:
Club de Deportes Náuticas Reloncaví, Camino a Chinquihue Km 7, T255022, www.nautico reloncavi.com. Marina, sailing lessons.
Marina del Sur (MDS), Camino a Chinquihue Km 4.5, T251958, www.marinadelsur.cl. Marina

with all facilities, restaurant, Wi-Fi, yacht charters with captain and crew, notice board for crew (tripulante) requests, specialists in cruising the Patagonian channels.

Tour operators
There are many tour operators. Some companies offer 2-day excursions along the Carretera Austral to Hornopirén, price includes food and accommodation. Most offer 1-day excursions to Chiloé and to Puerto Varas, Isla Loreley, Laguna Verde, and the Petrohué falls: both are much cheaper from bus company kiosks inside the bus terminal, eg Bohle. We have received good reports about:

Ecosub, Panamericana 510, T065-263939, www.ecosub.cl. Scuba-diving excursions.
Eureka Turismo, Gallardo 65, T065-250412, www.chile-travel.com/eureka.htm. Helpful, German and English spoken.

⊖ Transport

Puerto Montt p70
Air El Tepual Airport is 13 km northwest of town, T486200. **ETM** bus from terminal (T290100, www.busesetm.cl) 1½ hrs before departure, US$3.50; also meets incoming flights. **ETM** minibus service to/from hotels, US$10 for one person, US$15 for 2. Taxi US$20. **LAN** and **Sky** have several flights daily to **Santiago**, **Balmaceda** (for Coyhaique) and **Punta Arenas**. In Jan, Feb and Mar flights may be booked up, but cancellations may be available from the airport. Flights to **Chaitén** (or nearby Santa Bárbara) leave from the Aerodromo la Paloma on the outskirts of town. For flight details, see page 79.

Bus Terminal on sea front at Portales y Lota has been expanded with rural buses leaving from one side and long distance buses from the other. There are also telephones, restaurants, *casa de cambio* (left luggage, US$1-2 per item for 24 hrs). To **Puerto Varas** (US$1.50), **Llanquihue** (US$2), **Frutillar** (US$2.50 – minibuses every few mins), **Puerto Octay** (US$4), 5 daily. Expreso Puerto Varas,

Thaebus and **Full Express**. To **Ensenada** and **Petrohué**, **Buses JM** several daily. To **Cochamó** US$5, 3 hrs. To **Hornopirén**, 5 hrs, US$10. To **Osorno** US$5, 2 hrs, to **Valdivia**, US$7, 3½ hrs. To **Pucón**, US$16, 6 hrs. To **Temuco** US$10-18. **Concepción**, US$15-30. To **Valparaíso**, 14 hrs, US$30-55. To **Santiago**, 12 hrs, US$30-95, several companies including **Tur-Bus**. To **Punta Arenas**, **Pacheco**, **Turibus** and others, 1-3 a week (bus goes through Argentina via Bariloche, take US$ cash for Argentina expenses en route), 32-38 hrs. Also take plenty of food for this "nightmare" trip. Book well in advance in Jan-Feb and check if you need a multiple-entry Chilean visa. Also book any return journey before setting out.

To Argentina via Lago Todos Los Santos
The route is operated only by **Cruce Andino**, www.cruceandino.com. Bus from Puerto Montt daily at 0745 from **Turistour**, Antonio Varas 437 and selected hotels, and **Turistour**, Del Salvador 72, Puerto Varas, and hotels. The fare is US$230 for the one-day trip. From 1 May to 31 Aug the trip takes 2 days, with overnight in Peulla (Hotels **Natura** or **Peulla**, not included). Note that the trip may be cancelled if the weather is poor; difficulty in obtaining a refunds or assistance have been reported. If you take the boat from Petrohué to Peulla, you can cross to Argentina and carry on to Bariloche (check on the availability of public transport, bus and boat, across the border). In high season you must book ahead.

Buses to Argentina via Osorno and the Puyehue pass Daily services to Bariloche on this route via Osorno, 7 hrs, are run by **Vía Bariloche, Andesmar, Tas Choapa** and **Bus Norte Internacional**, US$30. Out of season, services are reduced. Buy tickets for international buses from the bus terminal. Book well in advance in Jan and Feb; ask for a seat on the right hand side for the best views.

Car hire Autovald, Sector Cardenal, Pasaje San Andrés 60, T215366, www.autovald.cl, cheap rates. **Egartur**, Benavente 575, loc 3,

T257336, www.egartur.cl, good service, recommended, will deliver your car to your hotel for free. **Full Famas**, Portales 506, T258060 and at airport, T263750. Helpful, good value, has vehicles that can be taken to Argentina. **Salfa Sur**, Pilpilco 800, also at Airport, T065-290226, www.salfasur.cl. Good value. See Essentials for international agencies.

Ferry To **Puerto Natales**: The **Evangelistas** or **Amadeo** of **Navimag** (Naviera Magallanes SA), Terminal Transbordadores, Angelmó 2187, T4423120, sail to Puerto Natales throughout the year on Fri at 1600, taking about 3 days, arriving Mon. It returns on Tue 0600, arriving Puerto Montt Fri morning. Check-in in Puerto Montt must be done 5 hrs before departure. In Puerto Natales check-in is 1300 to 2100 on Mon; dinner is not included. Confirm times and booking 48 hrs in advance. The fare, including meals, ranges from US$380 pp in C berth (sheets are extra, take your own or a sleeping bag; not available on **Amadeo**), to US$1,100 pp in double cabin (high season prices, Nov-Mar; fares 20-30% lower Apr-Oct). First class is recommended, but hardly luxurious. Check the website, www.navimag.com, for discounts and special offers. Cars are carried for US$500, motorcycles for US$150. Payment by credit card or foreign currency is accepted in all Navimag offices. The vessel is a mixed cargo/passenger ferry which includes live animals in the cargo. On board is a book exchange, video films are shown, there are guided talks and information sessions and you can play bingo. Food is good and plentiful and includes vegetarian options at lunch and dinner. Passengers tend to take their own alcohol and extra food. Standards of service and comfort vary, depending on the number of passengers and weather conditions. Take sea-sickness tablets, or buy them on board (you'll be advised when to take them!).

Booking Tickets can be booked through many travel agencies, **Navimag** offices throughout the country, or direct from www.navimag.com. Book well in advance for departures between mid-Dec and mid-Mar especially for the voyage south (Puerto Natales to Puerto Montt is less heavily booked and a little cheaper). It is well worth going to the port on the day of departure if you have no ticket. Departures are frequently delayed by weather conditions – or even advanced. For details and next season's fares see Navimag's website. **Note** It is cheaper to fly and quicker to go by bus via Argentina. The route does not pass Laguna San Rafael.

To Puerto Chacabuco: Navimag's ferries **Evangelistas** or **Amadeo** sail twice a week to Puerto Chacabuco (80 km west of Coyhaique). The cruise to Puerto Chacabuco lasts about 24 hrs. The high-season fares range from US$105 to US$165 pp, cars US$300, motorcycles US$135, bicycles US$65. There is a canteen; long queues if the boat is full. Food is expensive so take your own.

To Laguna San Rafael: The m/n *Skorpios 2* of Skorpios Cruises, Augusto Leguía Norte 118, Santiago, www.skorpios.cl, T02-477 1900, leaves Puerto Montt for a luxury cruise to San Rafael, via Chiloé and Puerto Aguirre. The fare varies according to season, type of cabin and number of occupants: double cabin from US$1900 pp. Generally service is excellent, the food superb, and at the glacier, you can chip ice off the face for your whisky. After the visit to San Rafael the ship visits Quitralco Fjord where there are thermal pools and boat trips on the fjord, and Chiloé. From Puerto Montt it's a 6-day/5-night cruise. The *Skorpios 3* sails from Puerto Natales to Glaciar Amalia and Fiordo Calvo in the Campo de Hielo Sur, 4 days, fares from US$1,500 pp, double cabin. An optional first day includes a visit to Torres del Paine or the Cueva del Milodón. **Navimag** (see above) 5-day/4-night cruises from Castro to Laguna San Rafael via Puerto Chacbuco on the *Mare Australis*, US$1350-1650 pp. See www.navimag.com.

Patagonia Connection SA, Fidel Oteíza 1921, of 1006, Providencia, Santiago, T02-225 6489, www.patagonia-connection.com. Operates Patagonia Express, a catamaran which runs from Puerto Chacabuco to Laguna San Rafael via Termas de Puyuhuapi, see page 81. Tours lasting 3 to 5 days start at Balmaceda airport and go to Puyuhuapi via Queu at by bus. Longer tours include the catamaran service from the Termas de Puyuhuapi to Laguna San Rafael, returning via Puerto Aisén. High season mid-Nov to 18 Mar, low season mid-Oct-mid Nov and 19 Mar-end Apr. High season price for a double cabin on the San Rafael trip: US$1,760 pp. Highly recommended. To **Chaitén**, via Ayacara, **Naviera Austral** runs this service, as well as Hornopirén–Chaitén, but check with the company first to see if it is running: Angelmó 1673, T270430, www.navieraustral.cl.

Directory

Puerto Montt *p70*

Airline offices Aerocord, La Paloma aerodrome, T262300. www.aerocord.cl. **Aerotaxis del Sur**, A Varas 70, T330726, www.aerotaxisdelsur.cl. **Cielo Mar Austral**, Quillota 245 loc 1, T254010. **LAN**, O'Higgins 167, T600-526 2000. **Sky**, Benavente 405, T437 557, or 600-600 2828 for information. **Banks** Many ATMs in the city. Commission charges vary widely. **Afex**, Portales 516 and at airport. **Inter**, Talca 84. For cash, TCs, no commission on Amex. **Note** The last city on the mainland with Visa ATM before Coyhaique. Obtain Argentine pesos before leaving Chile. There is a cambio at the bus terminal. **Consulates** Argentina, Pedro Montt 160, p 6, T253996, cpmontt@embargentina.cl, quick visa service. **Cycle repairs** Kiefer, Pedro Montt 129, T253079. 3 shops on Urmeneta, none very well stocked. **Motorcycle repairs** Miguel Schmuch, Urmeneta 985, T258877.

Carretera Austral

A third of Chile lies to the south of Puerto Montt, but until recently its inaccessible land and rainy climate meant that it was only sparsely populated and unvisited by tourism. The Carretera Austral, or Southern Highway, has now been extended south from Puerto Montt to Villa O'Higgins, giving access to the spectacular virgin landscapes of this wet and wild region, with its mountains, fjords and islands, hitherto isolated communities, and picturesque ports. Ships were the only means of access and remain important for exporting the timber grown here, and for bringing visitors; see page 71. The unexpected eruption of Chaitén volcano in 2008 caused major disruption to the northern part of the Carretera, not least to services in the town of Chaitén. Make enquiries before going to this area.

The only settlement of any size is Coyhaique and its nearby airport at Balmaceda and the equally nearby Puerto Chacabuco are the principal entry points. Coyhaique is a good starting point for exploring the Carretera, north to the thermal springs at Puyuhuapi and the unspoilt national park of Queulat, for trekking expeditions and for fishing. Coyhaique is also a good place for booking Parque Nacional Laguna San Rafael glacier trips, for which boats leave from Puerto Chacabuco.

The Carretera extends 575 km from Coyhaique to Villa O'Higgins, beyond which the southern icefields and their glaciers bring the roadway to a halt. This southernmost section of the Carretera is the wildest and most dramatic, with beautiful unspoilt landscapes around Lago General Carrera. The fairy tale peaks of Cerro Castillo offer challenging trekking, and there's world-class fishing in the turquoise waters of Río Baker. A road runs off to Puerto Ibáñez for lake crossings to Chile Chico, a convenient border crossing to Argentina, while a more adventurous cross-border route involves road, lake and foot or horseback travel to El Chaltén.

Getting to and travelling on the Carretera Austral

This road can be divided into three major sections: **Puerto Montt–Chaitén** (or however much of it is open), **Chaitén–Coyhaique**, and **Coyhaique–Villa O'Higgins**. The road is paved just south of Chaitén and around Coyhaique, from just north of Villa Amengual to Villa Cerro Castillo and Puerto Ibáñez. Currently, the rest is *ripio* (loose stones) and many sections are extremely rough and difficult after rain. The Carretera is very popular with cyclists, even though they can't expect to make fast progress. Motorists need to carry sufficient fuel and spares, especially if intending to detour along any of the highway's many side roads, and protect windscreens and headlamps from stones. Unleaded fuel is available all the way to Villa O'Higgins. There is now a road between Puerto El Vagabundo and Caleta Tortel, and the Carretera Austral is connected by a free ferry between Puerto Yungay and Río Bravo, where it continues to Villa O'Higgins. So far, there is little infrastructure for transport or accommodation among the rural hamlets, so allow plenty of time for bus connections, and bring cash, as there are few banking facilities along the whole route. Camping will give you more freedom for accommodation and there are many beautiful sites. Having your own transport here is definitely preferable. If you intend to hitchhike, **note** that it is essential to take up to three days' worth of supplies as you can be stuck for that long, especially in the far south. At the same time (for campers too), food supplies are limited and tend to be expensive. ▸▸ *See also Transport, pages 79, 89 and 96.*

Best time to visit The landscape throughout the region is lushly green because there is no real dry season. On the offshore islands and the western side of the Andes annual rainfall is over 2000 mm, though inland on the steppe the climate is drier and colder. Westerly winds are strong, especially in summer, but there's plenty of sunshine too, especially around Lago General Carrera (described in the Southern Section), which has a warm microclimate. January and February are probably the best months for a trip to this region.

Puerto Montt to Chaitén

This section of the Carretera Austral, 205 km, should include two ferry crossings. Before setting out, it is imperative to check which ferries are running and when and, if driving, make a reservation: do this in Puerto Montt (not Santiago), at the offices of Naviera Austral, Angelmó 1673, T065-270430, www.navieraustral.cl, and Transmarchilay, Angelmó 2187, T065-270700, www.transmarchilay.cl (Spanish only). An alternative route to Chaitén is by ferry from Puerto Montt or Quellón/Castro.

The road (Ruta 7) heads east out of Puerto Montt, through Pelluco, and follows the shore of the beautiful Seno Reloncaví. It passes the southern entrance of the **Parque Nacional Alerce Andino** ① *US$8, no camping within park boundaries,* which contains one of the best surviving areas of alerce trees, some over 1000 years old (the oldest is estimated at 4200 years old). Wildlife includes pudú, pumas, vizcachas, condors and black woodpeckers. There are two entrances: 2.5 km from Correntoso (35 km east of Puerto Montt) at the northern end of the park (with ranger station and campsite) and 7 km east of Lenca (40 km south of Puerto Montt) at the southern end. There are three other ranger posts, at Río Chaicas, Lago Chapo and Sargazo. Ranger posts have little information; map is available from CONAF in Puerto Montt.

At 46 km from Puerto Montt (allow one hour), is the first ferry at **La Arena**, across the Reloncaví Estuary to **Puelche**. See Transport, page 79, for ferry details. **Río Negro** is now called **Hornopirén** after the volcano above it. From here south, access is determined by the volcanic activity. In normal times a second ferry sails to Caleta Gonzalo, one of the centres for the Parque Pumalín (see below). At the mouth of the fjord is the small Isla Llanchahué, with a hotel and thermal springs (day entry US$14), good for hiking in the forests amid beautiful scenery. Boat to the island 50 minutes, US$60 one-way shared between passengers, T09-9642 4857; look out for dolphins and fur seals en route. If there is no ferry to Caleta Gonzalo, catch the ferry at Ayacara direct to Chaitén (see Transport, page 79).

Parque Pumalín

ⓘ *Open all year, free. Information centres: Klenner 299, Puerto Varas, T065-250079; Fiordo Reñihué, Caleta Gonzalo (not always open); Chaitén, O'Higgins 62, T065-731341. In USA T415-229-9339, www.pumalinpark.org (Spanish and English).*

Caleta Gonzalo is the entry point for Parque Pumalín for visitors from the north. The park, created by the US billionaire Douglas Tompkins, is a private reserve of 700,000 ha in two sections which has been given Nature Sanctuary status. Covering large areas of the western Andes, with virgin temperate rainforest, the park is spectacularly beautiful, and is seen by many as one of the most important conservation projects in the world. There are campsites and cabins throughout the park, a number of hot springs and hiking trails.

South of Caleta Gonzalo the Carretera Austral winds through the park's beautiful unspoilt scenery, and there is a steep climb on the *ripio* road to two lakes, Lago Río Blanco and Lago Río Negro, with panoramic views.

After the eruption of Volcán Chaitén, the government decided to abandon **Chaitén**, cutting off utilities, starting to rebuild the town 10 km north at Santa Bárbara and moving the seat of provincial government to Futaleufú. Chaitén, however, survived with running water, generators and fuel and in 2011 the government reversed former decisions and planned to rebuild the town in the northern part of the old town. There are shops, *hospedajes* and *cabañas* and all transport links: ferries to Puerto Montt and Chiloé, flights and buses.

Puerto Montt to Chaitén listings

For hotel and restaurant price codes and other relevant information, see pages 10-12.

Where to stay

Puerto Montt to Chaitén *p77*
$$$$ Alerce Mountain Lodge, Km 36 Carretera Austral, T286969, www.mountain lodge.cl. In Los Alerces de Lenca private reserve, beside Parque Nacional Alerce Andino, beautiful lodge with rooms and cabins, offering packages from 2 to 4 nights, with trekking, riding, fishing, guides speak English, good food, all-inclusive except drinks.

Hornopirén
$$$-$$ Hotel Termas de Llanchahué, sla Llanchahué. To get there, make arrangements by phoning T09-9642 4857, www.termasde llanchahue.cl. Price is per person for full board (excellent food), hot spring at the hotel. cheaper with shared bath.
$$ Hornopirén, Carrera Pinto 388, T217256. Rooms with shared bath, also *cabañas* and restaurant at the water's edge. Recommended.
$$ Hostería Catalina, Ingenieros Militares s/n, T217359, www.hosteriacatalina.cl. A good place to stay; comfortable rooms, bath and breakfast.

Chaitén

The following are open. all welcoming travellers, with not water and meals: **Cabañas Brisas del Mar** (Corcovado 278), **Cabañas Pudú**, **Casa de Rita** (Riveros y Pratt), **El Refugio** (Corcovado y Juan Todesco), **Hosp y Restaurante Corcovado** (Corcovado 410), **Hosp Don Carlos** (Almte Riveros y Pratt), **Hosp Llanos** (Corcovado 378), and **Shilling** (Corcovado 258).

▲ What to do

Puerto Montt to Chaitén *p77*
Chaitén

Chaitur, O'Higgins 67, T09-7468 5608, www.chaitur.com. General travel agent making bus, boat, plane and hotel reservations. Also offers tours to hot springs. glaciers, beaches, Carretera Austral, photography trips. Still **the** place to find about local conditions. English and French spoken, helpful, book exchange, internet when the phone lines are connected. Highly recommended.

⊖ Transport

Puerto Montt to Chaitén *p77*
Parque Nacional Alerce Andino

Bus To the north entrance: take a **Fierro** or **Río Pato** bus to **Correntoso** (or **Lago Chapo** bus which passes through Correntoso), several daily except Sun. then walk. To the south entrance: take any **Fierro** bus to **Chaicas, La Arena, Contau** and **Hornopirén**, US$2.50, getting off at Lenca sawmill, then walk (signposted).

La Arena to Puelche

Ferry Two ferries cross the Reloncaví Estuary, 30 mins, every 45 mins, US$20 for a car, US$14 for motorcycle, US$5.50 for bicycle, US$1 for foot passengers. 0715-2000 daily. Arrive at least 30 mins early to guarantee a place; buses have priority. Roll-on roll-off type operating all year.

Hornopirén

Bus Fierro (T253022) and **Jordán** (T254938) run Mon-Sat 0800 and 1330 (Sun 1500, 1730) from **Puerto Montt**. US$10; return 0530, 1330 Mon-Sat, 1245. 1500 Sun.

Ferry Hornopirén to **Chaitén** via Ayacara: check with **Naviera Austral**, www.navier austral.cl, for high season dates of this service: in Hornopirén T07-968 1646, in Ayacara T07-475 1168, in Chaitén T065-731012 or 07-975 0342. If there is no Hornopirén–Caleta Gonzalo ferry running, you can join Naviera Austral's Puerto Montt–Chaitén service at Ayacara, seat US$20, berth US$41-46, same price Ayacara-Chaitén or Ayacara–Puerto Montt.

Puerto Montt to Chaitén *p77*
Chaitén

Air Daily flights (except Sun) from **Puerto Montt** to Santa Bárbara with **Aerocord** (19 passengers), US$75.
Bus Terminal at **Chaitur**, O'Higgins 67. To **Coyhaique**, Thu 1000, direct in summer, 12 hrs otherwise overnight stop in La Junta, to which buses depart Mon, Tue, Fri, Sat 0930. Connections to Puyuhuapi and Coyhaique 0600 next day. Minibuses usually travel full, so can't pick up passengers en route. Buses to **Futaleufú**, daily except Thu, 0930; change here for buses to the Argentine border.

Ferry

The ferry port is about 1 km north of town. Schedules change frequently and ferries are infrequent off season. **Naviera Austral**, Corcovado 266, T065-731012 or 07-976 0342, www.navieraustral.cl. Check website for all future sailings.

To **Chiloé**, **Naviera Austral** operates ferry services to **Quellón** or **Castro** (Jan-Feb only), once a week, more in summer (Dec-Mar); fares given under Quellón, above.

To **Puerto Montt**, **Naviera Austral**, Mon-Fri via Ayacara, 10 hrs, passengers US$33. cabin US$60-65, car US$182, motorbike US$40, bicycle US$20.

Chaitén to Coyhaique

This section of the Carretera Austral, runs 422 km through breathtaking and varied scenery, passing tiny villages, most notably the idyllic Puyuhuapi, where there are thermal pools, and good trekking in Parque Nacional Queulat. While the northern part of the Carretera is disrupted, access is from the south. Roads which branch off east to the Argentine border at the picturesque Futaleufú and at Palena are subject to period closures because of volcanic ash, see page 78. Consequently, there may be disruption to services so before going to, or before crossing from Argentina in this region, check if there are travel restrictions.

Puerto Cárdenas, 44 km south of Chaitén, is on the northern tip of **Lago Yelcho**, a beautiful lake on Río Futaleufú surrounded by hills, much loved by anglers for its salmon and trout. Further south at Km 60, a path leads to **Ventisquero Yelcho** (two hours' walk there), a dramatic glacier with high waterfalls. Note that the path passes a campsite whose administrator charges walkers US$3.50 to go to the glacier. Whether he is legally entitled to do this is a contentious issue.

At **Villa Santa Lucía**, an uninspiring modern settlement 76 km south of Chaitén, with basic food and accommodation, a road branches east to the Argentine border. There are two crossings: Futaleufú and Palena, both reached from **Puerto Ramírez** past the southern end of Lago Yelcho, 24 km east of Santa Lucia. Here the road divides: the north branch runs along the valley of the Río Futaleufú to Futaleufú and the southern one to Palena. The scenery is spectacular, but the road is hard going: single track *ripio*, climbing steeply in places (tough for bikes; allow plenty of time).

Futaleufú → *Phone code: 065.*
The new provincial capital, 8 km west of the border, nestles in a bowl amid steep mountains on the Río Espolón. Its houses are neatly slatted with alerce wood and the wide streets are lined with shrubs and roses. Access to challenging whitewater rafting on the Río Futaleufú has made it into one of the southern hemisphere's prime centres for the sport, but with kayaking, riding, trekking, mountain biking and canyoning on offer Futaleufú now calls itself the capital of adventure tourism. **Lago Espolón**, west of Futaleufú, reached by a turning 41 km northeast of Villa Santa Lucía, is a beautiful lake in an area enjoying a warm microclimate: 30°C in the day in summer, 5°C at night, with excellent fishing at the lake's mouth. The lake is even warm enough for a quick dip, but beware of the currents. Banco del Estado on the plaza has a MasterCard ATM. **Tourist office** ① *on the plaza at O'Higgins and Prat, T721241, www.futaleufu.cl, daily in summer, 0900-2100,* for accommodation, maps and fishing licences.

Border with Argentina
Chilean immigration is at the border, 8 km east of Futaleufú. The border is just west of the bridge over the Río Grande: straightforward crossing, open 0800-2000. For Argentinian immigration, see Argentina chapter. Change money in Futaleufú; nowhere to change at the border but you can pay the bus fare to Esquel (Argentina) in US dollars. Alternatively, cross into Argentina further south near **Palena**, which is 8 km west of the border and has a Chilean immigration office. **Note** If entering from Argentina, no fresh produce may be brought into Chile. Check conditions locally before crossing at this border.

XI Región

La Junta in the XI (eleventh) Region is a village 151 km south of Chaitén. La Junta has a service station, where there's a minimarket. From the village you can visit **Lago Rosselot**, surrounded by forest in the **Reserva Nacional Lago Rosselot**, 9 km east of La Junta. The same road continues east, 74 km, to Lago Verde and the Argentine border: open summer 0800-2200, winter 0800-2000. Another road leads northwest, with a ferry crossing over the Río Palena (four daily), to the fishing village of **Puerto Raúl Marín Balmaceda** (hostels and camping). Different species of dolphin can be seen and Raúl Marín forms one apex of the blue whale triangle: the giant cetacean may be sighted on the ferry to Quellón in the summer. On clear days there are wonderful views of Volcán Melimoyu from the beach.

Puyuhuapi → *Phone code: 067. Population: 500.*

With the most idyllic setting along the whole Carretera Austral, Puyuhuapi lies in a tranquil bay at the northern end of the Puyuhuapi fjord, 46 km south of La Junta. The blissful thermal pools at Termas de Puyuhuapi are nearby. The village was founded by four German-speaking Sudeten families in 1935, and handwoven carpets are still made here, now to world renown. **Alfombras de Puyuhuapi** ① *T09-9359 9515, www.puyuhuapi.com, daily in summer 0830-1930, closed lunch, English spoken.* This is the best stopping point between Chaitén and Coyhaique with phone, fuel, shops, but no banks: hotels may change dollars. **Tourist office** ① *by the Municipalidad, main street, Mon-Sat in season, 1000-1400, 1600-1900,* helpful.

Termas del Ventisquero ① *6 km south of Puyuhuapi beside the Carretera overlooking the fjord, T09-7966 6862, www.termasventisqueropuyuhuapi.cl.* In season the baths are open until 2300 and during the day there is a café. See Where to stay below for the Termas de Puyuhuapi at the **Puyuhuapi Lodge and Spa**.

South of Puyuhuap , 24 km, is the 154,093-ha **Parque Nacional Queulat** ① *CONAF, La Junta, T314128, eladio.pinto@conaf.cl, daily Dec-Mar 0830-2100, rest of year 0830-1830, US$5, camping US$15 per site, CONAF campsite with cold showers.* It is most visited for the spectacular hanging glacier, **Ventisquero Colgante**. 2.5 km off the road passing the guardeparques' house, you'll find parking and camping areas. Three walks begin from here: a short stroll through the woodland to a viewpoint of the Ventisquero, or cross the river where the path begins to Laguna Tempanos, where boats cross the lake in summer. The third trail, 3.25 km, takes 2½ hours to climb to a panoramic viewpoint of the Ventisquero, where you can watch the ice fall into huge waterfalls like sifted sugar.

Puerto Cisnes

At 59 km south of Puyuhuapi, a winding road branches west and follows the Río Cisnes 33 km to Puerto Cisnes (*Population: 1784*), a fishing village and salmon-farming centre at the mouth of the river on Puyuhuapi fjord, set amongst steep mountains. The Río Cisnes, 160 km in length, is recommended for rafting or canoeing, with grand scenery and modest rapids except for the horrendous drop at Piedra del Gato. Good camping in the forest, and fuel is available in the village.

At 89 km south of Puyuhuapi is **Villa Amengual** and, at Km 92, a road branches east, 104 km to La Tapera and to the Argentine border. Chilean immigration is 12 km west of the border, open summer 0800-2200, winter 0800-2000. On the Argentine side the road continues to meet up with Ruta 40, a section with few services for fuel or food.

Coyhaique → *Phone code: 067. Population: 43,297.*

A growing centre for tourism, Coyhaique, 420 km south of Chaitén, is a busy small town perched on a hill between the Ríos Simpson and Coyhaique. It has a cinema and all main services, including stores selling hiking gear and warm clothes. It's a good idea to get cash here as there are no banks along the Carretera Austral. The **Museo Regional de la Patagonia Central** ① *Lillo 23, Tue-Sun winter 0830-1730, summer 0900-2000, US$1 is in the Casa de Cultura.* It traces local history through photos of the first pioneers, as well as sections on archaeology, mineralogy and zoology. From the bridge over the Río Simpson look for the **Piedra del Indio**, a rock outcrop which looks like a face in profile. **Tourist offices:** Sernatur office (very helpful, English spoken) ① *Bulnes 35, T231752, infoaisen@sernatur.cl. Mon-Fri 0830-1730, high season Mon-Fri 0830-2000, Sat-Sun 1000-1800.* See www.aysenpatagonia.cl. CONAF, Av Ogana 1060, T212109, aysen.oirs@conaf.cl.

Just outside the town, the **Reserva Nacional Coihaique** ① *0830-1700 Oct-Apr, US$1.75, information from CONAF,* has some trails for walking or biking, with picnic grounds, campsites and a *refugio.* A satisfying walk is up to Cerro Cinchao, and great views

Coyhaique

200 metres
200 yards

Where to stay 🛏
1 Cabañas Baquedano
2 Cabañas Mirador
3 Cabañas Río Simpson
4 Cabañas San Sebastián
5 El Reloj
6 Hosp Mondaca
7 Hostal Belisario Jara
8 Hostal Bon
9 Hostal Las Quintas
10 Hostal María Ester
11 Las Salamandras
12 Los Ñires
13 San Sebastián

Restaurants 🍽
1 Café Oriente
2 Casino de Bomberos
3 Club Sandwich Patagonia
4 Donde Ramiro
5 El Mastique
6 Histórico Ricer & Café Ricer
7 La Casona
8 Pizzería La Fiorentina

Bars & clubs 🍸
9 Pepe le Pub
10 Piel Roja

from Sendero Los Leñeros to Laguna Verde. Walk to Laguna Verde and Laguna Venus particularly recommended. Follow Baquedano to the end, over bridge, and past the guardeparque's hut where all the trails begin. There are well-marked walks of between 20 minutes and five hours. Ski centre El Fraile, 29 km from Coyhaique, is 1599 m above sea level, with five pistes. powder snow, in the middle of ñire (Antarctic beech) and lenga forests (1000 people capacity).

Border with Argentina: Coyhaique Alto

A 43 km road runs east to this crossing. On the Argentine side the road leads through Río Mayo and Sarmiento to Comodoro Rivadavia. **Chilean immigration** ① *6 km west of the border, open summer 0800-2200, winter 0800-2000*, is at Coyhaique Alto.

Puerto Aisén and Puerto Chacabuco → *Phone code: 067. Population: 13,050.*

The paved road between Coyhaique and Puerto Aisén passes through **Reserva Nacional Río Simpson**, with beautiful waterfalls, lovely views of the river and excellent fly-fishing. Administration/museum is at the entrance, 32 km west of Coyhaique, no marked trails; campsite opposite turning to Santuario San Sebastián, US$7.

   Puerto Aisén is 67 km west of Coyhaique at the meeting of the rivers Aisén and Palos. Formerly the region's major port, it has been replaced by Puerto Chacabuco, 15 km to the west, and though it remains an important centre for services, there's little of interest for the visitor. It's also very wet. In summer, the *Apulcheu* sails regularly down the northern shore of the Aisén Fjord to Termas de Chiconal, a spectacular one hour trip by boat, US$50 (take your own food) – book in the tourist office or **Turismo Rucaray**, on the plaza, rucaray@entelchile.net. **Tourist office** ① *in the Municipalidad. Prat y Sgto Aldea, www.portchacabuco.cl, Dec-Feb only*, gives information on shipping movements.

   The Puente President Ibáñez, once the longest suspension bridge in Chile, and a paved road lead to **Puerto Chacabuco** 15 km away; a regular bus service runs between the two. The harbour, rather a charmless place, is a short way from the town.

Balmaceda

From Coyhaique, the Carretera Austral heads south past huge bluffs, through deforested pasture (most dramatically on the slopes of Cerro Galera near El Blanco) and farmsteads edged with alamo (poplar) trees, before entering flatter plains and rolling hills. At around Km 41, a paved road runs east past the airport at Balmaceda to the Argentine border at Paso Huemules (no accommodation). Chilean immigration is open winter 0800-2000, summer 0800-2200.

Puerto Ibáñez

The Carretera Austral starts to climb again, past the entrance to the Reserva Nacional Cerro Castillo (see below). It winds up through the attractive narrow gorge of Río Horqueta, to a pass between Cerro Castillo and its neighbours, before dropping down a 6 km slalom into the breathtaking valley of Río Ibáñez. (This is currently the most southerly paved section and the road is safe and wide here). Here the road forks east to Puerto Ibáñez, a further 31 km away, for the ferry crossing of vast Lago General Carrera.

   Puerto Ibáñez (*Population: 828*) is the principal port on the Chilean section of the lake. As such you'll probably just pass through to reach the ferry. It is, however, a centre for distinctive pottery, leather production and vegetable growing (you can buy salad from greenhouses and visit potters). Local archaeology includes rock art and the largest Tehuelche cemetery in Patagonia. There are various hotels, but no other services. Fuel (sold in 5-litre containers) is available at Luis A Bolados 461 (house with five laburnum trees outside). Most shops and restaurants are closed Sunday. There are some fine waterfalls, including the Salto Río Ibáñez, 6 km north.

Villa Cerro Castillo

From the turning to Puerto Ibáñez the Carretera Austral goes through Villa Cerro Castillo (Km 8), a quiet village in a spectacular setting beneath the striking, jagged peaks of **Cerro Castillo**, overlooking the broad valley below. There's a petrol station, public phone, several food shops and a tiny tourist information kiosk by the road side (January and February only), with details of guides offering trekking and horse rides.

The village is a good place to stop for a few days with two appealing attractions. There are truly spectacular treks from one to four or five days in the **Reserva Nacional Cerro Castillo** (179,550 ha, US$1.60), whose entrance is 64 km south of Coyhaique. One goes around the fairytale castle peaks of Cerro Castillo, starting at Las Horquetas Grandes, a bend in the river Río Ibáñez, 8 km south of the park entrance, where any bus driver will let you off. It follows Río La Lima to the gorgeous Laguna Cerro Castillo, then animal trails around the peak itself, returning to the village (accommodation or bus back to Coyhaique). Another equally spectacular five-day trek goes around Lago Monreal. These are challenging walks: attempt only if fit, and ideally, take a guide, as trails are poorly marked (IGM map essential, purchase in advance in Coyhaique). The guardería is on the Senda Ibáñez, 50 m to the left of the main road (as you head south), opposite Laguna Chinguay to the right, with access to walks and campsite (US$7, take equipment – there are no *refugios*). The picnic ground is open summer 0830-2100, winter to 1830. Ask in Villa Cerro Castillo for details.

A few kilometres south of the village is the **Monumento Nacional Alero Las Manos de Cerro Castillo** ① *US$1 charged Dec-Apr*. In a shallow cave, a few handprints have been made on the side of vertical rocks high above the Río Ibáñez. There's no clue to their significance, but they're in a beautiful place with panoramic views. This makes a delightful two hours' walk. The site is accessible all year, signposted clearly from the road. There is also a small local museum, 2 km south of Villa Cerro Castillo ① *open Dec-Mar 0900-1200*.

◉ Chaitén to Coyhaique listings

Services in Futaleufú may be suspended due the eruption of the Chaitén volcano. Check the situation before going.

◉ Where to stay

Chaitén to Coyhaique *p80*
Villa Santa Lucía
$ pp Several places on main street: ask at **Nachito**, the café where the bus stops, which serves good breakfasts.

Futaleufú *p80*
$$$$ El Barranco, O'Higgins 172, T721314, www.elbarrancochile.cl. Elegant rustic rooms, luxurious, pool, good restaurant, and expert fishing guides, horses and bikes for hire, half and full board available.
$$$ Río Grande, O'Higgins y Aldea, T721320, www.pachile.com. Upmarket but not such good value, attractive rooms, internet, international restaurant, popular with rafting groups.

$$ Cabañas Río Espolón. Río Espolón, T9645 4172, follow Cerda to the end, www.futaleufu.cl/ locales/ crioespolon.html. Cosy *cabañas* in secluded riverside setting, also recommended *parrilla*, bar. Popular with river-rafting groups, book ahead.

$$ Cabañas Veranada, Sargento Aldea 430, T721266, www.turismofutaleufu.cl. Well-equipped cabins with excellent beds and good kitchens. All have slow-burning wood stoves except one with an open fireplace. Recommended.

$$-$ Adolfo B&B, O'Higgins 302, T721256, lodeva@surnet.cl. Best value in this range, comfortable rooms in family home, shared hot showers, kitchen, with breakfast. Warmly recommended.

$ pp Continental, Balmaceda 595, T721222. **$ singles**. Oldest in town, no breakfast, basic, but clean and welcoming.

Camping Aldea Puerto Espolón, Sector La Puntilla, 400m from town, T09-9447 7448, www.aldeapuertoespolon.blogspot.com Accommodation in pre-erected teepees and dome-tents. Several other campsites.

XI Región: La Junta *p81*

$$$$ Espacio y Tiempo, T314141, www.espacioytiempo.cl. Spacious rooms, warm and cosy atmosphere, restaurant, attractive gardens, fishing expeditions. Recommended.

$$ Res Copihue, Varas 611, T09-9501 8874. Some rooms with bath, with breakfast, good meals, changes money at poor rates.

$$-$ Hostería Valdera, Varas s/n, T314105, luslagos@hotmail.com. Breakfast and bath, meals served. Excellent value.

$$-$ Res Patagonia, Lynch 331, T09-7702 8181. Good meals, small rooms, limited bathrooms.

Puyuhuapi *p81*

$$$$ El Pangue, 18 km north, Km 240 at end of Lago Risopatrón, Parque Nacional Queulat, T526906, www.elpangue.com. Rooms and luxurious *cabañas* for 4 to 7 in splendid rural setting, with hot water and heating, horseriding, all meals extra, restaurant, trekking, mountain bikes, pool, great views, restful. Recommended.

$$$$ Puyuhuapi Lodge and Spa. Reservations: Patagonia Connection, Santiago, T02-225 6489, www.patagonia-connection.com, or directly at the hotel, T325103. Splendidly isolated on a nook in the sea fjord, the hotel owns the thermal baths: outdoors by the fjord so that you can dive in for a refreshing swim afterwards, or in the lovely indoor spa complex where there are jacuzzis of sea water, good for sufferers of arthritic and skin conditions, expert massage facilities. Good packages for de-stressing with all activities from riding, trekking, mountain biking, yoga and the thermals included. Price includes use of baths, boat transfer, full board US$50 extra, excellent restaurant. Guests met at Balmaceda airport, or arrive by boat from Puerto Chacabuco, taking in the San Rafael lake and glaciers (from US$170 for 2 for 3 nights, all included, depending on season and room category). Highly recommended. Boats leave frequently from a 2 hrs' walk from town, US$5 each way, 10 mins' crossing.

$$ Aonikenk, Hamburgo 16, T325208, aonikenkturismo@yahoo.com. Pleasant heated *cabañas* (not sound-proofed), good beds, helpful, informative, bike hire.

$$ Casa Ludwig, Otto Uebel s/n, T325220, www.casaludwig.cl. Cheaper with shared bath. Open Nov-Mar; enquire in advance at other times. In a beautiful 4-storey house built by first German settlers, wonderful views, a range of rooms, good breakfast, comfortable; charming owner Luisa is knowledgeable about the area, speaks German and English. Highly recommended.

$$ Hostería Alemana, Otto Uebel 450, T325118, hosteria_alemana@entelchile.net. A traditional wooden house on the main road by the water, very comfortable, lovely lake views and garden. Warmly recommended.

$ Sra Leontina Fuentes, Llantureo y Circunvalación, T325106. Clean, hot water, good breakfast for US$3.
Camping Campsite behind the general store.

Puerto Cisnes *p81*
$$$-$$ Cabañas Río Cisnes, Costanera 101, T346404. Cabins sleep 4 to 8. Owner, Juan Suazo, offers sea fishing trips in his boat.
$$ Hostería El Gaucho, Holmberg 140, T346514. With bath and breakfast, dinner available.

Also various *cabañas* and *residenciales*.

Villa Amengual
$ pp Res El Encanto, Fca Castro 33-A, T188-2-1964517. With restaurant and café, one of several cheap options in town, including **Res Bienvenido** and **Villa Mañihuales** (T234803), both **$**, on Ibar.

Coyhaique *p82, map p82*
Plentiful accommodation. The tourist office has a list.
$$$$-$$$ El Reloj, Baquedano 828, T231108, www.elrelojhotel.cl. Tasteful, quiet place in a former sawmill, with a good restaurant, charming, comfortable wood panelled rooms, some with wonderful views, nice lounge, Wi-Fi. Recommended as the best in town.
$$$ Cabañas Mirador, Baquedano 848, T233191. Attractive, well-equipped *cabañas*, also rooms, in lovely gardens with panoramic views of the Reserva Forestal, and Río Coyhaique below, book in advance. Recommended.
$$$ Hostal Belisario Jara, Bilbao 662, T234150. Most distinctive and delightful, an elegant and welcoming small place, with TV and excellent breakfast. Recommended.
$$$ Los Ñires, Baquedano 315, T233372, www.hotellosnires.cl. Small rooms, excellent gourmet restaurant, also serves breakfast, parking, free Wi-Fi.
$$$ San Sebastián, Baquedano 496, T233427. Modern, spacious rooms with great views over the Reserva, with breakfast, good value.

Recommended. Also **Cabañas San Sebastián**, Freire 554, T231762. Central, very good.
$$$-$$ Cabañas Río Simpson, 3 km north on road to Pto Aisén, T232183. Fully equipped cabins for 2-6 people plus 1 luxury cabin, **$$$$** sleeping 7. Horse riding, fishing and tours Tame alpacas in grounds.
$$ Cabañas Baquedano, Baquedano 20, T232520, Patricio y Gedra Guzmán, http://balasch.cl. Welcoming, well-maintained, lovely place, 7 *cabañas* of varying standards, with splendid views over the Reserva Forestal, very helpful hosts who speak English, access to river, great value. Recommended.
$$ Hostal Bon, Serrano 91, T231189, hostal_bon@hotmail.com. Simple but very welcoming place, with multilingual owner. They also have *cabañas* near Reserva Forestal 1 km away.
$$ Hostal Las Quintas, Bilbao 1208, T231173. Spartan, but clean and spacious rooms (some with bizarre design) with bath and breakfast.
$$ Hostal María Ester, Lautaro 544, T233023, www.hospedajemariaester.cl. With breakfast (extra), some rooms with bath and TV, use of kitchen (extra charge), laundry facilities, Wi-Fi, local information, car hire.
$ Hospedaje Mondaca, Av Simpson 571, T254676. Small (only 3 rooms) but spotless family home, hospitable, breakfast extra.
$ Las Salamandras, Sector Los Pinos, 2 km south in attractive forest, T211865, www.salamandras.cl. Double rooms, dorms (**$** pp, us$13.25) and 1 cabin (**$$$-$$**), kitchen facilities, winter sports and trekking (Jun-Oct), cycling information. Highly recommended.

Many more hospedajes and private houses with rooms; ask tourist office for a list.
Camping Tourist office on plaza or Sernatur in Coyhaique has a full list of all sites in XI Región. There are many camping sites in Coyhaique and on the road between Coyhaique and Puerto Aisén, eg **Camping Alborada**, at Km 2, T238868, US$14 per site, hot shower, and **Camping Río Correntoso**, Km 42, T232005, US$20 per site, showers, fishing. Camping in Reserva Nacional Río Simpson, US$7.

Puerto Aisén and Puerto Chacabuco p83

Accommodation is hard to find, most is taken up by fishing companies in both ports. There are several places to eat along The Merino and Aldea in Puerto Aisén.

$$$$ Loberías del Sur, José Miguel Carrera 50, Puerto Chacabuco, T351112, www.loberiascelsur.cl. Rebuilt 5-star hotel, the best around here and whose restaurant serves the best food in the area (handy for meal or a drink before boarding ferry – climb up steps direct from port). Same owner as Catamaranes del Sur (see Shipping, below), which also has a nearby nature reserve, Parque Aiken del Sur.

$$$ Patagonia Green, 400 m from bridge (on Pto Chacabuco side), T336796, www.patagoniagreen.cl. Nice cabins for up to 5, kitchen, heating, TV, gardens, arranges tours to Laguna San Rafael, fishing, mountain biking, riding, trekking, etc, English spoken

$$$-$$ Caicahues, Michimalonco 660, Puerto Aisén, T336633. The most recommended in this port, with heating and internet, book ahead.

$$ Hospedaje Mar Clara, Carrera 970, Puerto Aisén, T330945. More expensive with bath. Basic, clean, thin walls, looks nicer from outside than within.

Puerto Ibáñez p83

Various hotels in our **$** range, also a campsite.
$$ Cabañas Shehen Aike, Luis Riscpatrón 55, T423284, info@aike.cl. Swiss-Chilean owned, large cabins, lots of ideas for trips, bike rental, organizes tours, fine food, welcoming, English spoken, best to phone in advance.

$ Hosp Don Francisco, San Salvador y Lautaro. Very hospitable good food round the clock.

$ Vientos del Sur, Bertrán Dixon 282, T423208. Good, nice family, dormitories, check the bill, cheap meals (restaurant open till late) but not as good as the lodging; also adventure activities.

Villa Cerro Castillo p84

$ Cabañas Don Niba, Los Pioneros 872, T419920. Friendly but basic *hospedaje*, good value. Recommended.

$ Hostería Villarrica, O'Higgins 59, next to Supermercado Villarrica, T419500. Welcoming, basic, hot showers, and meals too, kind owners can arrange trekking guides and horse riding.

$ Res María, Padre O Ronchi, near the office of Mar del Sur and Fantasía supermarket.

❾ Restaurants

Futaleufú p80

$$ Futaleufú, Cerda 407, T721295. Serves typical Chilean meat dishes and local foods.
$$ Martín Pescador, Balmaceda y Rodríguez, T721279. For fish and meat dishes, rustic.
$$-$ Sur Andes, Cerda 308, T721405. Café serving cakes, sweets, light meals and real coffee Also sells handicrafts.

Puyuhuapi p81

$$ Café Rossbach, Costanera. Run by the descendants of the original German settlers, an attractive place by the water for delicious salmon, tea and *küchen*.
$$ Lluvia Marina, next to Casa Ludwig, veronet@entelchile.net. The best café, also selling handicrafts. Superb food in relaxed atmosphere, a great place to just hang out, owner Verónica is very helpful.

Coyhaique p82, map p82

$$$ Histórico Ricer, Horn 48 y 40, p 2, T232920. Central, warm and cosy, serving breakfast to dinner, regional specialities, with good vegetarian options, historical exhibits. Also has Café Ricer at No 48, serving light food.
$$ La Casona, Obispo Vielmo 77, T238894. Justly reputed as best in town, charming family restaurant serves excellent fish, congrio especially, but best known for grilled lamb.
$$-$ Casino de Bomberos next to the fire station Gral Parra 365, T231437. For great atmosphere and a filling lunch, can be slow when serving groups. Recommended.

$$-$ Donde Ramiro, Freire 319, T256885. Good set lunches, big-screen TV (watch football here).
$ Club Sandwich Patagonia, Moraleda 433. 24-hr fast food and huge Chilean sandwiches, a local institution.
$ El Mastique, Bilbao 141. Cheap but good pasta and Chilean food.
$ Pizzería La Fiorentina, Prat 230. Tasty pizzas, good service. Recommended.
Café Oriente, Condell 201. Serves a good lunch and tasty cakes.

🎵 Bars and clubs

Coyhaique *p82, map p82*
El Boliche, Moraleda 380. A beer-drinkers' bar. Many bars on the same street.
Pepe le Pub, Parra 72. Good cocktails and snacks, relaxed, live music at weekends.
Piel Roja, Moraleda y Condell. Good music, laid back, open Wed, Fri, Sat 1000-0500 for dancing, pub other nights. Recommended, but not cheap.

🛍 Shopping

Coyhaique *p82, map p82*
Camping equipment Condor Explorer, Dussen 357, T670349. Decent stock.
Bookshop Librería Rincón de Poeta, Moraleda y Parra. Good little place with some English books, maps and art books.
Handicrafts Artesanía Manos Azules, Riquelme 435. Sells fine handicrafts. **Feria de Artesanía** on the plaza. Kaienk, Plaza 219-A, T02245216, www.telaresdelapatagonia.cl, sells good-quality locally produced knitwear.

🚶 What to do

Futaleufú *p80*
Tour operators arrange whitewater rafting trips, prices starting from US$75 pp. Local fishing guides can also be found in the village.
Expediciones Chile, Mistral 296, T562639, www.exchile.com. Whitewater rafting, kayaking, etc. Offers the best multi-day trips, book in advance. Day trips can be booked at office.

Futaleufú Explore, O'Higgins 772, T721527, www.futaleufuexplore.com. A respected rafting company.
Rancho Las Ruedas, Pilota Carmona s/n, T8856 6339, rancholasruedas@hotmail.com. The best horseriding in the area.

Coyhaique *p82, map p82*
Many tours operate Sep-Apr, some Dec-Mar only. The surrounding area is famous for trout fishing with several estancias offering luxury accommodation and bilingual guides. Most tour operators also offer specialist fishing trips.
Andes Patagónicos, Horn 48 y 40, loc 11, T216711, www.ap.cl. Trips to local lakes, Tortel, historically based tours and bespoke trips all year round. Good, but not cheap.
Aysen Tour, Gral Parra 97, T237070, www.aysentour.cl. Tours along the Carretera Austral, also car rental.
Cabot, Lautaro 339, T230101. Horse-riding excursions to Cerro Castillo and other tours.
Camello Patagón, Moraleda 463, T244327, www.camellopatagon.cl. Trips to Capilla de Marmol in Río Tranquilo, also has a cosy café with good coffees. Closes 2000.
Casa del Turismo Rural, Dussen 357-B, T214031, www.casaturismorural.cl, Mon-Fri 1000-1330, 1530-2000 (also weekends in high season). An association of 40 families, mostly in the countryside, who offer activities such as horseriding and fishing. Many do not have telephones or internet, make reservations here.
Cóndor Explorer, Dussen 357, T573634, www.condorexplorer.com. Good small-scale agency specializing in trekking, but also Carretera tours, English spoken. Recommended.
Expediciones Coyhaique, Portales 195, T231783, www.coyhaiqueflyfishing.com. Fly-fishing experts.
Geo Turismo, Balmaceda 334, T573460, www.geoturismopatagonia.cl. Offers wide range of tours, English spoken, professional.
Turismo Prado, 21 de Mayo 417, T231271, www.turismoprado.cl. Tours of local lakes and other sights, Laguna San Rafael trips

and historical tours. Also offers general tourist information and accepts TCs

Transport

Futaleufú p80
Bus Bus to **Chaitén** 6 days a week, information from **Chaitur** in Chaitén. To **Puerto Montt** via Argentina, Mon 0630, 13 hrs, US$38, with Transporte Patagonia Norte.

Border with Argentina p80
Bus From west side of plaza in Futaleufú, a **Jacobsen** bus runs to the border, 3 times a week, and Mon-Fri in Jan-Feb, US$4, 30 mins, connecting with services to Trevelin and Esquel.

La Junta
Bus To **Chaitén** 4 a week, information from Chaitur. To **Coyhaique** with Daniela (T09-9512 3500), M&C (T242626), and Lagunas, 7 hrs, US$20. To **Puerto Cisnes**, with Empresa Entre Verde (T314275), US$10.

Puyuhuapi p81
Bus Daily to **Coyhaique**, US$18, 6 hrs, plus 2 weekly to **Lago Verde**.

Puerto Cisnes p81
Bus To **Coyhaique**, Transportes Terra Austral, T254335, Bus Alegría, T231350, run a daily (not Sun) service, US$15.

Coyhaique p82, map p82
Air Most flights from Balmaceda (see page 83), although Coyhaique has its own airport, Tte Vidal, about 5 km southwest of town. **Don Carlos**, to **Chile Chico** (Mon-Sat). **Cochrane** (Mon, Thu) and **Villa O'Higgins** (Mon, Thu, recommended only for those who like flying, with strong stomachs, or in a hurry).
Bus Full list of buses from tourist information. Terminal at Lautaro y Magallanes, T255726, but most buses leave from their own offices.
To **Puerto Aisén**, minibuses run every 45 mins, 1 hr **Suray** (A Prat 265, T2383871) and **São Paulo** (at terminal, T255726), US$3.

Change here for **Puerto Chacabuco**, 20 mins, US$1. To **Puerto Ibáñez** on Lago Gral Carrera, several minibus companies (connect with ferry to Chile Chico) pick-up 0530-0600 from your hotel, 1½ hrs, book the day before (eg Yamil Ali, Prat y Errázuriz, T219009, **Miguel Acuña**, M Moraleda 304, T251579 or 8900 4590, recommended).

Buses on the **Carretera Austral** vary according to demand, and they are always full so book early. Bikes can be taken by arrangement. North towards **Chaitén**: one service direct a week, US$35-40, otherwise change in La Junta: **Becker** (Parra 335, T232167) and **Queulat** (Parra 329, T242626); in winter these stop overnight in La Junta. These two companies also continue to **Futaleufú**, US$34. To **Puerto Cisnes**, Trans Austral (at terminal, T232057), Mon-Sat, Don Oscar (T254335), less frequent, US$14. South to **Cochrane** daily in summer with either **Don Carlos** (Subteniente Cruz 63, T232981), **Sao Paulo** (at terminal, T332918), or Acuario 13 (at terminal, T552143), US$27. All buses stop at **Cerro Castillo**. (US$8), **Bahía Murta** (US$12), **Puerto Tranquilo** (US$14) and **Puerto Bertrand** (US$16).
To Argentina: Giobbi/Trans Austral, T232067, at Terminal Municipal, run buses **Comodoro Rivadavia**, via Sarmiento, 2 daily. Daily buses from Com Rivadavia to Bariloche. Other options are given under Balmaceda and Chile Chico.
Car hire If renting a car, a high 4WD vehicle is recommended for Carretera Austral. Buy fuel in Coyhaique, several stations. There are several rental agencies in town, charging at least US$150 a day, including insurance, for 4WD or pick-up. Add another US$50 for paperwork to take a vehicle into Argentina.
Ferry office Navimag, Paseo Horn 47 D, T233306, www.navimag.com. Naviera Austral, Horn 40, of 101, T210727, www.navieraustral.cl.
Taxi US$7.50 to **Tte Vidal airport** (US$2 if sharing). Fares in town US$3, 50% extra after 2100. Colectivos (shared taxis) congregate at Prat y Bilbao, average fare US$1.

Puerto Aisén and Puerto Chacabuco *p83*
Bus See under **Coyhaique**, above.
Ferry Navimag's *Amadeo* and *Evangelistas*
sail each Fri from Puerto Chacabuco to Puerto
Montt, taking about 24 hrs (for details, see
Ferry, page 74). They divert from their
schedule in summer to run a 5-day trip from
Puerto Montt to Laguna San Rafael, calling at
Puerto Chacabuco. **Catamaranes del Sur** also
have sailings to Laguna San Rafael, US$1,080
for a 3-day trip (pp, double cabin), US$1,560
for 5 days, all-inclusive. Shipping Offices:
Agemar, Tte Merino 909, T332716, Puerto
Aisén. **Catamaranes del Sur**, J M Carrera 50,
T351115, www.catamaranesdel sur.cl.
Naviera Austral, Terminal de Transborda-
dores, T351493, www.navieraustral.cl.
Navimag, Terminal de Transbordadores,
Puerto Chacabuco, T351111,
www.navimag.com. It is best to make
reservations in these companies' offices in
Puerto Montt, Coyhaique or Santiago. For
trips to Laguna San Rafael, see page 75.

Balmaceda *p83*
Air Balmaceda airport is used for daily flights
to **Santiago** with LAN, via **Puerto Montt**, and
Sky, which sometimes makes several stops.
Landing can be dramatic owing to strong
winds. **Sky** also flies to **Punta Arenas**, 3 flights
weekly. Minibuses to/from hotels in Coyhaique
(56 km) US$8, 3 companies who all sell tickets
at baggage carousel. Taxi from airport to
Coyhaique, 1 hr, US$30. Car rental agencies at
the airport; very expensive, closed Sun.

Puerto Ibáñez *p83*
Bus Minibus to **Coyhaique**, 1½ hrs, US$7.55.
There is a road to **Perito Moreno**, Argentina,
but no public transport.
Ferry Two ferries, **Pilchero** and **Chelenco**
sail between Puerto Ibañez and **Chile Chico**,
daily except Saturday in summer, less often
otherwise. Both take passengers and vehicles,
fares about US$7.25 per adult (combined

minivan/ferry ticket from Coyhaique US$12,
with Miguel Acuña, see page 89), US$5 for
bikes, cars US$54 (62 on the Pilchero),
uncomfortable but beautiful 2½ hr crossing,
take food and warm clothing as the ferries are
completely open, but for a small cabin where
coffee is served and one can warm up.
Passports required, reservations essential:
Chelenco, in Coyhaique, T233466; in Chile
Chico T411864. **Pilchero** in Coyhaique,
Baquedano 146, T234240. At the quay, **Café
El Refugio** has toilets and sells sandwiches
and snacks. Minibuses meet the ferry in
Puerto Ibáñez for Coyhaique.

Villa Cerro Castillo *p84*
Bus 6 a week in summer to both **Coyhaique**
and **Cochrane**, companies as above under
Coyhaique. To **Río Tranquilo**, US$7.

❸ Directory

Coyhaique *p82, map p82*
Airline offices Don Carlos, address under
Bus, above. **LAN**, Moraleda 402, T600-526
2000. **Sky**, Prat 203, T240827 or 600-600
2828. **Banks** Several Redbanc ATMs in
centre. Casas de cambio: Turismo Prado, see
Tour operators. **Emperador**, Bilbao 222,
T233727. **Bicycle rental** Manuel Iduarte,
Parra y Bulnes, check condition first. **Bicycle
repairs** Tomás Madrid Urrea, Pasaje Foitzich
y Libertad, T252132. Recommended.
Language schools Baquedano
International Language School, Baquedano
20, at Cabañas of Sr Guzmán (see Where to
stay), T232520, www.balasch.cl. US$650 per
week course including lodging and all meals,
or US$40 for 4 hrs a day one-to-one tuition,
other lodging options and activities can
be arranged.

Puerto Aisén *p83*
Banks BCI, Prat, for Visa. **Banco de Chile**,
Plaza de Armas, cash only. **Redbanc** ATM
in Puerto Chacabuco.

Lago General Carrera and around

Southwest of Vila Cerro Castillo, the Carretera continues to afford stunning views, for instance minty-green Lago Verde and the meandering Río Manso, with swampy vegetation punctuated by the silver stumps of thousands of burnt trees, huge mountains behind. Lago General Carrera (Lago Buenos Aires in Argentina) straddles the border and, at 2240 sq km, is the second largest lake in South America. It's an area of outstanding beauty. Sheltered from the icy west winds by the Campo de Hielo Norte, the region also has the best climate in Southern Chile, with little rain, some 300 days of sunshine and a microclimate at Chile Chico that allows the cultivation of the same crops and fruit as in the Central Valley. Ferries cross the lake (see above), but it is worth taking time to follow the Carretera Austral around the lake's western shores.

Bahía Murta (*Km 198: Population: 586*), 5 km off the Camino, lies at the northern tip of the central 'arm' of the lake. There is a tiny tourist information hut, which opens summer 1000-1430, 1500-1930. Petrol is available from a house with a sign just before Puerto Murta. There's a public phone in the village.

Back on the Carretera Austral, **Puerto Río Tranquilo**, Km 223, is a slightly larger hamlet where the buses stop for lunch: fuel is available. Capilla del Marmol, in fact a limestone cliff vaguely resembling sculpted caves, is reached by a wonderful boat ride (ask at petrol station, to hire a boat US$45 with guide).

El Maitén, Km 277 south of Coihaique, an idyllic spot at the southwest tip of Lago General Carrera, is where a road branches off east along the south shore of the lake towards Chile Chico, while the Carretera Austral continues south to Puerto Bertand.

South of El Maitén the Carretera Austral becomes steeper and more winding (in winter this stretch, all the way to Cochrane, is icy and dangerous). At Km 294, is the hamlet of **Puerto Bertrand** lying by the dazzling turquoise waters of Río Baker. As this river is world renowned for fly fishing, good accommodation in Puerto Bertrand is either in one of the luxury *cabañas* that cater for wealthy anglers, or in a simple room in the village.

At **Puerto Guadal**, 13 km east of El Maitén, there are shops, accommodation, restaurants, a post office, petrol and a lovely stretch of lakeside beach. Further east is the villages of Mallín Grande (Km 40), **Paso de las Llaves**, a 30 km stretch carved out of the rock face on the edge of the lake, and Fachinal (turn off at Km 74). A further 5 km east is the **Garganta del Diablo**, a narrow gorge of 120 m with a fast-flowing stream below.

Chile Chico → *Population: 4500.*

This is a quiet town in a fruit-growing region, 125 km east of El Maitén. It has an annual fruit festival at the end of January and a small museum (open summer only). There are fine views from Cerro de las Banderas. It's 7 km to Los Antiguos, Argentina, where food and accommodation are preferable. **Laguna Jeinimeni**, 52 km from Chile Chico, is a beautiful place with excellent fishing, where you can also see flamingos and black-necked swans. The **tourist office** (helpful but usually closed) is in the Casa de la Cultura on O'Higgins. An unofficial purple tourist kiosk on the quay where the ferry arrives, sells bus tickets for Ruta 40 (Argentina), but has some accommodation information. Municipal website: www.chilechico.cl.

Border with Argentina

Chilean immigration 2 km east of Chile Chico. Open summer 0730-2200, winter 0800-2000. Argentine side closes for lunch 1300-1400. Remember that you can't take fresh food across in either direction, and you'll need ownership papers if crossing with a car. If entering Argentina here you will not have to fill in an immigration form (ask if you need entry papers).

Cochrane → *Population: 2996.*

From Puerto Bertand heading south, the road climbs up to high moorland, passing the confluence of the Ríos Neff and Baker (there is a mirador – lookout – here), before winding into Cochrane, 343 km south of Coyhaique. The scenery is splendid all the way; the road is generally rough but not treacherous. Watch out for cattle on the road and take blind corners slowly. Sitting in a hollow on the Río Cochrane, Cochrane is a simple place, sunny in summer, good for walking and fishing. The **Reserva Nacional Lago Cochrane**, 12 km east, surrounds Lago Cochrane. Campsite at Playa Vidal. Boat hire on the lake costs US$15 per person. Northeast of Cochrane is the beautiful **Reserva Nacional Tamango** ① *Dec-Mar 0830-2100, Apr-Nov 0830-1830. Ask in the CONAF office (Río Neff 417, T522164) about visiting because some access is through private land and tourist facilities are rudimentary, US$6.30, plus guided visits to see the huemules, Tue, Thu, Sat, US$80 for up to 6 people.* It has lenga forest, a few surviving huemul deer as well as guanaco, foxes and lots of birds including woodpeckers and hummingbirds. Access 9 km northeast of Cochrane, along Río Cochrane. There are marked paths for walks between 45 minutes and five hours, up to Cerro Tamango (1722 m) and Cerro Temanguito (1485 m). Take water and food, and windproof clothing if climbing the Cerros. The views from the reserve are superb, over the town, the nearby lakes and to the Campo de Hielo Norte to the west. It is inaccessible in the four winter months. **Tourist office** ① *on corner of plaza on Dr Steffen, T522115, www.cochranepatagonia.cl, summer Mon-Fri 0830-2000, Sat-Sun 1100-2000, off season Mon-Fri 0830-1730.* ATM for Mastercard only.

Caleta Tortel → *Population: 448.*

The Carretera Austral runs south of Cochrane and, after 105km, at the rather bleak looking Puerto Vagabundo, the road branches west to Caleta Tortel (see Transport, below). This quiet village at the mouth of the river, was until very recently accessible only by water and has no streets, only 7 km of walkways of cypress wood. Surrounded by mountainous land with abundant vegetation, it has a cool, rainy climate, and its main trade is logging, though this is declining as the town looks towards tourism. Located between the Northern and Southern Ice Fields, Tortel is within reach of two glaciers: **Glaciar Steffens** is to the north, a 2½-hour boat journey and three-hour walk, crossing a glacial river in a rowing boat. A boat for 10 people costs US$190. **Glaciar Jorge Montt** is to the southwest, five hours by boat, through landscapes of pure ice and water, US$300 for 10 people. Another boat trip is to the Isla de los Muertos, which has an interesting history, US$70 for 10. At the entrance to the village is a small tourist information office with information on lodging and a useful map. There is a post office, open Monday-Friday 0830-1330. The phone office number is T211876. **CONAF**, T211876, orlando.beltran@conaf.cl.

Villa O'Higgins

The Carretera Austral runs to Puerto Yungay (122 km from Cochrane), then another 110 km to **Villa O'Higgins**. There is one free ferry (*Padre Antonio Ronchi*) crossing between Yungay (military base) and Rio Bravo (1000, 1200, 1800, return to Yungay an hour later, 45 minutes, capacity four or five cars). The road beyond Río Bravo is very beautiful, but often closed by bad weather (take food – no shops or fuel on the entire route, few people and few vehicles for hitching). Tourist information is available from the Municipalidad. Lago Christie 121, T067-431821. See www.villaohiggins.cl.

It is possible to go from Villa O'Higgins to El Chaltén, Argentina. The road continues 7 km south to Bahía Bahamórdez on Lago O'Higgins (bus US$4), from where a boat leaves for Chilean immigration at **Candelario Mancilla** ① *Nov-Apr 0800-2200, 2¾ hours, US$86; departures vary each year, but usually one a week in Nov, 2 a week in Dec, 3 in Jan, Feb, then fewer in Mar; there may be other departures in Nov, even in Apr, but exact dates should be checked in advance.* A detour to Glaciar O'Higgins costs US$42 on the regular crossing or between US$90-150 for a day-long special trip, depending from which side of the lake you start (cheaper from Candelario Mancilla). Sailings may be cancelled if the weather is bad. Then it's 14 km to the Argentine border and a further 5 km to Argentine immigration at Punta Norte on Lago del Desierto. The first part can be done on foot, on horseback, or by 4WD service for US$30 (takes four passengers and luggage, call Hans Silva in Villa O'Higgins, T431821, to reserve car or horses). The next 5 km is a demanding hike, or you can take a horse for US$32 for the whole 19 km, with an extra horse to carry bags (Ricardo is great horseman with an excellent sense of humor).

The route descends sharply towards Lago de Desierto. Bridges are sometimes washed away. Make sure to wear good boots for crossing wetland. Panoramas on the descent are breathtaking, including of Cerro Fritz Roy. A short detour to Laguna Larga (on the right as you walk from the border) is worth it if you have the energy. The 40-minute boat crossing of the lake passes glaciers and ice fields on your right ① *daily except Mon, US$24.50 if bought in Argentina, US$29 if prepaid in Chile.* Finally it takes over an hour by bus or minivan on a gravel road to El Chaltén (37 km). Several companies including Transporte Las Lengas and JR Turismo Alternativo await the boat ① *US$30 if prepaid, may be cheaper if bought at the jetty.* There is no food available on either side of the lake, but Argentine immigration at Punta Norte are friendly and, if you are cold, may offer you coffee.

The best combination is to take 4WD from Candelario Mancilla to the border and then continue on horseback. This ensures that the trip can be done in a day (depart Villa O'Higgins 0800, arrive El Chatén 2115; full details on www.villaohiggins.cl, T067-431821). Allow for delays, though, especially if horses aren't available for hire. It's a good option to pay for each portion of the route separately. The route closes in late April. With the opening of this route it is possible to do the Carretera Austral and go on to Argentina's Parque Nacional Los Glaciares and Chile's Torres del Paine without doubling back on yourself.

Parque Nacional Laguna San Rafael

① *US$6, at the glacier there is a small ranger station which gives information; a pier and 2 paths have been built, one of which leads to the glacier.*

Some 150 nautical miles south of Puerto Aisén is the **Laguna San Rafael**, into which flows a glacier, 30 m above sea level and 45 km in length. The glacier has a deep blue colour, shimmering and reflecting the light. It calves small icebergs, which seem an unreal, translucent blue, and which are carried out to sea by wind and tide. The glacier is very noisy; there are frequent cracking and banging sounds, resembling a mixture of gunshots and thunder. When a hunk of ice breaks loose, a huge swell is created and the icebergs start rocking in the water. The glacier is disintegrating and is predicted to disappear entirely by 2013. Some suggest that the wake from tour boats is contributing to the erosion.

The thick vegetation on the shores, with snowy peaks above, is typical of Aisén. The only access is by plane or by boat. The glacier is equally spectacular from the air or the sea. The glacier is one of a group of four that flow in all directions from Monte San Valentín. This icefield is part of the **Parque Nacional Laguna San Rafael** (1,740,000 ha), regulated by CONAF. In the national park are puma, *pudú* (miniature deer), foxes, dolphins, occasional sealions and sea otters, and many species of bird. Walking trails are limited (about 10 km in all) but a lookout platform has been constructed, with fine views of the glacier.

Lago General Carrera and around listings

For hotel and restaurant price codes and other relevant information, see pages 10-12.

⊕ Where to stay

Lago General Carrera *p91*
Bahía Murta
$ Res Patagonia, Pje España 64, T419600. Comfortable, serves food. Free camping by lake at Bahía Murta.

Puerto Río Tranquilo
$$$ Hostal el Puesto, Pedro Lagos 258, T02-1964555, www.elpuesto.cl. No doubt the most comfortable place in Río Tranquilo, with breakfast, also organizes tours.
$$$ Hostal Los Pinos, Godoy 51, Puerto Río Tranquilo, T411576. Family run, well maintained, good mid-priced meals. Recommended.
$$ Cabañas Jacricalor, Carretera Austral 245, Puerto Río Tranquilo, T419500 (public phone). Tent-sized *cabañas*, hot shower, good meals, good information for climbers.
$$ Campo Alacaluf, Km 44 on the Río Tranquilo-Bahía Exploradores side road, T419500. Wonderful guesthouse hidden away from civilization. Run by very friendly German family. Recommended.
$$ Hostal Carretera Austral, 1 Sur 223, Río Tranquilo, T419500. Also serves mid-range/ cheap meals.

El Maitén
$$$$ Hacienda Tres Lagos, Carretera Austral Km 274, just west of cruce Maitén, T067-411323, T02-3334 4122 (Santiago), www.haciendatres lagos.com. Set in spacious grounds on the lakeshore. Small, boutique resort with bungalows, suites and less luxurious standard cabins. Good restaurant, wide range of excursions offered, sauna, jacuzzi, good service. English spoken. Recommended.
$$$$ Mallín Colorado Ecolodge, Carretera Austral Km 273, 2 km west of El Maitén, T02-919 6112/ 02-360 9742, www.mallincolorado.cl. Comfortable *cabañas* in sweeping gardens, complete tranquility, charming owners, 4- to 10-day packages available, including transfers from Balmaceda, horseriding, estancia trip, superb meals, open Oct-Apr. Highly recommended.

Puerto Bertrand
$$$ Lodge Río Baker, Puerto Bertrand, T411499, riobaker@hotmail.com. Full board, warmly recommended fishing lodge, also all-inclusive fishing packages.
$$$ Patagonia Baker Lodge and Restaurant, Puerto Bertrand, towards the south side of the lake, T411903, www.pbl.cl. Stylish *cabañas* in woodland, fishing lodge, birdwatching, fabulous views upriver towards rapids and the mountains beyond.

$$ Hostería Puerto Bertrand, Puerto Bertrand, T419900. With breakfast, other meals available, also *cabañas* activities.
$ Hospedaje Doña Ester, Casa 8, Puerto Bertrand, T09-9990 8541. Rooms in a pink house, good.
$ Turismo Hospedaje Campo de Hielo Norte, Ventisquero Neff s/n. Owned by Anselmo Soto, open in tourist season only, very hospitable and helpful.

Puerto Guadal

$$$ El Mirador Playa Guadal, 2 km towards Chile Chico, T09-9234 9130. www.patagonia playaguadal.cl. *Cabañas* near beach, fishing, walks to nearby waterfalls. meals extra, restaurant with fixed rate menus Sep-Nov, Mar-May, à la carte Jan-Feb. Recommended.
$$$ Terra Luna Lodge, on lakeside, 2 km from Puerto Guadal, T431263, www.terra-luna.cl. Welcoming well-run place with lodge, bungalows and camping huts (**$$**), also has restaurant, many activities offered.
$ Hostería Huemules, Las Magnolias 382, Puerto Guadal, T431212. Breakfast, good views.
Camping Site at east end of village.

Chile Chico *p91*

$$ Casa Quinta No me Olvides/Manor House Don't Forget Me, Sector Chacras, Camino Internacional s/n, T09-9833 8006. Hospedaje and camping, cooking facilities, shared bathrooms, hot showers, honey, eggs, fruit and vegetables for sale, tours arranged to Lago Jeinimeni and Cueva de las Manos.
$$ Hostería de la Patagonia Camino Internacional s/n, Casilla 91, T411337. Also camping; full-board available. Good food, English, French and Italian spoken, trekking, horse riding, whitewater rafting.
$$ Hospedaje Don Luis, Balmaceda 175, T411384. Meals available, laundry, helpful.
$ pp Hospedaje at Tel Sur phone centre, in the middle of O'Higgins. Use of kitchen, helpful owners also sell bus tickets for La Unión buses to Los Antiguos and Comodoro Rivadavia.

Camping Free site at Bahía Jara, 5 km west of Chile Chico, then turn north for 12 km.

Cochrane *p92*

$$$ Wellmann, Las Golondrinas 36, T/F522171. Comfortable, warm, hot water, good meals. Recommended.
$$$-$$ Cabañas Rogeri, Fío Maitén 80, T522264, rogeri3@hotmail.cl. *Cabañas* for 4, with kitchen facilities, price includes breakfast.
$$ Res Cero a Cero, Lago Brown 464, T522158, ceroacero@hotmail.com. With breakfast, welcoming. Recommended.
$$ Res Rubio, Tte Merino 871, T522173. Very nice, breakfast included, lunch and dinner extra.
$$ Res Sur Austral, Prat 334, T522150. Breakfast included, with bath, **$** pp shared bath, hot water, also very nice.
$ pp Res Cochrane, Dr Steffens 451, T522377. Also serves good meals, laundry, hot shower, breakfast. Recommended. Also camping.
$ pp Res El Fogón, San Valentín 65, T09-7644 7914. Its pub is the only eating place open in low season, it's the best restaurant at any time of year.

Caleta Tortel *p92*

There are several *hospedajes*. All prices are cheaper in the low season. For all T067-234815 (public phone) or 211876 (municipality).
$$$ Entre Hielos lodge, sector centro. T02-196 0271, www.entrehielostortel.cl. The only upmarket accommodation in town.
$$ Estilo, Sector Centro, Tortel, tortelhospe dajeestilo@yahoo.es. Warm and comfortable, good food. Entertaining, talkative host (if your Spanish is up to it). Recommended.
$$ Hospedaje Costanera, Sra Luisa Escobar Sanhueza. Cosy, warm, lovely garden, full board available, breakfast included.
Camping There is camping at sector Junquillo at the far end of town.

Villa O'Higgins *p93*

$$ Cabañas San Gabriel, Lago O'Higgins 310. Nice cabins. A good choice for small groups.

\$\$ El Mosco, at the northern entrance to the town, T431819, patagoniaelmosco@yahoo.es. **\$** pp in dorms. Spanish-run, kitchen facilities, games, laundry facilities, trekking maps and information. Help with bike repairs. Camping available, English spoken. More expensive than the rest, but best infrastructure. Recommended.
\$ Los Nirres, Lago O'Higgins 72, singles cheaper. Basic accommodation, goods meals. Several other similar places in town.
\$ Res Campanario, Lago O'Higgins 72. Friendly, kitchen facilities, camping.

🍴 Restaurants

Chile Chico *p91*
Café Refer, O'Higgins 416. Good, despite exterior.
Cafetería Loly y Elizabeth, PA González 25, on Plaza. Coffee, delicious ice cream and cakes.

Caleta Tortel *p92*
Café Celes Salom, bar/restaurant serving basic, cheap meals, disco on Sat, occasional live bands.

▲ What to do

Lago General Carrera and around *p91*
Patagonia Adventure Expeditions,
T09-8182 0608, www.adventurepatagonia. com. Professional outfit running exclusive fully supported treks to the Campo de Hielo Norte and the eastern side of Parque Nacional Laguna San Rafael. Expensive but a unique experience and recommended. Also organize rafting on the Río Baker and provide general help organizing tours, treks and expeditions.

🚍 Transport

Chile Chico *p91*
Bus Several minibuses daily to **Cochrane**, US\$27, 5 hrs. See above for ferry to Puerto Ibáñez and connecting minibus to Coyhaique. Ferry and minibus tickets from **Miguel Acuña**, Refugio Muelle Local, T411804 (for urgent enquiries call mobiles 9217 3520 or 8900 4590).

Border with Argentina: Chile Chico– Los Antiguos *p92*
Bus In summer, irregular minibuses from Chile Chico ferry to Los Antiguos on the Argentine side 0800-2200, US\$3.75 (in Chilean pesos), ½-1 hr including formalities: ask on quayside. **Minibus Jaime Acuña**, T411553.

Cochrane *p92*
Air Don Carlos to **Coyhaique**, Mon, Thu.
Bus Company agencies: **Don Carlos**, Prat 344, T522150; **Acuario 13** and **Sao Paulo**, Río Baker 349, T522143. There are 6 buses a week between Coyhaique and Cochrane, check with companies for current timetables, US\$27. To **Río Tranquilo**, US\$11. To **Villa O'Higgins**, **Acuario 13** (T067-255726), Sun, Thu 0900, return Mon, Fri 1000, 6-7 hrs, US\$25. To **Tortel**, **Acuario 13**, Tue, return Wed, and **Buses Aldea**, Tue, Thu, Fri, Sun, US\$12.50. Minibuses, including **Bus Ale**, Las Golondrinas 399, T522242, daily to **Chile Chico**, US\$27. Petrol is available at the **Esso** and **Copec** servicentros.

Caleta Tortel *p92*
Bus From **Cochrane**, see above. On Sun Dec-Mar a bus runs between Tortel and **Villa O'Higgins**, 4 hrs, US\$30, 0830 to Tortel, 1630 back to O'Higgins, T067-431821.

Parque Nacional Laguna San Rafael *p93*
Ferry Cruises are run by : Skorpios (see under Puerto Montt); Catamaranes del Sur, Compañía Naviera Puerto Montt and Navimag. Patagonia Express runs catamaran trips from Puerto Chacabuco to Laguna San Rafael via Termas de Puyuhuapi, in tours lasting 4-6 days, from Puerto Montt via Coyhaique including the catamaran service, the hotel stay at Termas de Puyuhuapi and the day excursion to Laguna San Rafael (see page 75).

🛈 Directory

Chile Chico *p91*
Banks Best to change money in Coyhaique.
Hospital Lautaro s/n, T411334.

Far south

This wild and wind-blown area, covering the glacial regions of southern Patagonia and Chilean Tierra del Fuego, is beautiful and bleak, with stark mountains and open steppe. Little vegetation survives here and few people; though it represents 17.5% of Chile's total area, it is inhabited by under 1% of the population. The southernmost city of Punta Arenas and the attractive, quiet port of Puerto Natales are the two main centres, the latter being the gateway to the Torres del Paine and Balmaceda national parks. In summer it is a wonderful region for climbing, hiking, boat trips and the southernmost crossings to Argentina.

Summers are sunny and very variable, with highs of 15° C. In winter snow covers the country, except those parts near the sea, making many roads more or less impassable, except on horseback. Cold, piercing winds blow, particularly in late spring, when they may exceed 100 kmph. Despite chilly temperatures, protect on against the sun's ultraviolet rays is essential here all year round and in summer, too, windproof clothing is a must.

Punta Arenas and around → *Phone code: 061. Population: 150,000.*

About 2140 km south of Santiago, Punta Arenas lies on the eastern shore of the Brunswick Peninsula facing the Straits of Magellan at almost equal distance from the Pacific and Atlantic oceans. Founded in 1843, it has grand neoclassical buildings and an opulent cemetery, testimony to its wealthy past as a major port and centre for exporting wool. In the late 19th century, Salesian Missions were established to control the indigenous population so sheep farming could flourish. The city's fortunes slumped when the Panama Canal opened in 1914, but it remains a pleasant place, with attractive, painted wooden buildings away from the centre and good fish restaurants. Paved roads connect the city with Puerto Natales, 247 km north, and with Río Gallegos in Argentina.

Arriving in Punta Arenas

Tourist office Sernatur ⓘ *Lautaro Navarro 999 y Pedro Montt, T225385, infomagallanes@ sernatur.cl, open Mon-Fri 0800-1800. See www.patagonia-chile.com.* In the plaza there is also the municipal tourist information kiosk ⓘ *opposite Centro Español, T200610, Mon-Thu 0800-1730, Fri 0800-1630, informacionturistica@puntaarenas.cl* has experienced staff, good town map with all hotels and internet places marked, English spoken, can book hotels. CONAF ⓘ *Av Bulnes 0309, p 4, T238554, magallanes.oirs@conaf.cl.*

Places in Punta Arenas

In the centre of the **Plaza Muñoz Gamero** is a striking statue of Magellan with a mermaid and two indigenous Fuegians at his feet. Around the plaza are a number of impressive neo-classical buildings, the former mansions of the great sheep ranching families of the late 19th century. **Palacio Sara Braun** ① *1000-1300, 1800-2030, US$2* (1895), part of which now houses the Hotel José Nogueira, has several elegant rooms which are open to the public. The fascinating **Museo de Historia Regional Braun Menéndez** ① *Magallanes 949, T244216, www.dibam.cl/sdm_mr_magallanes, Mon-Sat 1030-1700, 1030-1400 Sun (1030-1400 daily May-Sep), US$2, guided tours in Spanish, information in English*, was once the mansion of Mauricio Braun, built in 1905. It has fabulously decorated rooms, with ornate furniture, paintings and marble and crystal imported from Europe. Highly recommended. Further north, is the impressive **Cemetery** ① *Av Bulnes 929, daily, 0800-1800, later in summer*, charting a history of European immigration and shipping disasters through the huge mausoleums, divided by avenues of imposing sculpted cypress trees.

The perfect complement to this is **Museo Regional Salesiano Maggiorino Borgatello** ① *in the Colegio Salesiano, Av Bulnes 336 (entrance next to church), T221001, www.museo maggiorinoborgatello.cl, Tue-Sun 1000-1230, 1500-1730 (hours change frequently), US$4*. It covers the fascinating history of the indigenous peoples and their education by the Salesian missions, beside an array of stuffed birds and gas extraction machinery. The Italian priest, Alberto D'Agostini, who arrived in 1909 and presided over the missions, took wonderful photographs of the region and his 70-minute film can be seen on video (ask). Highly recommended. The **Instituto de la Patagonia** ① *Av Bulnes Km 4 north (opposite the University), T244216, outdoor exhibits Mon-Fri 0830-1130, 1430-1830, Sat 0830-1230, US$2*, has an open-air museum with artefacts used by the early settlers, pioneer homes, research library and botanical gardens.

Museo Naval y Marítimo ① *Pedro Montt 981, T205479, www.museonaval.cl/en/museo-de-p-arenas.html, Jan-Feb Tue-Sat 0930-1700; Mar-Dec Tue-Sat 0930-1230, 1400-1700, US$1*, has shipping instruments, maps, photos and relics from the Chilean navy and famous navigators. Recommended. West of the Plaza Muñoz Gamero on Calle Fagnano is the Mirador Cerro de La Cruz offering a view over the city and the Magellan Straits. The **Parque María Behety**, south of town along 21 de Mayo, features a scale model of Fuerte Bulnes and a campsite, popular for Sunday picnics; ice rink here in winter.

The city's waterfront has been given an extensive face-lift, with public boardwalks and outdoor spaces under special shelters giving protection from the sun's strong ultraviolet rays.

Around Punta Arenas

West of town (7 km) is the **Reserva Forestal Magallanes** ① *US$5, taxi US$7.50*, with nature trails from 45 minutes to 2 days, picnic areas. A recommended walk is a 4 hour circuit up to a lookout with beautiful views over town and the surroundings and back down along the Río Minas to Punta Arenas. Nearby is the Club Andino (see under skiing below). Some 56 km south, **Fuerte Bulnes** is a replica of the wooden fort erected in 1843 by the crew of the Chilean vessel *Ancud* to secure Chile's southernmost territories after Independence. Little to see but an interesting story. Nearby is **Puerto de Hambre**, a beautiful, panoramic spot where there are ruins of the church built in 1584 by Sarmiento de Gamboa's colonists. Tours by several agencies. Some 210 km to the northeast on Ruta 255, towards Argentina, is **Parque Nacional Pali Aike** ① *US$6*, near Punta Delgada. One

Punta Arenas

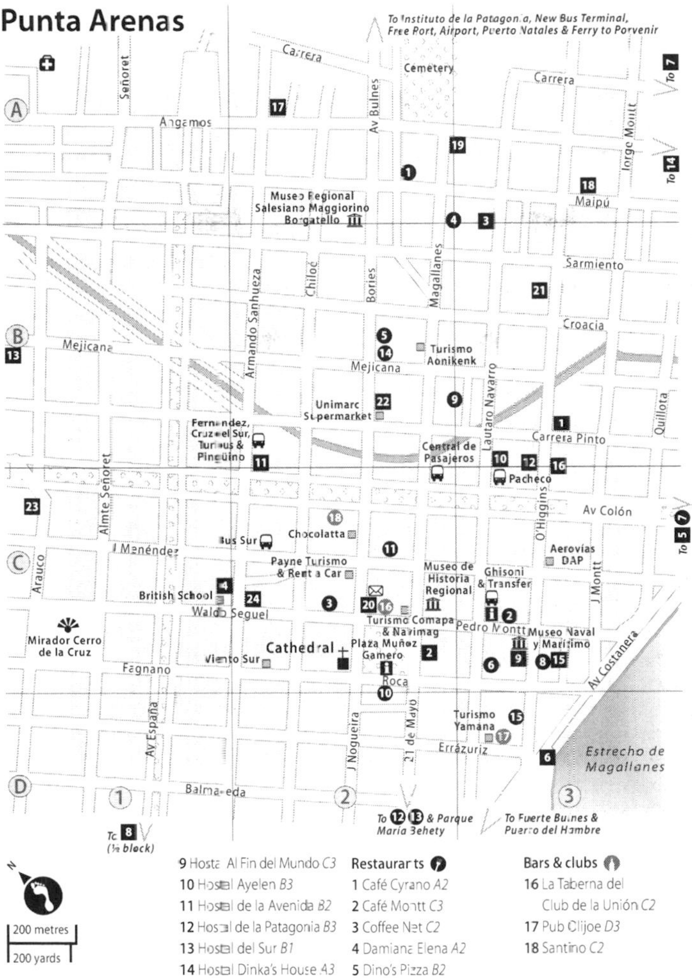

Map labels (as they appear on the map):

To Instituto de la Patagonia, New Bus Terminal, Free Port, Airport, Puerto Natales & Ferry to Porvenir

To 7

Carrera
Cemetery
Carrera
Av Bulnes
Señoret
Angamos
Jorge Montt
To 14
Maipú
Museo Regional Salesiano Maggiorino Borgatello
Sarmiento
Chiloé
Bories
Magallanes
Armando Sanhueza
Croacia
Mejicana
Turismo Aonikenk
Mejicana
Quillota
Unimarc Supermarket
Fernández, Cruz el Sur, Turibus & Pingüino
Central de Pasajeros
Carrera Pinto
Almte Señoret
Lautaro Navarro
Pacheco
Av Colón
Chocolatta
Bus Sur
Aerovías DAP
Arauco
I Menéndez
Payne Turismo & Rent a Car
Museo de Historia Regional
Ghisoni & Transfer
British School
Waldo Seguel
Turismo Comapa & Navimag
Museo Naval y Marítimo
Mirador Cerro de la Cruz
Fagnano
Viento Sur
Cathedral
Plaza Muñoz Gamero
Av Costanera
Roca
Av España
J Noguera
21 de Mayo
Turismo Yámana
Estrecho de Magallanes
Errázuriz
Balmaceda
To 12 13 & Parque María Behety
To Fuerte Bulnes & Puerto del Hambre

To 5 7

N
200 metres
200 yards

Tc 8 (½ block)

Where to stay 🛏

1 Backpackers' Paradise B3
2 Cabo de Hornos C2
3 Carpa Manzano A3
4 Chalet Chapital C1
5 Diego de Almagro C3
6 Dreams D3
7 Ely House A3
8 Hosp Independencia D1
9 Hostal Al Fin del Mundo C3
10 Hostal Ayelen B3
11 Hostal de la Avenida B2
12 Hostal de la Patagonia B3
13 Hostal del Sur B1
14 Hostal Dinka's House A3
15 Hostal El Conventillo C3
16 Hostal La Estancia B3
17 Hostal Sonia Kuscevic A2
18 Hostal Taty's House A3
19 Hostal Keoken A2
20 José Nogueira
   (Palacio Sara Braun) C2
21 Luna Hostal B3
22 Monterrey B2
23 Patagonia Pionera C1
24 Rey Don Felipe C2

Restaurants 🍴

1 Café Cyrano A2
2 Café Montt C3
3 Coffee Net C2
4 Damiana Elena A2
5 Dino's Pizza B2
6 El Quijote C3
7 Imago Café C3
8 La Luna C3
9 La Marmita B3
10 La Tasca D2
11 Lomit's C2
12 Mercado Municipal D2
13 Remezón D2
14 Sabores B2
15 Sotitos D3

Bars & clubs 🍸

16 La Taberna del
   Club de la Unión C2
17 Pub Olijoe D3
18 Santino C2

of the oldest archaeological sites in Patagonia (Pali Aike means 'desolate place of bad spirits' in Tehuelche). Evidence of aborigines from 10,000-12,000 years ago, in an extraordinary volcanic landscape pockmarked with countless tiny craters, rock of different colours and caves. Tour operators offer a full day trip, US$80; for more details, ask at CONAF, who manage the park.

Isla Magdalena, a small island 30 km northeast, is the location of the **Monumento Natural Los Pingüinos**, a spectacular colony of 60,000 pairs of Magellanic penguins, who come here to breed between November and January (also skuas, kelp gulls and other marine wildlife). Magdalena is one of a group of three islands (the others are Marta and Isabel), visited by Drake, whose men killed 3000 penguins for food. Boat trips to the island are run by **Comapa** and **Sólo Expediciones**, while **Cruceros Australis** call here (see What to do, below). Less spectacular but more easily accessible (70 km north of Punta Arenas by road), **Otway Sound** ① *Oct to mid-Mar, US$6,* has a colony of Magellanic penguins, viewed from walkways and bird hides, best seen in the morning. Rheas can also be seen. It is becoming a popular area for sea-kayaking and other adventure sports.

Punta Arenas and around listings

For hotel and restaurant price codes and other relevant information, see pages 10-12.

☉ Where to stay

Punta Arenas *p97, map p99*
Hotel prices are lower during winter months (Apr-Sep). For accommodation in private houses, usually **$** pp, ask at the tourist office. No campsites in or near the city.
$$$$ Cabo de Hornos, Muñoz Gamero 1025, on the plaza, T715000, www.hoteles-australis.com. 4-star, newly refurbished, comfy, bright and spacious rooms, with good views from 4th floor up.
$$$$ Dreams, O'Higgins 1235, T204648, www.mundodreams.com. New luxury hotel above the casino. Comfortable spacious rooms (many overlook the Magellan straights), spa, gym, pool, sauna.
$$$$ José Nogueira, Plaza de Armas, Bories 959 y P Montt, in former Palacio Sara Braun, T711000, www.hotelnogueira.com. Best in town, stylish rooms, warm atmosphere, excellent service. Smart restaurant in the beautiful loggia. A few original rooms now a 'small museum', with a portrait of Sara Braun.
$$$$-$$$ Diego de Almagro, Colón 1290, T208800, www.dahoteles.com. Very modern,

good international standard, on waterfront, many rooms with view, heated pool, small gym, big bright rooms, good value. Highly recommended.
$$$$-$$$ Rey Don Felipe, Sanhueza 965, T295000, www.hotelreydonfelipe.cl. Small standard 4-star. Good-sized rooms, bar, restaurant, parking. A decent choice.
$$$ Carpa Manzano, Lautaro Navarro 336, T710744, www.hotelcarpamanzano.com. Small hotel with comfortable, somewhat cramped carpeted rooms (superior rooms have king-size beds). Basic English spoken.
$$$ Chalet Chapital, Sanhueza 974, T730100, www.hotelchaletchapital.cl. Small well-run hotel, smallish rooms, helpful staff, a good choice in this price range.
$$$ Hostal de la Avenida, Colón 534, T247532. Attractive rooms, central heating, cable TV, pretty courtyard with plants and apple tree, breakfasts.
$$$ Hostal de la Patagonia, O'Higgins 730, T249970, www.ecotourpatagonia.com.
$$ in low season, heating, TV, Wi-Fi, buffet breakfast, afternoon tea/onces, smart, comfy, well appointed.
$$$ Patagonia Pionera, Arauco 786, T222045, www.hotelpatagoniapionera.cl.

Beautiful 1930s wooden casona carefully restored and converted into a comfortable high end B&B. Helpful staff, onsite parking. Recommended. Insalubrious neighbourhood at night.

$$ Ely House, Caupolicán 75, T226660, www.residencialely.com. Some rooms with bath, welcoming, laberynthine hostel, with breakfast, comfortable, heating and hot water, kitchen, thin walls, good value.

$$ Hostal Al Fin del Mundo O'Higgins 1026, T710185, www.alfindelmundo.cl. **$** pp in dorms. With breakfast, bright, cosy, shared baths, central, helpful, laundry service, book exchange, internet, pool table, cooking facilities, English spoken. Recommended.

$$ Hostal Ayelen, Lautarro Navarro 763, T242413, www.ayelenresidencial.com. Family atmosphere, very helpful, 120-year old house with some new rooms at the back, bathroom a bit small but super clean, comfy, hot water, TV, heating, breakfast at any hour, Wi-Fi.

$$ Hostal del Sur, Mejicana 151, T227249, www.hostaldelsur.cl. Impeccable old house with modern rooms in residential area, welcoming, excellent breakfast, heating, advance booking in summer, basic English spoken. Recommended.

$$ Hostal Dinka's House, Caupolicán 169, T244292, www.dinkashouse.cl. With breakfast, use of kitchen, heating, laundry, internet, welcoming, very colourful, painted deep red with lots of real and imitation flowers, gnomes, etc, attended by Dinka herself.

$$ Hostal El Conventillo, FaEje Korner 1034, T242311, www.hostalelconventillo.com. With breakfast, 'hip' hostel with rooms for 2-6 with shared bath, cheerful, good value, free internet.

$$ Hostel Keoken, Magallanes 209, T244086, www.hostelkeoken.cl. Bizarre construction on 3 floors each with its own entrance up rickety outside staircases. With breakfast, some rooms with bath, kitchen facilities, Wi-Fi. Good value, some info. Recommended, though top floor rooms with shared bathroom have paper thin walls.

$$ Hostal La Estancia, O'Higgins 765, T249 30, www.estancia.cl. Simple but comfortable rooms, some with bath. **$** pp in dorms. Heating in passageways but not in rooms. Very good kitchen facilities, internet, lots of information, English spoken. Excellent breakfast with real coffee. Recommended.

$$ Hostal Sonia Kuscevic, Pasaje Darwin 175, T248543, www.hostalsk.cl. One of the city's oldest guesthouses, with breakfast, kitchen facilities, hot water, heating, parking. Better value for longer than short stays, good discount with Hostelling International card.

$$ Hostal Taty's House, Maipu 1070, T241 525, www.hostaltatyshouse.cl. Nice rooms with cable TV, good beds, decent choice in this price bracket, basic English spoken.

$$ Luna Hostal, O'Higgins 424, T221764, hostalluna@hotmail.com. Quiet house with delightful rooms with or without bath, comfy beds with duvets, or **$** in dorms, use of kitchen, laundry facilities.

$ Backpackers' Paradise, Carrera Pinto 1022, T240104, backpackersparadise@ hotmail.com. Popular, limited bathroom facilities, only curtains dividing the large dorms, not exactly comfortable, cooking and laundry facilities, internet, luggage store.

$ Hospedaje Independencia, Independencia 374, T227572. www.chileaustral.com/ independencia. Cheaper in shared rooms. Use of kitchen, laundry, bike rental, internet, good value. Highly recommended. Also good-value *cabañas* away from the centre.

$ pp **Monterrey**, Bories 621, T220636, monterrey@turismoaventura.net. Cheaper without breakfast (which is good), tiny rooms with TV, heating, clothes washing, use of kitchen, comfortable but a bit tatty in public areas, discounts for long stay, charming people.

🍴 Restaurants

Punta Arenas *p97, map p99*
Many eating places close Sun. **Note** *Centolla* (king crab) is caught illegally by some fishermen using dolphin, porpoise and penguin as

live bait. There are seasonal bans on *centolla* fishing to protect dwindling stocks; out of season *centolla* served in restaurants will probably be frozen. If there is an infestation of red tide (*marea roja*), a disease which is fatal to humans, bivalve shellfish must not be eaten. Mussels should not be picked along the shore because of pollution and *marea roja*. Sernatur and Centros de Salud have leaflets.

$$$ Remezón, 21 de Mayo 1469, T241029. Regional specialities such as krill. Very good, but should be, given sky-high prices.

$$$-$$ Damiana Elena, Magallanes 341, T222818. Stylish restaurant serving Mediterranean food with a Patagonian touch, popular with locals, book ahead at weekends, open Mon-Sat from 2000.

$$$-$$ Sabores, Mejicana y Bories, www.restaurantsabores.cl. Upstairs, pleasant, quite traditional, comfy, varied menu of well-cooked seafood, fish, pastas, meats, etc. Service can be slow.

$$$-$$ Sotitos, O'Higgins 1138. An institution, famous for seafood in elegant surroundings, excellent. Book ahead in season.

$$$-$$ La Tasca, Plaza Muñoz Gamero 771, above Teatro Cervantes in Casa Español. Large helpings, limited selection, decent set lunch, views over the plaza.

$$ La Luna, O'Higgins 1017, T228555. Fish, shellfish and local specialities, huge pisco sours, popular, reasonable.

$$ La Marmita, Plaza Sampiao 678. Regional dishes with international twist, vegetarian options, good sized portions, prettily presented, chatty owner, open 1230-1500, 1830-2330, generally very good.

$$-$ El Quijote, Lautaro Navarro 1087, T241225. Meat dishes, fish, soups, salads, good burgers and sandwiches, daily lunch specials, bright atmosphere, happy hour 1900-2100. Recommended.

$ Dino's Pizza, Bories 557. Good-value pizza in a cheerful fast food atmosphere, lots of choice, irregular opening hours.

$ Lomit's, Menéndez 722. A fast-food institution, cheap snacks and drinks, open when the others are closed, good.

$ Mercado Municipal, 21 de Mayo 1465. Wide range of cocinerías offering cheap empanadas and seafood on the upper floor of the municipal market.

Cafés

Café Cyrano, Bulnes 297 y Maipú, T242749. Popular in evening, less busy at lunchtime, teas, coffee and sandwiches, tortas and cakes.

Café Montt, Pedro Montt 976. Coffees, teas, cakes, pastries and snacks, Wi-Fi.

Coffee Net, Waldo Seguel 670, www.coffeenet.cl. Big internet café/bar opposite the police HQ, good service and music, occasional live acts, hot chocolate and coffee.

Imago Café, Costanera y Colón. Tiny, laid back café hidden away in a beachfront bunker overlooking the straights.

Bars and clubs

Punta Arenas *p97, map p99*
La Taberna del Club de la Unión, on the plaza in the basement of the Hotel Nogueira. Smoky but atmospheric bar, good for evening drinks, open Mon-Sat from 1830.

Pub Olijoe, Errázuriz 970. Like a traditional British pub, for beer in a lively atmosphere, plush leather interior. Recommended.

Santino, Colón 657, www.santino.cl. Also serves pizzas and other snacks, large bar, good service, open Mon-Sat till 0300.

Sky Bar, O'Higgins 1235. Bar with panoramic views on the top floor of **Dreams Hotel**.

Shopping

Punta Arenas *p97, map p99*
Punta Arenas has certain free-port facilities; Zona Franca, 3.5 km north of the centre, opposite Museo Instituto de la Patagonia, is cheaper than elsewhere. Closed 1230-1500 and Sun (bus E or A from Plaza Muñoz Gamero; many *colectivos*; taxi US$3).

Food and drink Chocolatta, Bories 852.
Tasty handmade chocolate, good coffee. Also
Chocolates Norweisser, Carrera 663, open
0930-1230, 1430-1930, Sat 1300-1300.
Secreto de la Patagonia, Sarmiento de
Gamboa 1029. Local produce, chocolates,
cheese, jams, delicatessen, souvenirs.
Handicrafts Chile Típico, Carrera Pinto
1015, T225827.
Supermarkets Unimarc (Abu-Gosch),
Bories 647, open daily 0900-2200. Others
such as **Cofrima 2**, España 01375 and **Líder**
2 km northwest of centre.

▲ What to do

Punta Arenas *p97, map p99*
Patagonia Expedition Race An exteme,
multi-sport challenge held each Feb, the
Wenger Patagonia Expedition Race,
www.patagonianexpeditionrace.com,
is hosted by **Nomadas**, T613893,
www.nomadas.cl, who offer customized
adventure trips in the wilderness, have an
outdoor school, a shop and equipment rental.
Skiing Cerro Mirador, only 9 km west of
Punta Arenas in the Reserva Nacional
Magallanes, one of the few places in the
world where you can ski with a sea view.
Taxi US$8. Daily lift pass, US$35 (high season);
equipment rental available. Mid-way lodge
with food, drink and equipment. Season
Jul-Sep, weather and snow permitting.
In summer there is a good 2-hr walk on the
hill, with labelled flora. Contact **Club
Andino**, T241479, www.clubandino.cl.

Tour operators
Most tour operators organize trips to Torres
del Paine, Fuerte Bulnes, the pingüineras on
Isla Magdalena and Otway sound and Tierra
del Fuego; shop around.
Arka Patagonia, Manuel Señoret 1597,
T248167, www.arkapatagonia.com.
All types of tours, rafting, fishing, etc.
Cruceros Australis, at Comapa, Magallanes
990, T200200, www.australis.com (in Santiago

Av El Bosque Norte 0440, p 11, T02-442 3115,
in Buenos Aires T011-4787 3752). Runs cruises
on the *Via Australis* and the brand new, larger
Stella Australis between Punta Arenas and
Ushuaia, through the Magellan Straits and the
'avenue of glaciers', with stops at Cape Horn
and Isla Navarino, glaciers and Isla Magdalena
(the itinerary varies according to route). There
are opportunities to disembark and see
wildlife. 4 nights from Punta Arenas, 3 nights
from Ushuaia, service from Sep-Apr, 2012-2013
fares start at US$1989 pp (US$1258 low
season), inclusive of all but port tax and
national park fees (US$30 from Punta Arenas,
US$30 Ushuaia); check website for promotions.
Very safe and comfortable, first-class service,
fine dining, daily lectures, an unforgettable
experience. Advance booking is essential;
check-in is at **Comapa**. Consistently highly
recommended.
Frieda Lange & Co., Errázuriz 950, T613991,
www.friedalange.com. Two-hour city tours
charting Punta Arenas's golden age by
visiting various sites of historical interest,
English spoken. Recommended.
Magallanes Adventure, Errázuriz 950, p2,
www.magallanesadventure.com. New
kayaking company based 27 km south of the
city, with own *hostería*, a variety of programmes,
good guides and equipment. Also offers
horseriding trips by the Magellan straights.
Turismo Aonikenk, Magallanes 57C,
T228616, www.aonikenk.com. Expensive but
excellent tailor-made, multi adventure and
trekking tours for all levels of fitness, top of
the market, French, German, English spoken.
Recommended. Also has **$$ Hosp
Magallanes** at same address, T228616.
Turismo Aventour, Patagonia 779, T241197,
http://aventourpatagonia.cl. Specialize in
fishing trips, organize tours to Tierra del
Fuego helpful, English spoken.
Turismo Comapa Magallanes 990, T200200,
www.comapa.com. Tours to Torres del Paine
(responsible, well-informed guides), Tierra del
Fuego and to see penguins at Isla Magdalena

(3 times a week Nov-Mar, 5 hrs in all, US$53 on Broom's vessel *Melinka*). Sell tickets for sailings Puerto Montt to Puerto Natales. Agents for **Cruceros Australis** (see above).
Turismo Laguna Azul, Menendez 786, T225200, www.turismolagunaazul.com. Full-day trips to a colony of King Penguins on Tierra del Fuego. Trips run all year round.
Turismo Yamana, Errázuriz 932, T240056, www.yamana.cl. Conventional tours, trekking in Torres del Paine, kayaking in the fjords of Parque Nacional De Agostini (Tierra del Fuego), multilingual guides, camping equipment provided.
Viento Sur, Fagnano 585, T222590, www.vientosur.com. Horse riding, trekking, kayaking in the Magellan straits and elsewhere, plus Torres del Paine, good tours.
Whale Sound, Lautaro Navarro 1191, T223725, www.whalesound.com. Whale-watching trips in the Magellan Straits.

⊜ Transport

Punta Arenas *p97, map p99*
All transport is heavily booked from Christmas to Mar: advance booking strongly advised.
Air Carlos Ibáñez del Campo Airport, 20 km north of town. Minibus service by **Transfer Austral**, Lautaro Navarro 975, T615100, US$6. DAP have their own bus service to town, US$6. Taxi US$14 to city, US$10 to airport. Note that in most taxis much of the luggage space is taken up by natural gas fuel tanks. To **Santiago**, LAN, via **Puerto Montt** and **Sky** (several stops) daily. To **Porvenir**, Aerovías DAP 3 times daily Mon-Fri, 2 on Sat, 9 passengers, 12 mins, US$35. To **Puerto Williams**, daily except Sun, 1¼ hrs, US$95 one way (book a week in advance for Porvenir, 2 in advance for Puerto Williams). Services to Argentina: To **Ushuaia**, 1 hr, **LAN** three a week in summer (schedules change frequently). **Note** Take passport when booking tickets to Argentina.
Bus A new bus terminal has been built at the northern edge of town by the Zona Franca. At the time of writing bus companies are still choosing to leave from their own offices in the city centre. **Cruz del Sur, Fernández, Pingüino** and **Turibus**, Sanhueza 745, T221429, www.buses fernandez.com. **Pacheco**, Colón 900, T242174, www.buses pacheco.com; **Pullman**, Colón 568, T223359, tickets for all Chile. **Central de Pasajeros**, Colón y Magallanes, T245811, office for booking all tickets, also cambio and tour operator. **Bus Sur**, Menéndez 552, T222938, www.bus-sur.cl. **Ghisoni** and **Tecni Austral**, Lautaro Navarro 975, T613422. Full and up to date timetables are published daily in the *Prensa Austral* newspaper. Bus services: To **Puerto Natales**, 3-3½ hrs, **Fernández, Bus Sur** and **Pacheco**, up to 8 daily, last departure 2015, US$8, US$15 return, look out for special offers and connections to Torres del Paine. Buses may pick up at the airport with advance booking and payment. **Pacheco** have services through Argentina to **Osorno, Puerto Montt** and **Castro**, US$60-75, several weekly, 36 hrs, also **Sur**.

To **Río Grande** and **Ushuaia** via **Punta Delgada** (route is described in Argentina, Arriving in Tierra del Fuego; no buses via Porvenir) **Pacheco, Sur, Tecni-Austral** and others, 8-10 hrs, US$30, heavily booked; US$46-50 to Ushuaia, 12 hrs. Some services have to change in Río Grande for Ushuaia, others direct. Check companies for frequencies. Book well in advance in Jan-Feb. To **Río Gallegos**, Argentina, via Punta Delgada, **Pingüino** daily; **Pacheco**, Sun, Tue, Fri; **Ghisoni**, Mon, Wed, Thu, Sat. Fares US$20, 5-8 hrs, depending on customs, 15 mins on Chilean side, up to 2 hrs on Argentine side.

Ghisoni sell tickets to many Argentine destinations: **El Calafate** US$30, **Comodoro Rivadavia** US$52, **Puerto Madryn** US$76, **Bariloche** US$100, **Buenos Aires** US$140.
To **Otway Sound**: Bus with **Fernández** 1500, return 1900, US$13.50. Tours by several agencies, US$20, entry extra, taxi US$50 return.
Car hire **Payne**, Menéndez 631, T240852, www.payne.cl, also tours, treks, birdwatching, etc. **Lubag**, Colón 975, T710484, www.lubag.cl.

Also multinational companies. **Note** You need a hire company's authorization to take a car into Argentina. This takes 24 hrs (not Sat or Sun) and involves mandatory international insurance at US$30 per week, plus notary fees.
Ferry For services to **Porvenir** (Tierra del Fuego), see page 123.
Shipping offices: Navimag in the same office as **Comapa**, Magallanes 990, T200263, www.navimag.com, www.comapa.com.
Shipping services: For Navimag services Puerto Montt-Puerto Natales, see under Puerto Montt (confirmation of reservations is advised). For **Cruceros Australis** to Cape Horn and Ushuaia, see above.

To **Antarctica:** Most cruise ships leave from Ushuaia, but a few operators are based in Punta Arenas. Try **Antarctic Dream Shipping**, Ebro 2740 Suite 602, Las Conces, Santiago, T02-48 6910, www.antarctic.cl (in UK **Senderos**, T0208-144 8335, info@senderos.co.uk). The ship Antarctic Dream has daily landings and wildlife observation. Or **Antarctic XXI**, O'Higgins 1170, T61410C, www.antarcticaxxi.com, flight/cruise packages. Otherwise, another possibility is with the Chilean Navy. The Navy does not encourage passengers, so you must approach the captain direct. Spanish is essential. Two vessels, Galvarino and Lautaro, sail regularly (no schedule); iscop@mitierra.cl.

To **Monumento Natural Los Pingüinos**: The boat of Agencia Broom (see Ferries to Tierra del Fuego) booked through **Comapa** (see What to do), at 1600, schedules vary monthly, US$40. Take your own

refreshments, as they are expensive on board. Recommended, but the trip may be cancelled if it's windy. **Solo Expediciones**, Nogueira 1255, T262281, www.solo expediciones.com, operate their own service on a faster, smaller boat, also passing by Isla Marta, US$50, also recommended.
Taxi Ordinary taxis have yellow roofs. *Colectivos* (all black) run on fixed routes, US$0.70 for anywhere on route. Reliable service from **Radio Taxi Austral**, T247710/244409.

❶ Directory

Punta Arenas *p97, map p99*
Airline offices Aerovías DAP, O'Higgins 891, T616100, www.aeroviasdap.cl. Open 0900-1230, 1430-1930. Helpful. LAN, Bories 884, T500-526 2000. Sky, Roca 933, T710645, or 600-600 2828. **Banks** Most banks and some supermarkets have ATMs; many on the Plaza. Banks open Mon-Fri 0830-1400. **Casas de cambio** open Mon-Fri 0900-1230. 1500-1900, Sat 0900-1230, many on Lautaro Navarro 1000 block. **Consulates** Argentina, 21 de Mayo 1878, T261912/261264, cparenas@embargentina.cl, open Mon-Fri 0900-1800, visas take 24 hrs. **Medical services** Hospitals: Hospital Regional Lautaro Navarro, Angamos 180, T244040. Public hospital, for emergency room ask for La Posta. Has good dentists. **Clínica Magallanes**, Bulnes 01448, T211527. Private clinic, minimum charge US$45. **Hospital Naval**, Av Bulnes 200 esq Capitán Guillermos. Open 24 hrs, good, friendly staff. Recommended.

Puerto Natales and around

Beautifully situated on the calm waters of Canal Señoret fjord, an arm of the Ultima Esperanza Sound, edged with spectacular mountains, Puerto Natales, 247 km north of Punta Arenas, is a quiet town of brightly painted corrugated-tin houses. It's the base for exploring the magnificent O'Higgins and Torres de Paine national parks, and even when inundated with visitors in the summer, retains an unhurried feel, and is a place to relax for a few days.

Arriving in Puerto Natales → *Population: 20,500.*

Tourist office At the Sernatur office ① *on the waterfront, Av Pedro Montt 19, T412125, info natales@sernatur.cl, Mon-Fri 0830-1300, 1430-1730, Sat 1000-1800,* there's no English spoken, but good leaflets available on Puerto Natales and Torres del Paine in English, and bus and boat information in the park. **Municipal tourist office** ① *Bulnes 285, T411263.* CONAF ① *Baquedano 847, T411843, patricio.salinas@conaf.cl.*

Places in Puerto Natales

Museo Histórico Municipal ① *Bulnes 285, T411263, Mon-Fri 0900-1300, 1500-2000, US$2,* has displays and photos of early colonizers, as well as a small collection of archaeological and natural history exhibits. There are lovely walks along the waterfront or up to Cerro Dorotea, which dominates the town, with superb views (watch out for high winds). Take any bus going east and alight at the road for summit (Km 9.5).

Puerto Natales

200 metres
200 yards

Where to stay 🛏
1 Aquaterra *C2*
2 Blanquita *C2*
3 Capitán Eberhard *B1*
4 Casa Cecilia *B2*
5 Casa Teresa *C2*
6 Costaustralis *C1*
7 Hosp Casa Lili *B1*
8 Hosp Nancy *C3*
9 Hostal Las Carretas *C3*
10 Hostal Sir Francis Drake *A2*
11 Hostel Natales *B1*
12 Indigo Patagonia *B1*
13 Josmar 2 Camping *C2*
14 Keoken *B1*
15 Lady Florence Dixie *B3*
16 Lili Patagónico's *C3*
17 Martín Gusinde *B2*
18 Niko's *C3*
19 Niko's II *A2*
20 Patagonia Adventure &
   Sendero Aventura *B2*
21 Remota *A2*
22 Res Dickson *C2*
23 The Singing Lamb *C3*
24 Weskar Patagonian
   Lodge *A2*

Restaurants 🍴
1 Afrigonia *B2*
2 Andrés *C1*
3 Angelica's *B2*
4 Cormorán de las Rocas *A2*
5 El Asador Patagónico *B2*
6 El Living *B2*
7 La Mesita Grande *B2*
8 La Picada de Carlitos *C3*
9 Parrilla Don Jorge *B2*
10 Patagonia Dulce *B1*
11 Ultima Esperanza *B2*

Bars & clubs 🍸
12 Baguales Brewery *B2*
13 El Bar de Ruperto *B2*

Monumento Natural Cueva Milodón ① *25 km north, 0830-2030, US$6 to enter park (US$3 low season), getting there: regular bus from Prat 517, T412540, leaves 0945 and 1500, returns 1200 and 1700. US$8; taxi US$30 return or check if you can get a ride with a tour; some full-day tour buses to Torres del Paine stop at the cave.* In this cave (70 m wide, 30 m high and 220 m deep), formed by ice-age glacial lakes, remains were found of a prehistoric ground-sloth, together with evidence of occupation by early Patagonian humans some 11,000 years ago. There is a small, well-presented visitor centre, with restaurant, shop and toilets.

Parque Nacional Bernardo O'Higgins

Usually referred to as the **Parque Nacional Monte Balmaceda** ① *US$6*, the park is at the north end of Ultima Esperanza Sound and can only be reached on boat trips from Puerto Natales. After a three-hour journey up the Sound, the boat passes the Balmaceda Glacier which drops steeply from the eastern slopes of Monte Balmaceda (2035 m). The glacier is retreating; in 1986 its foot was at sea level. The boat docks further north at Puerto Toro, from where it's a 1-km walk to the base of Serrano Glacier on the north slope of Monte Balmaceda. On the trip dolphins, sea-lions (in season), black-necked swans, flightless steamer ducks and cormorants can be seen. The boat then returns to Puerto Natales. There is a route from Puerto Toro on the eastern side of the Río Serrano for 35 km to the Torres del Paine administration centre; guided tours are available on foot or on horseback. It is also possible to travel onwards to the Paine administration centre along the river by boat or zodiac. Better going to the park than from the park (the view suddenly opens up and then just gets better and better).

Border with Argentina

There are three crossing points: **Dorotea**, 16 km east of Puerto Natales. On the Argentine side the road continues to a junction, with alternatives to Río Turbio and north to La Esperanza and Río Gallegos. Chilean immigration is open all year 0800-2400. **Paso Casas Viejas/Laurita**, 16 km northeast of Puerto Natales. On the Argentine side this joins the Río Turbio–La Esperanza road. Chilean immigration is open 0800-2200. **Río Don Guillermo/Cerro Castillo**, 65 km north of Puerto Natales on the road to Torres del Paine, 7 km from the border, open 0800-2200. On the Argentine side, Paso Río Don Guillermo (Cancha Carrera 14 km), the road leads to La Esperanza and Río Gallegos. All buses from El Calafate go via Cerro Castillo, making it possible to transfer to a bus passing from Puerto Natales to Torres del Paine. The small settlement has several hospedajes and cafeterías. Sheep shearing in December, and rodeo and rural festival third weekend in January. See www.pasosfronterizos.gov.cl and Argentina chapter.

Puerto Natales and around listings

For hotel and restaurant price codes and other relevant information, see pages 10-12.

⊙ Where to stay

Puerto Natales *p105, map p106*
In season cheaper accommodation fills up quickly after the arrival of the Navimag ship from Puerto Montt. Hotels in the countryside open only in summer months; dates vary. Good deals in upper range hotels may be available; out of season prices may be 50% lower.
$$$$ Costaustralis, Pedro Montt 262, T412000, www.hoteles-australis.com. Very comfortable, tranquil, lovely views (but not

from inland-facing rooms), lift, English spoken, waterfront restaurant serves international and local seafood.

$$$$ Indigo Patagonia, Ladrilleros 105, T413609, www.indigopatagonia.com. Relaxed atmosphere, on the water front, great views, a boutique hotel with roof-top spa, rooms and suites, breakfast included, café/restaurant serves good seafood and vegetarian dishes, internet access.

$$$$ Remota, Ruta 9 Norte, Km 1.5, Huerto 279, T414040, www.remota.cl. Boutique hotel just outside town, unique design with big windows, lots of trips, activities and treks offered, spa, all-inclusive packages, good food, first-class.

$$$$ Weskar Patagonian Lodge, Ruta 9, Km 1, T414168, www.weskar.cl. Quiet lodge overlooking the fjord, simple rooms with good views, onces and dinner served, internet, bicycle rental, many activities offered, helpful.

$$$$-$$$ Martín Gusinde, Bories 278, T412770, www.hotelmartingusinde.com. American buffet breakfast included, modern 3-star standard, smart, parking, expensive restaurant.

$$$ Aquaterra, Bulnes 299, T412239, www.aquaterrapatagonia.com. Good restaurant with vegetarian options, 'resto-bar' downstairs, alternative therapy centre, understated design, safe, warm and comfortable but not cheap, very helpful staff.

$$$ Capitán Eberhard, Pedro Montt 58, T411208, www.busesfernandez.com/hotel.html. Great location, has seen better days, but most rooms have some of the best views in town, Wi-Fi, cable TV, laundry, café. Good deals off season.

$$$ Hostal Sir Francis Drake, Phillipi 383, T411553, www.hostalfrancisdrake.com. Calm and welcoming, tastefully decorated, smallish rooms with cable TV, filling breakfast, good views. Recommended.

$$$ Hostel Natales, Ladrilleros 209, T414731, www.hostelnatales.cl. **$** pp in dorms in this high-end hostel, comfortable, with breakfast, internet.

$$$ Keoken, Señoret 267, T413670, www.keokenpatagonia.com. New cosy, upmarket B&B, spacious living room, some rooms with views. All rooms have bathroom but not all are en suite, English spoken, helpful staff.

$$$ Lady Florence Dixie, Bulnes 655, T411158, www. hotelflorencedixie.cl. Modern 3-star hotel, hospitable, variable room standards, superior are good value.

$$ Blanquita, Carrera Pinto 409, T411674, www.hotelblanquita.cl. Looks like a giant portacabin from the outside but is quiet, simple rooms, heating, stores luggage. Recommended.

$$ Casa Cecilia, Tomás Rogers 60, T613560, www.casaceciliahostal.com. **$$-$** singles. Welcoming, popular, with small simple rooms, some with bath, great breakfast. English, French and German spoken, Wi-Fi, rents camping gear and bicycles, booking for tours and information for Torres del Paine. Warmly recommended.

$$ Hospedaje Nancy, Ramírez 540, T410022, www.nateslodge.cl. Good breakfast, some rooms with bath, warm and hospitable, use of kitchen, information, internet, laundry service, runs tours. Recommended.

$$ Hostal Las Carretas, Galvarino 745, T414584, www.portalmagallanes.com/lascarretas. Tastefully decorated and spotless B&B 15 mins' walk to the centre, comfortable rooms, some with bath, good beds, kitchen facilities, Wi-Fi, English spoken. Recommended.

$$ Lili Patagónico's, Prat 479, T414063, www.lilipatagonicos.com. **$** pp in dorms. Small but pleasant heated rooms, good breakfast, helpful staff. Lots of information, good quality equipment rented. Tours offered. Indoor climbing wall. Recommended.

$$ Niko's II, Phillipi 528, ½ block from Plaza de Armas, T411500, www.nikostwo adventure.com. Breakfast included, some rooms with bath, heating, English spoken, book exchange, kitchen, internet for guests if staff/family not using it, information, tours, tent hire. Recommended.

$$ Patagonia Adventure, Tomás Rogers 179, T411028, www.apatagonia.com. Lovely old house, bohemian feel shared bath, **$** pp in dorms, good value, home-made bread for breakfast, luggage store, internet, Wi-Fi, equipment hire, bike and kayak tours and tour arrangements for Torres del Paine (see Sendero Aventura, page 110); no kitchen. Recommended.

$$-$ Niko's, Ramírez 669, T412810, niko residencial@hotmail.com. With breakfast, basic rooms, some rooms with bath, good meals. also dorm accom modation. Recommended.

$$-$ Res Dickson, Bulnes 307 T411871, www.hostaldickson.com. Good value, with good breakfasts, helpful, internet, cooking and laundry facilities.

$ Casa Teresa, Esmeralda 463. T410472. freepatagonia@hotmail.com. Good value, warm and quiet, breakfast included, also cheap meals, tours to Torres del Paine arranged.

$ Hospedaje Casa Lili, Bories 153, T410463, lilinatales@latinmail.com. Dorms are cheaper than private rooms, small, family-run, use of kitchen, internet, breakfast from 0630, rents equipment and can arrange tickets to Paine.

$ pp **The Singing Lamb**, Arauco 779, T410958, www.thesinginglamb.com. Very hospitable New Zealand-run backpackers dorm accommocation only. Great breakfasts with home-made bread, home-from-home feel. Good information. Highly recommended.

Camping Josmar 2, Esmeralda 517, in centre, T414417. Family-run, convenient, hot showers, parking, barbecues, electricity, café, US$7.50 per site or **$** pp in double room.

Border with Argentina p107

$$$$-$$$ Hostería El Pionero, Cerro Castillo, 56 km north of Puerto Nata es, T613530, www.baqueanozamora.cl. Comfortable country house ambience, good service, horse riding.

$ pp **Hospedaje Loreto Belén**, Cerro Castillo, T413063, or 691932 (public phone, ask to speak to Loreto Belén). Rooms for 4, all with bath, break fast included, also offers meals, good home cooking.

Puerto Natales p105, map p106

$$$ Afrigonia, Eberhard 323, T412232. An unexpected mixture of Patagonia meets East Africa in this Kenyan/Chilean-owned fusion restaurant, considered by many to be the best, and certainly the most innovative, in town.

$$$ Angelica's, Bulnes 501, T410365. Elegant Mediterranean style, well-prepared food with quality ingredients. Pricy but recommended.

$$$-$$ Cormorán de las Rocas, Miguel Sánchez 72, T413723, www.cormoran delasrocas.com. Patagonian specialties with an innovative twist, wide variety of well-prepared dishes, pisco sours, good service and attention to detail, incomparable views. Recommended.

$$$-$$ El Asador Patagónico, Prat 158 on the Plaza. Spit-roast lamb, salads, home-made puddings. Recommended, book in advance.

$$$-$$ Parrilla Don Jorge, Bories 430, on Plaza, T410999. Also specia izes in spit-roast lamb, but serves fish too, good service.

$$ La Mesita Grande, Prat 169 on the Plaza, T411571. Fresh pizzas from the wood-burning oven, also pasta and good desserts.

$$ Ultima Esperanza, Eberhard 354, T411391. Classic seafood restaurant. Not the most imaginative menu but consistently good.

$$-$ La Picada de Carlitos, Blanco Encalada y Esmeralda. Good, cheap traditional Chilean food, popular with locals at lunchtime, when service can be slow.

$ Andrés, Ladrilleros 381. Recommended for fish, nice owner, good service.

$ El Living, Prat 156, Plaza de Armas, www.el-living.com. Just what you need: comfy sofas, good tea, magazines in all languages, book exchange, good music, delicious vegetarian food, British-run, popular.

Cafés

Patagonia Dulce, Barros Arana 233, T415285, www.patagoniadulce.cl. Mon-Sat 1400-2030. For the best hot chocolate in town, good coffee and chocolates.

🎵 Bars and clubs

Puerto Natales *p105, map p106*
Baguales Brewery, Bories 430, on the plaza.
Pub with microbrewery attached. Also serves
hamburgers and other snacks. Open
weekends only off season.
El Bar de Ruperto, Bulnes 371, T414302.
Open 2100-0500. Lively place with DJs,
live music, lots of drinks and some food.
Murciélagos, Bulnes 731. Popular bar with
late-night music and dancing.

🛍 Shopping

Puerto Natales *p105, map p106*
Camping equipment Check all camping
equipment and prices carefully. Average
charges per day: whole set US$15, tent
US$6-8, sleeping bag US$3-6, mat US$1-2,
raincoat US$1, also cooking gear, US$2.
(**Note** Deposits required: tent US$200,
sleeping bag US$100.) Camping gas is widely
available in hardware stores. See under Where
to stay and What to do for places that hire
equipment, eg **Casa Cecilia**, **Lili Patagónico's**,
Patagonia Adventure, **Erratic Rock**.
Supermarkets Several in town, including at
Bulnes y Ramírez and **Don Bosco**, Baquedano
358. The town markets are also good.

🅰 What to do

Puerto Natales *p105, map p106*
Many agencies along Eberhard. It is better to
book tours direct with operators in Puerto
Natales than through agents in Punta Arenas
or Santiago. Several agencies offer tours to
the Perito Moreno glacier in Argentina, 1 day,
US$90, 14-hr trip, 2 hrs at the glacier, without
food or park entry fee. You can then leave the
tour in Calafate to continue into Argentina.
Baguales Group, Galvarino 661, T412654,
www.baguualesgroup.com. Specialists in the
route from the park back to Puerto Natales.
Tailor-made tours that can incorporate
zodiacs, horse riding, kayaking and trekking,
mostly off the beaten track. Recommended.

Blue Green Adventures, M Bulnes 1200,
T410009, www.bluegreenadventures.com.
Adventure tour specialist and travel agent,
with trekking, riding, kayaking, fishing and
multi-activity options, estancia, whale
watching, wine and yoga programmes.
Also caters for families.
Comapa, Eberhard 555, T414300,
www.comapa.com. Large regional operator
offering decent day tours to Torres del Paine.
Criollo Expeditions, Huerto 157-B, T09-8528
4225, www.criolloexpeditions.com. Guided
horse rides around Natales and Last Hope
Sound as well as the edge of Parque Nacional
Torres del Paine, multi-day trips to the Sierra
Baguales, US/Chilean-run, attentive guides,
well-kept horses. Recommended.
Erratic Rock, Baquedano 719, T410355,
www.erraticrock.com. Trekking experts
offering interesting expeditions from half a
day to 2 weeks. Also hire out good-quality
equipment and hold a daily trekking seminar
at 1500. They have B&B lodging, too.
Estancia Travel, Casa 13-b, Puerto Bories,
Puerto Natales, T412221, www.estancia
travel.com. Based at the Estancia Puerto
Consuelo, 5 km north of Puerto Natales.
Horse riding trips from 1 to 10 days around
southern Patagonia/Torres del Paine, with
accommodation at traditional estancias. Also
kayaking trips, British/Chilean-run, bilingual,
professional guides, at the top end of the
price range.
Indómita Patagonia, Bories 206, T414525,
www.indomitapatagonia.com. Considered
the best choice for kayak trips in the area.
Sendero Aventura, at Hostal Patagonia
Adventure, Tomás Rogers 179, T415636,
www.senderoaventura.com. Adventure tours,
including trekking to Torres del Paine, boats
in Balmaceda PN, camping equipment,
bike hire.
Skorpios, www.skorpios.cl. 2- to 3-day
cruises up the southern fjords to Puerto Edén
and the Pío XI Glacier. No office in Puerto
Natales; book online or through an agency.

⊕ Transport

Puerto Natales *p105, map p106*
Air Aerodromo Teniente Julio Gallardo,
5 km north of town. **Sky** airline has services
in summer from Santiago via Puerto Montt.
Also charter services from Punta Arenas with
Aerovías DAP. Work is underway (2012) to
lengthen the runway which should allow
more long-distance flights soon.
Bus In summer book ahead. Full and up-to-
date timetables are published daily in the
Prensa Austral newspaper. In theory there is a
municipal bus terminal on Santiago Bueras,
20 mins walk from the centre, but at present,
bus companies are refusing to use it and
leave from their own offices: **Bus Fernández**,
E Ramírez 399, T411111. **Facheco**, Ramírez
224, T414800. **Bus Sur**, Baquedano 668,
T614220. **Transfer**, Bulnes 518, T421616.
Zaahj, Prat 236, T412260

To **Punta Arenas**, several daily, 3-3½ hrs,
US$9, Fernández Pacheco, Bus Sur and
others. To Argentina: to **Río Gallegos** direct,
Bus Sur, and **El Pingüino**, 2-3 weekly each,
US$18, 4-5 hrs. Hourly to **Río Turbio**, Cootra,
and other companies, US$5, 2 hrs (depending
on Customs – change bus at border). To **El
Calafate**, US$20, **Cootra** via Río Turbio, daily,
4 hrs; or **Zaahj** (3 a week, 4½ hrs) via Cerro
Castillo. Otherwise travel agencies run several
times a week depending on demand, US$60
one way, not including Perito Moreno glacier
entry fee (12 hr trip), shop around, reserve
1 day ahead. **Bus Sur** also runs 3 buses a
week to **Ushuaia** Oct-Ap , 15 hrs, US$63.

Note See Torres del Paine section for
buses from Puerto Natales into the park,
page 118.

Car hire EMSA Avis, Bulnes 632, T410775.
Punta Alta, Blanco Encalada 244, T410115,
www.puntaalta.cl good reports. Hire agents
can arrange permission to drive into
Argentina, takes 24 hrs to arrange,
extra insurance required.
Ferry See services from Puerto Montt.
Comapa, see above. **Navimag**, Pedro Montt
308, T411642, www.navimag.com.

To **Parque Nacional Bernardo O'Higgins**:
Sailings to **Balmaceda Glacier** daily at 0815
in summer, returning 1630, Sun only in winter
(minimum 10 passengers), US$135. Heavily
booked in high season. Take warm clothes,
hat and gloves. All agencies can arrange boat
trips. Punta Alta, see Car Hire, above, and
21 de Mayo (www.turismo21demayo.cl)
take the same route. but the former in a faster
boat. Both offer the possibility to continue
by zodiac to the Pueblito Serrano at the Park's
southern edge (US$190 one way from Puerto
Natales to the Pueblito Serrano). **Punta Alta**
also has an option to return to Natales on the
same day by minibus along the southern
access road, thus avoiding park entry fees.

⊙ Directory

Puerto Natales *p105, map p106*
Banks Rates for TCs, which can't be changed
into US$ cash, are poor. **Banco Santiago**,
ATM; several others. Casas de cambio on
Blanco Encalada, eg 266 (**Enio América**).
Others on Bulnes and Prat. **Bicycle**
repairs **El Rey de la Bicicleta**, Ramírez 540.
Good, helpful.

Parque Nacional Torres del Paine → *For listings, see pages 116-118.*

Nothing prepares you for the spectacular beauty of Parque Nacional Torres del Paine. World renowned for its challenging trekking, the park's 242,242 ha contain 15 peaks above 2000 m. At its centre is the glacier-topped granite massif Macizo Paine, from which rise the vertical pink granite Torres (Towers) del Paine and, below them, the Cuernos (Horns) del Paine, swooping buttresses of lighter granite under caps of darker sedimentary rock. From the vast Campo de Hielo Sur icecap on its western edge, four main glaciers (ventisqueros), Grey, Dickson, Zapata and Tyndall, drop into vividly coloured lakes formed by their meltwater: turquoise, ultramarine and pistachio expanses, some filled with wind-sculpted royal blue icebergs. Wherever you explore, there are constantly changing views of dramatic peaks and ice fields. The park enjoys a micro-climate especially favourable to wildlife and plants: there are 105 species of bird including condors, ibis, flamingos and austral parakeets, and 25 species of mammals including guanaco, hares, foxes, pumas and skunks. A day tour from Puerto Natales will give a broad overview of the park, but seven to 10 days are needed to see it all properly.

Arriving in Torres del Paine

Information The park is administered by CONAF: the Administration Centre (T691931, ptpaine@conaf.cl) is in the south of the park at the northwest end of Lago del Toro (0830-2030 in summer, 0830-1230, 1400-1830 off season). There are entrances at Laguna Amarga, Lago Sarmiento, Laguna Azul and the Puente Serrano, and you are required to **register** and show your passport when entering the park, since rangers (*guardaparques*) keep a check on the whereabouts of all visitors. Phone the administration centre for information (in Spanish) on weather conditions. It also has videos and exhibitions with summaries in English of flora and fauna. There are six ranger stations (*guarderías*) staffed by rangers, who give help and advice. Entry for foreigners: US\$32 (low season US\$17, Chilean pesos only; proceeds are shared between all Chilean national parks), includes a reasonable trail map to take with you (not waterproof); climbing fees US\$1000. If you are based outside the park and plan on entering and leaving several times explain this when paying your entrance to be given a multiple-entry stamp valid for three consecutive days. The impact of huge numbers of visitors to the park, over 100,000 a year, is often visible in litter around the *refugios* and camping areas. Take all your rubbish out of the park including toilet paper.

Getting around and accommodation The park is well set up for tourism, with frequent bus services running from Puerto Natales through the park, to pick up and drop off walkers at various hotels, to start treks, and to connect with boat trips. For details, see Transport, below. Accommodation is available on three levels: there are hotels (expensive, over US\$300 for a double room per night), six privately run *refugios*, well-equipped, staffed, offering meals and free hot water for tea, soup, etc, and 10 campsites with amenities and 10 basic *campamentos*. All options fill up quickly in peak summer months, January and February, so plan your trip and book hotels and *refugios* in advance. Pay in dollars to avoid IVA (tax).

Safety warning It is vital to be aware of the unpredictability of the weather (which can change in a few minutes, see Climate below) and the arduousness of some of the stretches on the long hikes. Rain and snowfall are heavier the further west you go and bad weather sweeps off the Campo de Hielo Sur without warning. The only means of rescue are on horseback or by boat; the nearest helicopter is in Punta Arenas and high winds usually prevent its operation in the park.

Parque Nacional Torres del Paine

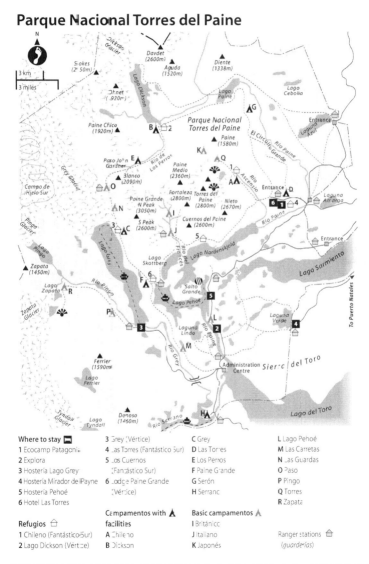

Where to stay 🏠
1 Ecocamp Patagonia
2 Explora
3 Hostería Lago Grey
4 Hostería Mirador del Payne
5 Hostería Pehoé
6 Hotel Las Torres

Refugios 🏠
1 Chileno (Fantástico Sur)
2 Lago Dickson (Vértice)

3 Grey (Vértice)
4 Las Torres (Fantástico Sur)
5 Los Cuernos
  (Fantástico Sur)
6 Lodge Paine Grande
  (Vértice)

Campamentos with ⛺
facilities
A Chileno
B Dickson

C Grey
D Las Torres
E Los Perros
F Paine Grande
G Serón
H Serrano

Basic campamentos ⛺
I Británico
J Italiano
K Japonés

L Lago Pehoé
M Las Carretas
N Las Guardas
O Paso
P Pingo
Q Torres
R Zapata

Ranger stations 🏠
  (guarderías)

Forest fires are a serious hazard. Follow all instructions about lighting fires to the letter. Unauthorized campfires in 2005 and 2011 led to the destruction of 160 sq km and 110 sq km respectively.

Equipment and maps A strong, streamlined, waterproof tent gives you more freedom than crowded *refugios* and is essential if doing the complete circuit. Also essential at all times of year are protective clothing against cold, wind and rain, strong waterproof footwear, a compass, a good sleeping bag, sleeping mat, camping stove and cooking equipment. Most *refugios* will hire camping equipment for a single night. Sun-screen and sunglasses are also necessary, and you'll want shorts in summer. Take your own food: the small shops at the *refugios* and at the Posada Río Serrano are expensive and have a limited selection Maps (US$7), published by Mattassi and (more accurate) Cartografía Digital and Patagonia Interactiva, are obtainable in shops in Punta Arenas or Puerto Natales. All three have a few mistakes, however.

Climate Do not underestimate the severity of the weather here. The Park is open all year round, although snow may prevent access in the winter. The warmest time is December to March, but also the most unstable; strong winds often blow off the glaciers, and rainfall can be heavy. It is most crowded in the summer holiday season, January to mid-February, less so in December or March. October and November are recommended for wild flowers. In winter there can be good, stable conditions and well-equipped hikers can do some good walking, but some treks may be closed and boats may not be running.

Hikes
There are about 250 km of well-marked trails, and walkers must keep to the paths: cross-country trekking is not permitted. The times indicated should be treated with caution: allow for personal fitness and weather conditions.

El Circuito (Allow at least seven days) The park's emblematic hike is a circuit round the Torres and Cuernos del Paine: it is usually done anticlockwise starting from the Laguna Amarga *guardería*. From Laguna Amarga the route is north along the west side of the Río Paine to Lago Paine, before turning west to follow the Río Paine to the south end of Lago Dickson. From here the path runs along the wooded valley of the Río de los Perros before climbing steeply to Paso John Gardner (1241 m, the highest point on the route), then dropping to follow the Grey Glacier southeast to Lago Grey, continuing to Lago Pehoé and before joining up with the 'W' (see below) back to the Hostería Las Torres or Laguna Amarga. There are superb views, particularly from the top of Paso John Gardner.

Camping gear must be carried. The circuit is often closed in winter because of snow. Walking times between campsites is four to six hours. The most difficult section is the very steep slippery slope between Paso John Gardner and Campamento Paso, a poorly-signed section exposed to strong westerly winds. The major rivers are crossed by footbridges, which are occasionally washed away.

The 'W' (Allow four to five days) A more popular alternative to El Circuito, it can be completed without camping equipment by staying in *refugios*, and can be done in either direction. It combines several of the hikes described separately below. From Laguna

Amarga the first stage runs west via Hotel Las Torres and up the valley of the Río Ascensio via Refugio Chileno to the base of the Torres del Paine (see below). From here return to the Hotel Las Torres and then walk along the northern shore of Lago Nordenskjold via Refugio Los Cuernos to Campamento Italiano. From here climb the Valley of the Río del Francés (see below) before continuing to Lodge Paine Grande. From here you can complete the third part of the 'W' by walking west along the northern shore of Lago Grey to Refugio Grey and Glaciar Grey before returning to Lodge Paine Grande. To do the hike from west to east, either take the scheduled catamaran service across Lago Pehoé to Lodge Paine Grande and start from there or take the trail to Paine Grande from the administration centre. This precursor to the main hike passes Campamento Las Carretas and for all but the last hour is easy, with views of what you will be undertaking or the W.

The Valley of the Río del Francés (Allow five hours each way) From Lodge Paine Grande this route leads northeast across undulating country along the west edge of Lago Skottberg to Campamento Italiano and then follows the valley of the Río del Francés, which climbs between to the west) Cerro Paine Grande and the Ventisquero del Francés, and (to the east) the Cuernos del Paine to Campamento Británico. Allow 2½ hours from Lodge Paine Grande to Campamento Italiano, 2½ hours further to Campamento Británico. The views from the mirador, 20 minutes above Campamento Británico, are superb.

To the base of the Torres del Paine (Allow five to six hours each way) From Laguna Amarga the route follows the road west to Hotel Las Torres before climbing along the west side of the Río Ascensio via Campamento Chileno to Campamento Las Torres, close to the base of the Torres and near a small lake. Allow 1½ hours to Hotel Las Torres, then two hours to Campamento Chileno, two hours further to Campamento Torres where there is a fork: the path to the base of the Torres is well marked, but these last 30 minutes are up the moraine; to see the towers lit by sunrise (spectacular, but you must have good weather), it's well worth humping camping gear up to Campamento Torres and spending the night (no *refugio*). One hour beyond Campamento Torres is the good site at Campamento Japonés (for climbers only).

Up the Río Pingo valley (Allow five hours each way) From Guardería Grey (18 km west by road from the Administration Centre) follow the Río Pingo, via Refugio Pingo and Refugio Zapata (four hours), with views south over Ventisquero Zapata (plenty of wildlife, icebergs in the lake). It is not possible to reach Lago Pingo as a bridge – marked on many maps – has been washed away. Ventisquero Pingo can be seen 3 km away over the lake.

To Laguna Verde (Allow four hours each way) From the administration centre follow the road north 2 km, before taking the path east over the Sierra del Toro and then along the south side of Laguna Verde to the Guardería Laguna Verde. This is one of the easiest walks in the park and may be a good first hike.

To Laguna Azul and Lago Paine (Allow 8½ hours each way) This route runs north from Laguna Amarga to the west tip of Laguna Azul (following the road for 7 km), from where it continues across the sheltered Río Paine valley past Laguna Cebolla to the Refugio Lago Paine (now closed) at the west end of the lake.

Parque Nacional Torres del Paine listings

For hotel and restaurant price codes and other relevant information, see pages 10-12.

🟢 Where to stay

Parque Nacional Torres del Paine
p112, map p113

All the park's hotels are expensive, many feel overpriced. Agencies in Puerto Natales offer accommodation and transfers or car hire.

$$$$ EcoCamp Patagonia (Don Carlos 3227C, Las Condes, Santiago, T02-923 5950), www.ecocamp.travel. Upscale comfort in the Pataginian wilderness at the foot of the mighty granite towers. Chile's first ISO 14001 environmentally certified hotel includes hydro and solar power, state-of-the-art composting devices and low-impact geodesic dome design inspired by the ancient Kaweskar inhabitants.

$$$$ Explora, T411247. The park's most expensive and exclusive is nestled into a nook at Salto Chico on edge of Lago Pehoé, spectacular views. Everything is included: pool, gym, horse riding, boat trips, tours, can arrange packages from Punta Arenas (reservations: Av Américo Vespucci 80, p 7, Santiago, T02-206 6060, www.explora.com).

$$$$ Hostería Lago Grey, head office Lautaro Navarro 1077, Punta Arenas, T712100, www.turismolagogrey.com. Great views over Lago Grey, but small rooms, glacier walks, decent restaurant.

$$$$ Hostería Mirador del Payne, Estancia Lazo, lovely location on Laguna Verde on east edge of the park, 52 km from Sarmiento entrance, reservations from Fagnano 585, Punta Arenas, T226930, www.miradordelpayne.com. Comfortable, meals extra, but inconvenient for park itself, riding, hiking, birdwatching. Private transport essential, or hike there from the park.

$$$$ Hostería Pehoé, T411390, www.pehoe.com, 5 km south of Pehoé ranger station, 11 km north of park administration. Beautifully situated on an island with spectacular view across Lago Pehoé, but rather run-down, restaurant.

$$$$ Hotel Las Torres, T617450, www.lastorres.cl. Comfortable rooms, beautiful lounge with wood fire and great views of the Macizo, excellent restaurant with evening buffet, good service, horse riding, transport from Laguna Amarga ranger station, spa, disabled access. Visitor centre and *confitería* open to non-residents

$$$$ Tierra Patagonia, T02-263 0606, www.tierrapatagonia.com. Luxury hotel and spa on the edge of the national park overlooking Lago Sarmiento, opened late 2011, sister hotel of **Tierra Atacama**. Guided excursions on foot and horseback.

Refugios

Two companies between them run the *refugios* in the park, comfortable dormitory accommodation (bring your own sleeping bag, or hire one for US$8-10 per night). Prices are US$45-50 pp bed only, breakfast US$10, packed lunch US$15, dinner US$18, full board US$82-100. Restaurants open to non-residents. *Refugios* have good hot showers and space for camping, US$7.50-11. All *refugios* hire tents for US$13-15 per night, plus US$3 per sleeping mat (book in advance for Vértice Refugios as they have very few tents available). Kitchen facilities are available in some Vértice Refugios. Fantástico Sur will not let you prepare your own hot food unless you are camping. Most close in winter, although one or 2 may stay open, depending on the weather. Advance booking essential in high season.

Fantástico Sur Refugios Book in agencies in Puerto Natales or direct at Esmeralda 661, Puerto Natales, T061-614134, www.fslodges.com:

Refugio Chileno, in the Valley of Río Ascencio, at the foot of the Torres.

Refugio Las Torres, 2 *refugios* next to the Hotel Las Torres (see above), good facilities, especially in the newer **Torre Central**.

Refugio Los Cuernos, on the northern shore of Lago Nordenskjold. Also has 8 cabins (US$134 double occupancy without board).

Vértice Refugios (agencies in Puerto Natales, or Casilla 3, Puerto Natales, T061-613550, via www.verticepatagonia.com) runs:

Lodge Paine Grande, on the northwest tip of Lago Pehoé (kitchen facilities, internet). Also semi-permanent 'luxury' dome tents.

Refugio Grey, on the eastern shore of Lago Grey (similar facilities to Lodge Paine Grande).

Refugio Lago Dickson, a more basic *refugio* on the northern part of the circuit.

Camping

Fires may only be lit at organized camping sites, not at *campamentos*. The *guardaparaues* expect people to have a stove if camping. In addition to sites at the above *refugios* there are the following sites: **Camping Lago Pehoé**, www.campingpehoe.com, US$16 pp, tent rental US$24 for 2 including sleeping mat, also pre-pitched dome tents (US$90 bed and breakfast for 2), hot showers, shop, restaurant. **Camping Los Perros** (run by Vértice Patagonia, US$9 pp, tent US$15, sleeping bag US$9), shop and cold showers. **Camping Serón** and **Camping Las Torres** (by the Refugio Las Torres) both run by **Fantástico Sur** (see above), US$9-11, hot showers. Free camping is permitted in 10 other locations in the park: these sites are known as *campamentos* and are generally extremely basic. The wind tends to rise in the evening so pitch tent early. Mice can be a problem around camping sites; do not leave food in packs on the ground. Equipment hire in Puerto Natales (see above). Other campsites in or near the park: fixed sites, such as the indigenous Kaweskar-influenced domes of **Ecocamp Patagonia** (Don Carlos 3219. Las Condes, Santiago, T02-232 9878, www.eco camp.travel), the only ISO14001, environmental sustainability-certified hotel in Chile, and the luxury yurts of **Patagonia Camp** at Lago Toro, www.patagoniacamp.com. **Camping Río Serrano**, just outside the park's southern entrance, www.campingchile.com, also has a cosy *cabaña*, horse rides and hikes.

▲ What to do

Parque Nacional Torres del Paine
p112, map p113

See page 110, for recommendations. Reports of tours are increasingly mixed. Before booking, check details carefully and get them in writing. **Experience Chile**, T570 9436, www.torres delpaine.org, www.experiencechile.org. Specialize in tailor-made itineraries for individuals, couples and small groups.

Boat trips From Refugio Lago Pehoé to Refugio Pudeto, US$24 one way with a backpack (US$8 for extra backpacks), US$38 return, from Pudeto 0930, 1200, 1800, from Paine Grande 1000, 1230, 1830, 30 mins in high season, reserve in advance at the *refugios* at either end or at Catamarán Hielos Patagónicos, Los Arrieros 1517, Puerto Natales, T411380, maclean@entelchile.net. Reduced service off season (also Christmas Day and New Year's Day), no service May-Sep. At all times check in advance that boats are running. See Parque Nacional Bernardo O'Higgins above for entry by 3-hr zodiac trip up the Río Serrano from Balmaceda glacier. Boat to face of glacier from **Hostería Grey**, twice daily, 3½ hrs, US$90 return. A one-way trip can be made via the glacier face to/ from the Hostería to **Refugio Grey** for US$60.

⊖ Transport

Parque Nacional Torres del Paine
p112, map p113

Bus The park administration is 147 km north-west of Puerto Natales by the old road, with a shorter new road, 85 km, opened to the south side of the park in 2007. After mid-Mar there is little public transport and trucks are irregular. From early Oct to mid-Apr, there are several companies running daily services into the park, leaving Puerto Natales between 0630 and 0800, and again (Nov-Mar) at around 1430, using the old road, with a 20-min stop at Cerro Castillo (3 cafés and some shops), 2½ hrs to Laguna Amarga, 3½ hrs to Guardería Pudeto and 4½ hrs the administration centre. Transport on the new road takes 1½ hrs to park. To go to the Administration centre, all charge US$16 one way, US$30 open return (return tickets are not interchangeable between different companies). Buses will stop anywhere en route, but all stop at Laguna Amarga entrance, Salto Grande del Paine and the administration centre. Return buses to Puerto Natales stop at Laguna Amarga from 1430 to 2000. Services are provided by **Bus Gómez**, Prat 234, T411971; **JB**, Prat 258, T410242; and **Trans Via Paine**, Bulnes 518, T413672. In high season the buses fill quickly so it is best to board at Administration for the return to Puerto Natales. All buses wait at Refugio Pudeto until the 1200 boat from Refugio Paine Grande arrives. Travel between 2 points within the park US$6.

In season there are frequent minibus connections within the park: from Laguna Amarga to Hotel Las Torres, US$5, and from the administration centre to Hostería Lago Grey, US$15. Other than these routes getting around the park without your own transport is difficult and expensive. From Torres del Paine to **Calafate** (Argentina): take the direct bus run by **Chaltén Travel**, US$80, or take services from Puerto Natales (see above); alternatively take a bus from the park to Cerro Castillo (106 km south of administration centre) then catch a direct service to Calafate (see Puerto Natales Buses). **Car hire** Hiring a pick-up in Punta Arenas is an economical proposition for a group (up to 9 people): US$400-420 for 4 days. If driving there yourself, the shorter new road from Puerto Natales is narrow with lots of blind corners and sudden gusts of wind and can be rough in patches. In the park, the roads are also narrow and winding with blind corners: use your horn a lot. Petrol available at Río Serrano, but fill up in Puerto Natales to be safe.

Tierra del Fuego

The western side of this, the largest island off the extreme south of South America, belongs to Chile and the eastern to Argentina. Here the Andes cordillera runs from west to east, so that the north of the island is flat, covered with vast sheep farms, while the south has mountains, glaciers, lakes and forests. The major population centres, Ushuaia and Río Grande, are on the Argentine side, but Chile has the most southerly town in the world, Puerto Williams, on the island Isla Navarino below Tierra del Fuego.

Porvenir and around → *Phone code: 061. Population: 5100.*

Porvenir is a quiet, pleasant place with many inhabitants of Croatian descent. Founded in 1894 in the gold boom, when many people came seeking fortunes from Croatia and Chiloé, it's a quiet, pleasant place with neat, painted tin houses and neatly trimmed yew trees lining the main avenue. There is a small museum, the **Museo Fernando Cordero Rusque** ⓘ *Jorge Schythe y Zavattaro 402, Mon-Thu 0800-1700, Fri 0800-1600, Sat-Sun 1030-1330, 1500-1700, US$1,* with archaeological and photographic displays on the Selk'nam (Onas); good displays on natural history and the early colonisers. **Mirador de la Ciudad** is a walkable excursion round the bay from Porvenir and uphill to the radio aerials. There is a bank just below the Plaza on Phillippi (Monday to Friday 0900-1400, changes cash and has a Maestro ATM. Post office on Plaza, on Phillipi. **Tourist information**: the best information is at the Museum. There are tourist notice boards outside the Municipalidad, on seafront and elsewhere; they wrongly suggest that ferries dock in town. A handicrafts stall in a kiosk on the seafront gives tourist information (opposite Comercial Tuto, No 588).

Porvenir is the base for exploring the wonderfully wild virgin territory of Tierra del Fuego. Excursions in the south, the more interesting half, must be totally self-sufficient. There are no hotels, shops, petrol stations or public transport. The only town in the south is Cameron, on the southern shore of Bahía Inútil. In the north, there is fuel and lodging at **Cerro Sombrero**, 46 km south of Primera Angostura, a village built to administrate oil drilling in the area, and a *hostal* and a place to eat in San Sebastián. There is no car hire on the island and no public transport to Argentina.

North of Porvenir, 6 km, is the **Monumento Natural Laguna de los Cisnes**. Access is across private land; the owner will give permission. Another place to see wildfowl, including black-necked swans from December is **Laguna Santa María**, not far from Porvenir on road to **Bahía Inútil**, a wonderful windswept bay. Cabo Boquerón, the headland at the start of Bahía Inútil, has great views on a clear day, as far as Cabo Froward, Isla Dawson and the distant Cordillera Darwin's snow peaks. Driving east along the bay you pass Los Canelos, with trees, a rare sight, and then the junction for the Cordón Baquedano, on the **Circuito de Oro**. This is a recommended tour, on which you can see gold panning using the same techniques since mining began in 1881, a four-hour, 115-km round trip. Miner Sr Jorge

Gesell Díaz is happy to show tourists his workings (very enthusiastic), in summer only. Write in his visitors' book and leave a tip.

The main road east goes to **Onaisin**, 99 km east of Porvenir, and the Argentine border at San Sebastián. A road south at Onaisin passes Caleta Josefina, a handsome ex-estancia built in 1833, where some old buildings remain. To the most southerly point by road, Estancia Lago Fagnano, and the most southerly habitation at Río Azopardo is four hours. The government is hoping to complete the road to **Yendegaia** with a view to having a summer route, including ferry, to Puerto Navarino, for Puerto Williams; work was underway in 2012. See www.theconservation landtrust.org for information on Yendegaia and its conservation. Other options are sailing from Porvenir to **Río Cóndor** across Bahía Inútil, south of Cameron, with trekking or riding from Cameron to **Seno Almirantazgo**, a beautiful, wild and treeless place, where mountains sink into blue fjords with icebergs. A large part of the peninsula between Bahía Inútil and Seno Almirantazgo is the **Karukinka** nature reserve, www.karukinkanatural.cl, run by the Wildlife Conservation Society. Also sailing to **Marinelli glacier**, where you can sail, kayak and dive. Fly fishing, until recently the secret of Hollywood stars, is becoming world-renowned. The area is rich in brown trout, sea-run brook trout and steelheads, weighing 2-14 kg.

Border with Argentina → *Argentine time is 1 hr ahead of Chilean time, Mar-Oct.*

The only legal border crossing between the Chilean and Argentine parts of Tierra del Fuego is 142 km east of Porvenir at **San Sebastián**; open 0800-2200. On the Argentine side the road continues to Río Grande. **Note** There are two settlements called San Sebastián, on each side of the border but they are 14 km apart; taxis are not allowed to cross. No fruit, vegetables, dairy produce or meat permitted on entry to Chile. For entry to Argentina, see Argentina chapter.

Puerto Williams → *Phone code: 061. Population: 2300, less than ½ civilian.*

Puerto Williams is a Chilean naval base on **Isla Navarino**, south of the Beagle Channel. About 50 km south east of Ushuaia (Argentina) at 54° 55' 41" south, 67° 37' 58" west, it is small, friendly and remote. The island is totally unspoilt and beautiful, offering great geographical diversity, thanks to **Dientes de Navarino** range, with peaks over 1000 m, covered with southern beech forest up to 500 m, and, south of that, great plains covered in peat bogs, with many lagoons and abundant in flora. The island was the centre of the indigenous Yaganes culture and there are 500 archaeological sites, the oldest from 3000 years ago. The town is a mixture of neat naval housing and the more haphazard civilian building with some impressive, modern municipal and school buildings. On an inlet at western edge is the Micalvi, an old naval vessel which is now HQ of the yacht club. **Museo Martín Gusinde** ① *Mon-Thu 1000-1300, 1500-1800, Sat-Sun1500-1800, Fri closed (subject to change), US$1*, is also known as the Museo del Fin del Mundo ('End of the World Museum'). It is full of information about vanished tribes, local wildlife, and voyages including Charles Darwin and Fitzroy of the Beagle, a must. Businesses in town accept US dollars; there are minimarkets and a hospital. **Tourist information** ① *Municipalidad de Cabos de Hornos, O'Higgins y Prat, T621011, isotop@mitierra.cl, closed in winter*. They may have maps and details on hiking, but it is probably as good, if not better, to get information from agencies, such as Shila (see What to do, below). **CONAF** ① *Carabinero M Leal 106, T621303, area.cabodehornos@gmail.com*.

Around Puerto Williams

For superb views, climb Cerro Bandera (three to four hours' round trip, steep, take warm clothes). Villa Ukika, 2 km east of town, is where the last descendants of the Yaganes people live, relocated from their original homes at Caleta Mejillones (an old, overgrown cemetery marks the spot on the road to Puerto Navarino). There is excellent trekking around the Dientes de Navarino, the southernmost trail in the world, through impressive mountain landscapes, with superb views of Beagle Channel (challenging, 53 km in five days, November to March, snowfall permitting, good level of fitness needed). Also to Laguna Windhond, four cays, and others all over island.

Cape Horn

It is possible to catch a boat south from Isla Navarino to Cape Horn (the most southerly piece of land on earth apart from Antarctica). There is one pebbly beach on the north side of the island; boats anchor in the bay and passengers are taken ashore by motorized dinghy. A stairway climbs the cliff above the beach, up to the building where a naval officer and his family run the lighthouse and naval post. A path leads from here to the impressive monument of an albatross overlooking the wild, churning waters of the Drake Passage below. Cruceros Australis ships call here (see page 103).

Tierra del Fuego listings

For hotel and restaurant price codes and other relevant information, see pages 10-12.

⊜ Where to stay

Porvenir *p119*

$$ España, Croacia 698, T530160. Expanded and upgraded, with bath, hot water, cable TV, central heating, internet, helpful and friendly. Good restaurant with fixed price lunch and dinner, also serves tea.

$$ Rosas, Phillipi 296, T580088. hotelrosas@chile.com. Heating, hot water, with breakfast, restaurant and bar, internet. Recommended.

$ Central, Phillipi 298, T580077, opposite Rosas. All rooms with bath, TV, heating and breakfast.

$ pp Hostal Kawi. Pedro Silva 144, T581638, hostalkawi@yahoo.com. Comfortable, rooms for 3, with bath, TV, meals available, breakfast included, heating, offers fly-fishing trips.

Elsewhere in Chilean Tierra del Fuego

$$-$ Hostería Tunkelen, Arturo Prat Chacón 101, Cerro Sombrero, TC61-212757, hosteria_tunkelen@hotmail.com. A so dorm **$** pp. Recommended.

Border with Argentina: San Sebastián *p120*

$$-$ Hostería de la Frontera, T061-696004, frontera@entelchi e.net. Where some buses stop for meals and cakes, cosy, with bath (the annex is much more basic), good food.

Puerto Williams *p120*

$$$$ Lakutaia, 2 km west of town. T621721, www.lakutaia.cl. A 'base camp' for a range of activities and packages (riding, trekking, birdwatching, sailing, flights), 24 double rooms in simple but attractive style, good bath, no TV, lovely views from spacious public areas, library, maps, internet, uses local personnel and produce, bikes for hire, modern stables, 3 golf 'holes' – most southerly in world! Sailing on SV *Victory* (1986 wooden schooner), 3 crew, 10 pax on overnight trips, 23 on day trips. Everyone becomes a crew member.

$$ Hostal Akainij. Austral 22, T621173, www.turismoakainij.cl. Smallish but comfortable rooms, very helpful, excellent, filling meals, kitchen facilities, basic English spoken, adventure tours and transfers. Recommended.

$$ pp Hostería Camblor, Vía 2 s/n, a bit out of town, T621033, hostalcamblor@ hotmail.com. Full board, full choice at meals, all wine included, also a short tour, free airport pick-up, for 4-passengers will include tour of Cementerio Indígeno. 2 backpacker rooms available, **$** with breakfast.

$ pp Forjadores de Cabo de Hornos, Uspashun 64, Plaza B O'Higgins, near Centro Cómercial, T621140, www.hostal forjadoresdelcabode hornos.cl. With breakfast, bath, TV, heating, agency for tours and transport, welcoming.

$ pp Hostal Coirón, Ricardo Maragaño 168, T621227, or through **Ushaia Boating** or **Sim Ltda** (see What to do). With breakfast, shared bath, helpful, good food, relaxed, quite basic, but OK.

$ pp Hostal Pusaki, Piloto Pardo 222, T621116. Breakfast, cheaper without bath, use of kitchen, heated by stove, good meals available, laundry, luggage store, internet, owner Patty is helpful and fun.

$ pp Hostal Yagan, Piloto Pardo 260, T621118, 8749 0166, hostalyagan@ hotmail.com. Comfortable, some rooms with bath, central heating, includes breakfast, lunch and dinner available US$12, run by Daniel Yevenes, who offers tours and transport to Ushuaia.

$ pp Refugio El Padrino, Costanera 262, T621136, 8438 0843, ceciliamancillao@ yahoo.com.ar. The vivacious Cecilia Mancilla is great fun, good food. Recommended.

Camping
At **Hostal Bella Vista**, Tte Muñoz 118, T621010, US$10 per night (also has rooms). See **Victory Adventures**, below.

Porvenir *p119*

$$ Club Croata, Señoret entre Phillippi y Muñoz Gamero, next to the bus stop on the waterfront. A lively place where you can get a good lunch.

$$-$ El Chispa, Señoret 202, T580054. Good restaurant for seafood and other Chilean dishes.

$$-$ La Picá de Pechuga, Bahía Chilote s/n, by ferry dock. Good fresh seafood and fish. Owner Juan Bahamonde runs **Cordillero de Darwin** tours (see below):

$ Panadería El Paine, Sampaio 368. Shop and tea room, very friendly.

Puerto Williams *p120*

$$-$ Café Angelus, Centro Comercial Norte 151, T621080. Also travel agent and transport. Run by Loreto Camino, friendly cheerful atmosphere, small, good simple cooking, coffee (including Irish), beer. Best place for tourists.

$ Los Dientes de Navarino, Centro Comercial Sur. Popular with locals, limited fare.

Panaderías and minimarkets: **Simón & Simón** and **Temuco** are opposite each other on Piloto Pardo, junction Condell. The former seems to be centre of reference in town.

Porvenir *p119*
For adventure tourism and trekking activities contact tour operators in Punta Arenas (see What to do, page 103).

Turismo Cordillera de Darwin, run by Juan 'Pechuga' Bahamonde, T09-9888 6380, or 061-580167, gerencia@cordilleradarwin.com or jebr_darwin@hotmail.com. Runs land, fishing and boating tours. Oro circuit costs US$120 for 4 without lunch, 4 hrs; US$60 pp with lunch, 0800-1700 including Laguna Santa María. Costs of tours to far south vary according to circumstances. Boat and fishing trips, 6 days allowing a day for unforeseen delays.

Puerto Williams p120

Boat trips Victory Adventures, Tte Muñoz 118, Casilla 70, T061-621010, www.victory-cruises.com, Captain Ben Garrett and his family run this recommended online travel agency for many tours and expeditions around Tierra del Fuego, Patagonia and the southern oceans to Antarctica. They also have the **$$$ Hostal Bella Vista ($$** without bath, **$** pp in bunks) B&B, internet services and a minimarket. **Cruceros Australis**, Av El Bosque Norte 0440, p 11, Las Corces, Santiago, T02-442 3115, www.australis. com (see page 103), call at Wula a Bay on the west side of Isla Navarino after visiting Cape Horn; you can disembark to visit the museum and take a short trek.

Trekking You must register first with Carabineros on C Piloto Pardo, near Brito. Tell them when you get back, too. Sometimes they will not allow lone trekking.

Tour operators

Akainij, see Where to stay.

Sea, Ice and Mountains Ricardo Maragaño 168, T621150, www.simld.com. Sailing trips, trekking tours and many other adventure activities, including kayaking and wildlife spotting.

Shila, O'Higgins 322 (a hut at entrance to Centro Comercial), T621366, www.turismo shila.cl. Luis Tiznado Gonzales is an adventure guide, trekking and fishing equipment hire (bikes, tents, sleeping bags, stoves, and more). Lots of trekking information, sells photocopied maps.

⊖ Transport

Ferries to Tierra del Fuego

There are 2 crossings. The ferry company accepts no responsibility for damage to vehicles.

Punta Arenas to Porvenir The Crux Australis, sails from Tres Puentes (5 km north of Punta Arenas, bus A or E from Av Magallanes, or *colectivo* 15, US$1; taxi US$5) at 0900 or 1500-1600, no service Mon in season; less frequent sailings off season. **Tabsa/ Transboradora Austral Broom**, Bulnes 5075 (Tres Puentes), T218100, www.tabsa.cl or through **Comapa**, see Punta Arenas Tour operators. 2½-hr crossing (can be rough and cold, watch for dolphins), US$11.50 pp, US$72 per vehicle. Boat disembarks at Bahía Chilota, 5 km from Porvenir, bus US$1.50; bus drops you where you want to go in town. Return from Porvenir varying times in afternoon between 1400 and 1900, daily except Mon. Timetable dependent on tides and subject to change; check in advance. **Tabsa** website gives monthly schedules. Reservations for cars essential, especially in summer. Tabsa have an office on Señoret, seafront in Porvenir, T580089, Mon-Fri 0900-1200, 1400-1830.

Punta Delgada to Punta Espora (Bahía Azul) This crossing is via the Primera Angostura (First Narrows), 170 km northeast of Punta Arenas (Punta Espora is 80 km north of Porvenir). There are 3 boats working continuously. On board is a café, lounge, toilets and decks for getting splashed. Buses can wait up to 90 mins to board. Boats run 0830-2345, 20 mins' crossing, US$29 per vehicle, foot passengers US$3.45, www.tabsa.cl. The ferries takes about 4 trucks and 20 cars; before 1000 most space is taken by trucks. There is no bus service to or from this crossing. If hitching, this route is preferable as there is more traffic.

Porvenir p119

Air From Punta Arenas (weather and bookings permitting), **Aerovías DAP**, Señoret s/n, T580089, Porvenir, www.aeroviasdap.cl, details under Punta Arenas, Transport. Heavly booked so make sure you have your return reservation confirmed.

Bus The only public transport on Chilean Tierra del Fuego is Jorge Bastian's minibus Porvenir–Cerro Sombrero, T345406/ 8503-3662, jorgebastian@hotmail.com, or the driver axelvig20@hotmail.com. Mon, Wed, Fri, leaves Sombrero 0830, 0700 on Mon, returns from Porvenir Municipalidad, 2 hrs, US$4.50.
Road All roads are good *ripio* except paved from Bahía Chilota to Porvenir and in Porvenir itself.

Puerto Williams *p120*
Air From Punta Arenas with DAP (details under Punta Arenas). Book well in advance; long waiting lists (be persistent). The flight is beautiful (sit on right from Punta Arenas) with superb views of Tierra del Fuego, the Cordillera Darwin, the Beagle Channel, and the islands stretching south to Cape Horn. Also army flights available (they are cheaper), but the ticket has to be bought through DAP. Also from the Aeroclub in Ushuaia (see Ushuaia, Transport). Airport is in town.
Boat Yaghan ferry of Broom, www.tabsa.cl, from **Punta Arenas** once a week, 24 passengers, US$186 for chair, US$258 for bunk, 34-hr trip through beautiful channels. Will not take passengers if carrying petrol, so

ask in advance. From **Ushuaia** with **Ushuaia Boating**, US$120 each way, which includes a 20-40 min crossing in a semi-rigid boat to Puerto Navarino, a jetty, the Alcaldía del Mar and 4 more houses, plus a few horses and cows. Despite Ushuaia Boating dealing with documents when you buy the ticket, there is a lot of hanging around at Puerto Navarino, but the setting is nice and they sometimes offer coffee and pastries for impatient passengers. Then it's a 1-hr ride in a combi on a lovely, *ripio* road past inlets and forests, river outflows, Bahía Mejillones and birdlife to Williams. For return make sure you are clear about transport arrangements. Also **Fernández Campbell** have a 1½-hr crossing from **Ushuaia**, Fri, Sat, Sun 1000, return 1500, US$125 for foreigners, tickets sold at **Naviera RFC** in Puerto Williams and **Zenit Explorer**, Juana Fadul 126, Ushuaia, T02901-433232.

Directory

Puerto Williams *p120*
Centro Comercial has **Aerovías DAP**, T621051, internet services, **post office** selling postcards, stamps and maps, and a **telephone office**, Mon-Sat 0930-2230, 1000-1300, 1600-2200.

Contents

Footnotes

Index